{DESIGN}
[CODE]
<BUILD>
[PLAY]

THE GAMER'S GUIDE TO
CODING

GORDON McCOMB

STERLING
New York

STERLING
New York

An Imprint of Sterling Publishing Co., Inc.
1166 Avenue of the Americas
New York, NY 10036

ISBN 978-1-4549-2234-6

Distributed in Canada by Sterling Publishing Co., Inc.
c/o Canadian Manda Group, 664 Annette Street
Toronto, Ontario, Canada M6S 2C8
Distributed in the United Kingdom by GMC Distribution Services
Castle Place, 166 High Street, Lewes, East Sussex, England BN7 1XU
Distributed in Australia by NewSouth Books
45 Beach Street, Coogee, NSW 2034, Australia

For information about custom editions, special sales, and
premium and corporate purchases, please contact Sterling Special Sales
at 800-805-5489 or specialsales@sterlingpublishing.com.

Manufactured in Canada

2 4 6 8 10 9 7 5 3 1

www.sterlingpublishing.com

Interior design by Sharon Jacobs

{CONTENTS}

➤ PART ONE: GETTING STARTED ➤

PART THREE: STEPPING UP YOUR GAME

[INTRODUCTION]

In a world where computers are built into toasters, learning to program means learning how to build just about anything.

With *The Gamer's Guide to Coding*, you'll discover how to create, test, and play colorful and fun 2-D computer games—and learn vital computer programming skills while doing it.

Here's some good news: No prior programming skills are required. Just open the book at Chapter 1 and begin.

▶ Free Tools, Simplified Steps

Think it might be too complicated to begin? Think again. Special programs and fancy computer systems are absolutely not required. You don't have to pay an extra dime to get started. All you need is a reasonably current Windows® or Macintosh® PC and an Internet connection. The software to develop your games is free.

▶ **Use this book to discover what coding is all about**

You'll see how easy it is to begin. Follow the step-by-step examples for learning how to code, then publish your own games that you can play by yourself, or share with family and friends.

There's more good news: No need to retype tons of text . . . all examples and exclusive game artwork are provided free online. Just download and go!

▶ **Use this book as a guide to unleash your creative talent**

You've got bright ideas—now learn how to turn those ideas into reality. Tweak, rearrange, or transform the examples to your heart's content. Or take what you've learned and create your own games from scratch.

Now here's the best news of all: It's all here—everything you need to get started on learning how cool coding can be!

Time to begin.
And time to learn some coding!

▶ Why Learn Game Coding?

Simple: Coding for games is a fun and productive way to learn about programming.

Writing games involves all the core coding skills required to master the art of computer programming. Games are the perfect springboard for learning any coding skill. And because your games will use the same tools and technologies modern websites use, you'll be learning the lucrative field of Web development while you play!

Here are some of the topics you'll explore:

- Using graphics to build colorful and interactive pages
- Animating to create motion
- Designing the exact look you want
- Generating and displaying text messages at any size and in any font
- Waiting for and reacting to the player's input—keyboard, mouse, and touch
- Making decisions using programming logic
- Integrating code with other technologies; namely, HTML5 and Cascading Style Sheets
- Working with system resources, like clocks, timers, and sound
- Learning how to troubleshoot and debug your programs
- Working with numbers: performing math calculations during game play
  . . . and more.

Start with simple games that demonstrate basic concepts. As each chapter unfolds, you'll be introduced to new ideas, allowing you to build games of increasing complexity. And remember: All coding examples and game art are provided online for free, speeding your expedition into the land of coding.

▶ Playground Scripts for Interactive Discovery

There's no better way to learn than by rolling up your shirt sleeves and actually doing it. Most chapters include what I call *playground scripts*. These are working examples that let you experiment using a premade framework. All are available online; you don't have to retype them from scratch.

Change things, try new concepts, dare to make a mistake and learn from it—these are playgrounds . . . so play and have some fun!

▶ 12+ Bonus Games, Ready to Go

You'll find over a dozen bonus games exclusively created for this book. Each game demonstrates important JavaScript™ coding concepts. Here's a short rundown of some of the bonus games—read more about them on the Online Support Site (see Appendix A, page 310):

Kaylee Saves the World ▶ Explore this 2-D first-person shooter where you ready-aim-fire at rapidly moving Martians who've just landed on Earth. Oh, the joy of hearing that sizzle sound when you zap 'em!

Kitteh in Space ▶ Here's a side-scrolling outer-space adventure where you help Kitteh navigate a dangerous asteroid belt. Watch out for tumbling asteroids and other obstacles—Kitteh likes to keep a clean spaceship, so do your best steering clear.

The Ruins of Ramic ▶ Give your memory a stress test with this matchup card game. *Ruins* is one of many "build-as-you-learn" games, presented in several versions from start to finish. These innovative examples demonstrate the progression of how JavaScript games can be developed by building up features one at a time.

Zombie Girl Dressup ▶ Help newly-dead Jessica get ready for her big date. Learn important graphics coding techniques while helping her try on different tops, bottoms, shoes, and accessories.

All of the playground scripts and bonus games are provided for free on the Online Support Site for this book. See Appendix A (page 310) for more details. Example code is organized by chapter.

▶ What Makes This Book Special

This isn't your ordinary book on learning JavaScript. Here are just some of the reasons it's unique. First, the examples in *The Gamer's Guide to Coding* are based on the same technologies that drive websites, making it widely applicable to all sorts of fun stuff you may want to do, now or in the future. While you're learning about coding, you'll have fun creating 2-D games that you can play and share with others. Sort of a 2-for-1 deal!

Second, this book doesn't require lots of JavaScript add-in libraries, like jQuery®, to make things work. While some of these libraries provide coding shortcuts, being shortcuts, they're not the best way for beginners to study. They can complicate the learning process for newcomers. Only a few very special add-in libraries are used for important functions, like adding sound.

And third, it doesn't try to talk past you by bringing up concepts not critical for learning core coding concepts. It's not a super-duper advanced book—it's designed for readers just starting out in JavaScript or coding, readers who want to learn the ropes before graduating to more elaborate ventures.

PART ONE

GETTING STARTED

STARTING AT SQUARE ONE: SETTING UP SHOP

Every journey starts somewhere.

For Dorothy in *The Wizard of Oz*, it was a brightly colored brick road that eventually wound its way to the magical Emerald City. For those of us not wearing ruby slippers, we begin our journey into the land of coding by starting right here, on this page.

As with any journey, you must first:

- **Decide where you're headed** ▶ No problem; you want to learn more about computer coding.

- **Collect some supplies before starting off** ▶ You might already have a few of these supplies in your knapsack. But even if you don't, everything is *free* and just a download away.

▶ Learning to Code with HTML + CSS + JavaScript

Coding starts with a *programming language.* You can learn programming by studying any of several different languages: Python, BASIC, Forth®, C++, COBOL, Lisp, Delphi, Fortran. . . . The list goes on.

For this book, the programming language you'll learn about is *JavaScript.* First introduced around the mid-1990s, it is now arguably the most widely used programming language on the planet. (That's planet Earth, for those readers from Tau Upsilon IV.) For proof: Go to a website.

Any website will do.

Odds are, that page uses JavaScript to provide a richer user experience.

Or play a game on the Web, like the one in Figure 1-1. It's quite likely that the game you play uses JavaScript.

JavaScript is often paired with two other technologies: HTML and CSS. The trio is both ubiquitous and standardized throughout the globe. What's more, knowledge of how to use these technologies is a golden ticket to a well-paying job (if you're interested in that sort of thing).

Figure 1-1. A game written entirely with JavaScript.

HTML

▶ Serves as a road map of *elements*—elements are things like text and pictures—displayed on a web page. For the inquisitive, HTML stands for *HyperText Markup Language*. It's a way of defining the words, images, animation, media, and other content of the page using just text and a couple of symbols.

CSS

▶ Defines the visual look of that page. Text can be tiny, or it can loom large. It's all done with a set of styles defined in a *Cascading Style Sheet*, or CSS. I reserve why it's so named for a later chapter.

JavaScript

▶ Enhances the layout and action of a web page. Though now an independent programming language all on its own, implemented in all sorts of things—including little robots—JavaScript began its life intimately connected to the Internet experience.

Although this book is primarily about learning to code with JavaScript, all three of these technologies are tightly wound around each other. So naturally, you'll learn about all three throughout your journey.

▶ Tools for Writing and Viewing Your Code

You don't need anything special to develop code using JavaScript. You need only a text editor program to write the code and a web browser to view the result.

For the sake of standardization, this book relies on two free and commonly available applications, as shown in Figure 1-2:

GOOGLE CHROME WEB BROWSER
(https://www.google.com/chrome/)

▶ If you don't already have it, you can download it from the Google™ website. For desktop computers, Chrome™ is available for modern versions of Windows, Apple® OS X, and Linux®. Chrome serves as the environment for *rendering* (displaying) the results of your code.

ATOM EDITOR
(https://atom.io)

▶ Atom® is likewise available for modern versions of Windows, OS X, and Linux. Atom is a glorified text editor specifically made for programming. Included among its varied benefits are the ability to display numbers on each line of text and the ability to color-code important parts of your program. If you have a preference for another code editor, you can certainly use it. But throughout this book, Atom is the one I'll assume you're using.

The Chrome browser is also available for Android™ and Apple iOS mobile devices. Although much of the code you write will run on Chrome in these devices, mobile devices are not great platforms to develop on—even the pros don't code games using just a mobile device. For this book, it's assumed you're using a desktop or laptop computer to write and test your programming endeavors.

When installing either or both of these tools, download the program file from its website and follow the installation procedure.

▶ Make Sure Your Tools Are Up to Date

Be sure you have the latest versions of both Chrome and Atom. Updating is easy for both:

For Chrome, type `chrome://help` in the address bar. Chrome reports the current version and, as needed, prompts you to update if it's old (or updates automatically, depending on your settings).

For Atom, choose Help > Check For Update. It'll tell if you have the latest version.

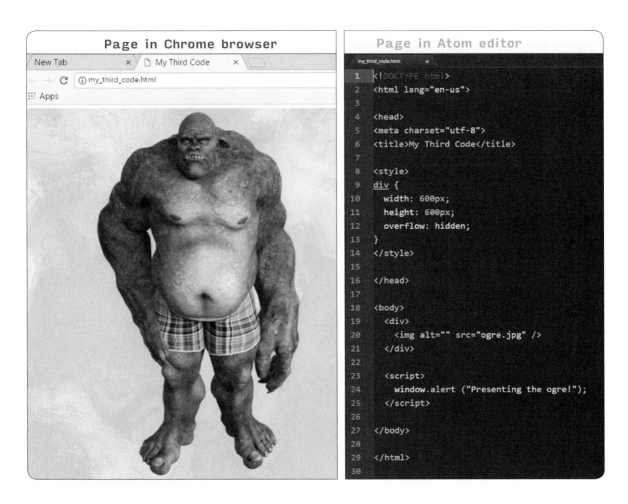

Figure 1-2. Chrome and Atom, the primary tools for developing web pages with JavaScript.

▶ Writing Your First Page of Code

You have to learn basic arithmetic before moving on to calculus. The same is true of writing programming code: Start simple and move up from there. So let's do just that. Start the Atom text editor:

1. Choose File > New File. A new blank document appears.

2. Carefully type the text that appears below (starting with <!DOCTYPE . . .).
    Press the Tab key to indent. Be sure your version looks just like the one in this book.

3. When you're done, look over your work and then choose File > Save As.

4. Locate a convenient place on your computer to save the file (your personal documents directory is a good place) and name it *my_first_code.html*. Don't forget the *.html* part at the end.

5. Click Save.

Why am I having you type this by hand rather than just download it readymade? By actually typing it out yourself, you get a better sense of the "rhythm" of an HTML page and of the information that goes inside.

Still, not to worry: This and the next example in this chapter are the only scripts in this book that you are expected to type yourself. All of the examples and demonstration games that accompany this book are provided online for easy download. For details, see Appendix A (page 310).

```
my_first_code.html
```

```html
<!DOCTYPE html>
<html lang="en-us">

<head>
<meta charset="utf-8" />
<title>My First Code</title>
</head>

<body>
  <p>This is my first page of code!</p>
</body>

</html>
```

Now start the Chrome browser, and:

1. Press Ctrl+O (the CTRL key and the letter *O*, not the number zero). If you're using a Macintosh, use Cmd+O.

2. A dialog box appears asking you which file you want to open. Navigate to the location where you saved the code page you made above, and select the *my_first_code.html* file.

3. Click Open to open the file. Your browser window should say, in proud text, "This is my first page of code!" (Figure 1-3).

Figure 1-3. How the *my_first_code.html* example should look on the screen.

Oops! Your example doesn't look like mine? Odds are there's a mistake someplace on the page. Examine your version very carefully in the Atom editor. Be sure all the < and > characters are where they're supposed to be. Missing parts could cause the page to not load or display an unintentional result.

Make any corrections and resave the file. Go back to Chrome. Hit the Reload button (circular arrow to the left of the address bar), and see if that corrected the problem.

▶ Deconstructing the First Example

The *my_first_code.html* example contains only HTML markup—*markup* refers to the special codes that Chrome or any other browser interprets as instructions for how the page is to appear on the screen. For the sake of simplicity, this example doesn't include any JavaScript or CSS; these elements come later.

HTML markup is composed of tags, identified by < and > angle brackets. Each tag has a specific purpose in the construction of the visual page. Some things to know about tags:

Many tags come in pairs ▶ The pairings denote the *start* and the *end* of an *HTML element*. An element is a kind of self-contained entity that—as you'll see in later chapters—can be manipulated using JavaScript. An example pairing is the <p> tag (see Figure 1-4), so-called because it defines a paragraph of text. The *start tag* is <p>, and its matching *end tag* is </p>. The text between is what you want to display as text in the browser window.

▨ Not all HTML elements have separate start and end tags ▶ As you'll see later in this chapter, the <img> tag, for displaying an image, is one such "single-tag" element.

▨ A special type of tag at the top of the document—<!DOCTYPE html>—also does not have a start/end pairing ▶ The reason: It's not really a tag per se but what's known as a *document declaration*. It's used to tell the browser what kind of file it's been handed; in this case, it's an HTML document.

Figure 1-4. The makeup of an HTML tag.

HTML elements can, and often do, enclose one another. The *root* of the document is defined by the <html> tag. Inside the <html> and </html> tags are several more enclosing (paired) tags:

▨ <head></head> defines content that is generally not displayed as part of the page itself, such as the title and the character set used for any text. (**Note:** While not directly displayed, what goes into the <head> section often plays an important role in *how* content appears. Just keep that in mind as you go along.)

▨ <body></body> defines content that you see in the browser's main window.

▶ Adding Some More Features

This first example is admittedly pretty boring, so let's move up a notch and add more functionality. For this second example, begin by opening a new window in Atom (File > New Window). Then,

1. Type the text as it appears in the listing below.

2. When done, save the file as *my_second_code.html*.

3. Open the file in Chrome by pressing Ctrl+O (Cmd+O on Mac), selecting the file, and clicking Open.

```
my_second_code.html

<!DOCTYPE html>
<html lang="en-us">

<head>
<meta charset="utf-8" />
<title>My Second Code</title>

<style>
div {
   width: 600px;
   height: 600px;
   background-color: lightgray;
   opacity: 0.8;
   font-size: 72px;
   overflow: hidden;
}
</style>

</head>

<body>
  <div>
    <p>This is my second page of code</p>
  </div>

</body>

</html>
```

The resulting page in Chrome should look like that in Figure 1-5.

Notice that when you save the document, Atom updates the colors used for the text and elements of your document. When you give the document the *.html* extension, Atom identifies it as an HTML document. The program assigns a preset HTML color scheme to it, which makes it easier for you to pick out the elements.

Right off you can see several new things in the second example:

New <style> Tag ▶
The <style> tag provides a convenient way to define how the parts of the page are shown on-screen. With this tag, you've now added CSS to the page.

New <div> Tag ▶
The <p> paragraph element holding the text has been moved into a <div> container. The role of a container is to hold other things as a collective unit. They are an incredibly useful feature of HTML and one that's used throughout this book.

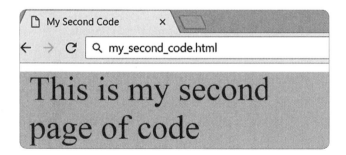

Figure 1–5. How the *my_second_code.html* example should look on the screen.

Style Rule for the <div> Tag ▶ The style sheet has a single rule: The style definition for the <div> tag. This rule states that any text in the <div> is to be sized at a whopping 72 pixels tall; the <div> itself is to be 600 pixels wide by 600 pixels high; and its background color is to be light gray, with an opacity (the inverse of transparency) of 80 percent.

▶ Adding JavaScript to the Mix

A third and final example for this chapter is provided in *my_third_code.html*. This one you don't have to type yourself. You can download it from the Online Support Site (refer to Appendix A, page 310). For reference, the code is below.

my_third_code.html

```
<!DOCTYPE html>
<html lang="en-us">

<head>
<meta charset="utf-8" />
<title>My Third Code</title>

<style>
div {
  width: 600px;
  height: 600px;
  overflow: hidden;
}
</style>

</head>

<body>
  <div>
    <img alt="" src="ogre.jpg" />
  </div>

  <script>
    window.alert ("Presenting the ogre!");
  </script>

</body>

</html>
```

Follow these steps when downloading:

1. Go to the examples page on the Online Support Site. The examples are organized by chapter. All of the examples for each chapter are combined together in a single zip file.

2. Right-click over the file link, and choose Save As.

3. Navigate to a place on your computer's hard drive to store the zip. Create a folder named *GamersGuide*, and put all the zips you download in there.

4. On your computer, go to the folder where you saved the zip file and unzip it.

5. After all the files have been unzipped, open the *my_third_code.html* file in Chrome.

The browser loads the file and immediately displays an alert box with the text "Presenting the ogre!" Click the box and the ogre appears on the page, shown in Figure 1-6.

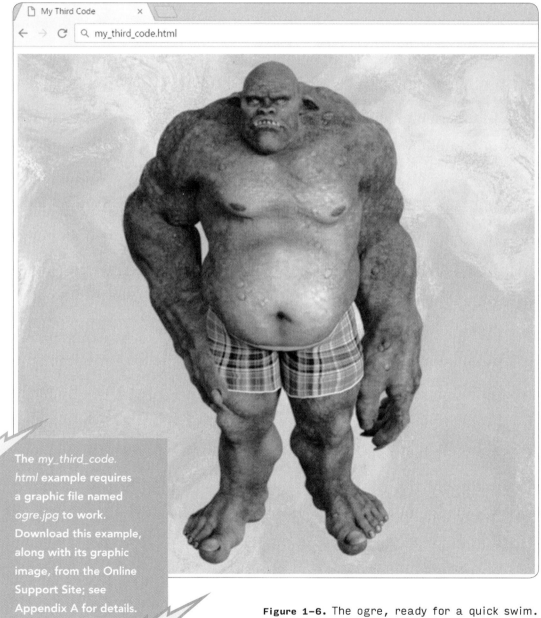

The *my_third_code. html* example requires a graphic file named *ogre.jpg* to work. Download this example, along with its graphic image, from the Online Support Site; see Appendix A for details.

Figure 1-6. The ogre, ready for a quick swim.

Some versions of Chrome and some other browsers may display the alert box after the ogre has already appeared. That's okay. Future chapters show how to precisely control the sequence of events when loading pages, but for now, what's important is that you've created a web page that combines text and graphics with HTML, CSS styles, and JavaScript.

If, instead of the ogre graphic, you get a small icon of a broken picture on the screen, it means the browser couldn't find the *ogre.jpg* image file. Be sure this file is in the same folder as *the my_third_code. html* example (see Figure 1-7).

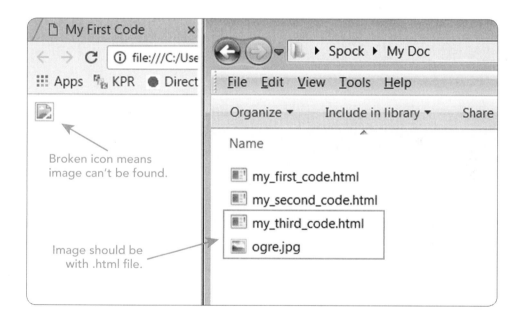

Figure 1-7. The broken image icon: The browser can't find the picture file.

Learn more about tags and get a detailed tour
at what's inside an HTML document in Chapter 2.

A CLOSER LOOK AT
HTML SCRIPT PAGES

Script pages—your games are made of these.

Combining the talented triad of HTML, CSS, and JavaScript, script pages contain all the information necessary for colorful, immersive animated games that think on their own and react to players' actions.

Center stage to any script page are the bits and pieces known as HTML elements, which a browser uses to define the things that appear on-screen. You learned a little bit about them in Chapter 1; in this chapter, discover more details about HTML and how it's used to define both the layout and the overall appearance of your games.

▶ Of Tags and Elements

Remember the all-in-one example from Chapter 1 that combined HTML, CSS, and JavaScript? Let's look at that one again and explore it in a bit more detail. This time, I've added line numbers that correspond with those shown in a script editor like Atom. The line numbers make it easier to detail the parts of the code.

ogre-revisited.html

```
1  <!DOCTYPE html>
2  <html lang="en-us">
3
4  <head>
5    <meta charset="utf-8" />
6    <title>Ogre Revisited</title>
7    <meta name="description" content="Sample"/>
8
9    <style>
10     #mainContent {
11       width: 600px;
12       height: 600px;
13       overflow: hidden;
14     }
15   </style>
16
17 </head>
18
19 <body>
20   <div id="mainContent">
21     <img alt="" src="ogre.jpg" />
22   </div>
23
24   <script>
25     window.alert ("Presenting the ogre!");
26   </script>
27
28 </body>
29
30 </html>
```

Examples:

Going forward, I refer to HTML elements using their widely accepted ALL-CAPS names, without the clunky < and > stuff. (Examples are shown in the chart on the right.) Many online resources and books follow this practice, so I will, too—it improves readability.

TAGS	ELEMENT NAME
<html></html>	HTML
<head></head>	HEAD
<style></style>	STYLE
<body></body>	BODY
<div></div>	DIV
<img />	IMG
<script></script>	SCRIPT

Recall from Chapter 1 that all the elements and other content in an HTML page are collectively called *markup* (the *M* in HT*ML*). Markup allows you to use just words and symbols to define a feature-rich web page that contains text, graphics, animation, thinking scripts, and interactive content. See Figure 2-1 for an overview of how the page is constructed.

Declaration

▩ Line 1 is a *document declaration*. It defines this file as an HTML5 document. *HTML5* is version 5 of the HTML specification, a worldwide standard. By specifying an HTML5 document, the browser can better interpret the content the way you intend to have it displayed.

HTML Element

▩ Lines 2 and 30 form the HTML element. Everything between the start and end tags of this element defines the actual web page. Other than the document declaration, noted above, no tags should appear outside the HTML element.

HEAD Element

The *HEAD element* specifies a number of important pieces of an HTML script page. It serves as a container for other elements.

▩ Lines 4 through 17 comprise the HEAD element, where important information about the document is kept. This info may not appear inside the browser window, although, as you'll see throughout this book, it may influence the appearance of that content.

▩ Text between the TITLE tags on line 6 displays the title of the page at the top of the browser or in a tab. This information is indeed "displayed"; it's not part of the page content itself.

▩ Lines 5 and 7 provide common metadata about the document. I'm using just two metadata tags for this example. (If you're interested, the *charset* metadata tells the browser that text should conform to the UFT-8 Unicode alphabet set. The *description* metadata describes the page so that it can be cataloged by search engines.)

STYLE Element

Also inside the HEAD element is the STYLE *element* (lines 9 through 15). This one bears special consideration because it's so important to the games you create. The STYLE element defines one or more *style rules* for the visible components of the document, the things you see in the browser's main window. For this page, there's only one style rule—a rule for an element named `mainContent`. More about it on the following page.

BODY Element

Lines 19 through 28 comprise the BODY element. Markup between these lines appears as part of the browser window.

Lines 20 through 22 are a DIV element, a container that holds other elements. Though it only contains one thing—the IMG element defined on line 21—it has the ability to hold multiple sub-elements at a time and all those elements are treated as a unit. Note that this element has been given a unique ID, or name: mainContent.

SCRIPT Element

Lines 24 through 26 is a SCRIPT element; it's in here that JavaScript code goes.

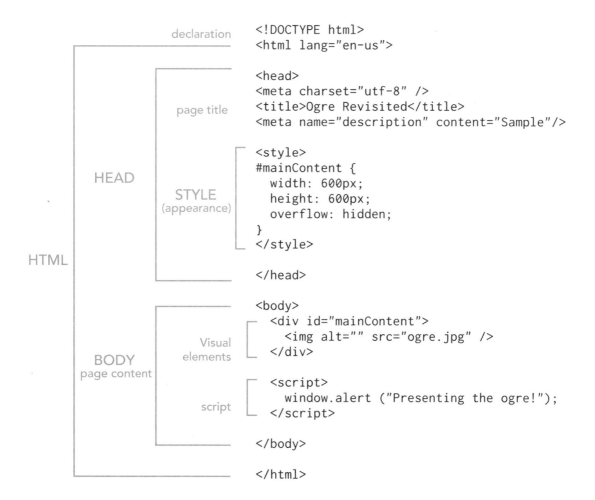

Figure 2-1. Script pages are structured with text and tags.

Notice some of the tags have additional information between the < and > brackets. These are called *attributes*. Some tags have them; some don't. Example: The IMG tag contains two such attributes, named `alt` and `src`. *Alt* means *alternate text* (left empty in this example); src means the *source* (file name) of the image. Throughout the book, I introduce various tag attributes as they come up.

When an HTML document is loaded and processed in a browser, its elements get *parsed* (analyzed and divvied up) into a hierarchical structure somewhat like an upside-down tree (Figure 2-2). This allows the browser to keep track of each and every "branch" of the tree and it's a crucial part of coding pages with JavaScript. JavaScript can interact with the individual branches.

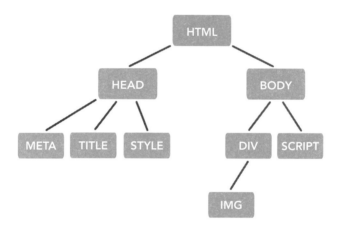

Figure 2-2. HTML elements are processed in a tree-like structure.

There's a term for the way browsers break down HTML elements and store them for later manipulation: It's called the *document object model*, or *DOM*. Branches of the DOM tree are referred to as *nodes* and it's the ability to alter the size, position, and other attributes of these nodes that makes using JavaScript such a great tool for creating fun and colorful games.

▶ Getting Down and Dirty with the SCRIPT Element

All JavaScript goodness happens inside the SCRIPT element, that part between the `<script>` and `</script>` tags. JavaScript code can be placed most anywhere in the HTML document, though in practice, it's often limited to just a few areas. Its location at the end of the BODY element is typical. More about this in a bit.

The example uses a very simple script comprising just one JavaScript *method*:

```
window.alert ("Presenting the ogre!");
```

This script causes a pop-up box to appear in the browser with the text, "Presenting the ogre!" You may have seen similar pop-ups on some web pages you've visited. Apart from a crude method of demonstrating JavaScript, it's used on the occasional web page to grab your attention—sometimes refusing to let go! Because of its potential for misuse, this is one of the only times I use it in this book. I show you a better way of displaying feedback messages at the end of this chapter.

In any case, the alert box is a good way to learn the *syntax* of JavaScript code. *Syntax* is the special rules for using the language. I provide just the basics here and reserve the more thorough discussion of syntax for Chapter 5: Getting Started with JavaScript—Part 1 (page 67).

Here's what makes up the statement line for the alert (see Figure 2-3):

- Name of the method, in this case, `alert`

- One or more *parameters* for use by the method, enclosed in parentheses

- The ; (semi-colon) *line-terminator* character

```
        alert method              parameter
                                                        line
window.alert("Presenting the ogre!");  ←  terminator

                 statement line
```

Figure 2-3. The parts of the JavaScript alert box.

Some JavaScript resources refer to alert and similar methods as *commands, statements, program instructions, functions, keywords,* or other such names. I try to be as specific as possible in the use of these terms, while hopefully avoiding the trap of nitpicking. Just know that, although there are nuances between these words, it's what they do that's important.

More elaborate JavaScript merely adds more lines of code. Some scripts comprise just a small handful of code lines, whereas others span hundreds and hundreds of lines. Don't worry if this sounds daunting; as with any language, the more you practice, the easier it gets.

▶ Better Feedback with the Console

I promised I'd use the pop-up alert method only sparingly in this book. There is a much better way to get feedback from your scripts: The browser's console. The *console* is an otherwise hidden feature of Chrome (and, for that matter, most modern browsers). The console has many uses, but among the most important for JavaScripters is its ability to

- Display errors
- Have your script give feedback while it's running

Opening the Console

The console is available for any HTML page you view in Chrome. To display it: Press Ctrl+Shift+J (Windows or Linux), or Cmd+Shift+J (Mac). This displays the DevTools panel. If this is the first time you've displayed the panel. it may be docked to the right side of the browser window. I find it's easier to work with the console when it's docked at the bottom. Do this by clicking the three vertical dots at the right of the panel, then choose Dock to Bottom for the *Dock Side* option.

When the DevTools panel is opened using these steps, the Console tab should already be selected. If it's not, just click on the tab.

Getting Feedback from Your Script

My scripts talk back to me. No, really! This is a good thing, because I use this communication to get useful information from the script while it's running. It's much better than guessing what's going on. The console provides a seamless and unobtrusive way of accomplishing this.

To send a message from your script to the console, you use the console.log JavaScript method. Just put the text (or other information) you want to see between the parentheses.

1. In Chrome, open the *ogre-console.html* page.
2. Open the console.
3. The feedback text will have already been inserted into the console. You can rerun the page by clicking the Reload button. Example output is shown in the *ogre-console.html* playground script.

In place of the alert pop-up, the script uses the console.log method. You can see that the way you use console.log is similar to the pop-up method:

- The console.log method name
- The text you want to print out in quotes and parentheses
- The ; character to end the line of code

The next example is from the *ogre-console.html* playground script. I'm only showing the important part that has changed—on line 25. I use snips like this often throughout the book in order to save space. The numbered lines correspond to those shown in the Atom (or similar) code editor.

snipped from: ogre-console.html

```
24 <script>
25   console.log ("This is your script speaking!");
26 </script>
```

Note that you must enter the method as console.log, with the dot between. It won't work if you enter just console, or combine the text into one word, consollog.

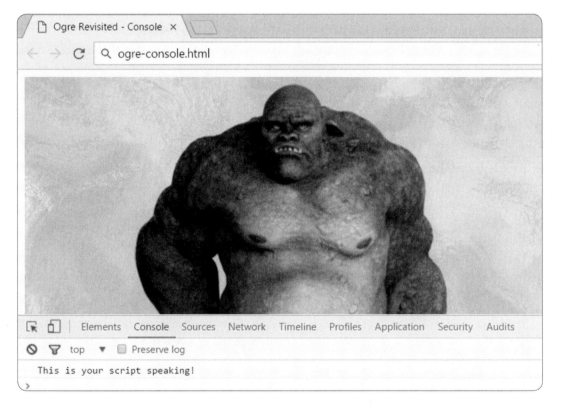

Figure 2-4. Messages from your script can be displayed in the console window.

I've been using the term *method* to describe numerous JavaScript code instructions. At this stage in the book, for the sake of brevity, I'll just say that a method is a kind of programming entity that uses an *object*. In JavaScript, objects are pieces of code that represent things. Objects can be either built-in or self-made by you. Using dots—like in `console.log`—to connect up the various parts of objects is a common thing to do in JavaScript coding.

I cover methods, objects and other related topics much more extensively in Chapters 5 and 6. I bring up the subject now because you'll encounter numerous hands-on examples of these subjects throughout the book.

Viewing Errors

The world would be a poorer place if we couldn't view the errors caused by some glitchy JavaScript we just wrote. Errors are the bane of coding; error messages are the way to challenge and overcome this evil villain.

The best way to demonstrate an error is to intentionally cause one.

1. Open the *ogre-console.html* example in the Atom editor.

2. Modify line 25 by removing the parenthesis near the end of the line. Save the file.

3. With the console window open in Chrome, reload the page. The browser detects an error in the syntax of the script, as shown in Figure 2-6, and duly reports it in big, bold red, telling you "Uncaught SyntaxError: missing) after argument list." As a nice convenience, it also tells you the line number where the error occurred—on line 25—so you know where to go to fix it.

Enough demonstration. You may return the example to its normal self by adding the closing parenthesis back in.

Figure 2-5. Use the console to check for errors.

▶ Talking To Yourself: Using Comments in Script Pages

Comments are notes you can write to yourself about what your script does. Comments are effectively ignored by the browser, so they are a terrific way of writing notes and reminders about the code you develop.

Different parts of the HTML document use different forms of comments:

STYLE Element Comments

Multiple line comments within a STYLE element use the symbols /* and */ for the beginning and ending of the comment. Anything between these symbols is considered a comment.

```
/* Multiple line comments */
/* Can span one

or more lines */
```

HTML Comments

For HTML, insert a comment starting with <!-- and ending with -->. Text between these characters is considered a comment.

```
<!-- HTML can span one line -->
<!--Or can span
multiple lines -->
```

JavaScript Comments

JavaScript supports two kinds of comments, single line and multiple line:

- Single line comments begin with two slash characters, //

  ```
  // This is a single line comment
  ```

- Multiple line comments begin and end with the same /* and */ symbols as the STYLE element. Anything between these symbols is considered a comment.

  ```
  /* This is a multiple line comment-it can span one line */
  /* Or it can go on two
  or more lines */
  ```

Below is a playground file you can open and experiment with:

snipped from: ogre-revisited-commented.html

```
9   <style>
10  #mainContent {
11    width: 600px;
12    height: 600px;      /* Height & width to 600 pixels */
13    overflow: hidden;
14  }
15  /* STYLE comments
16  can span one or
17  more lines */
18  </style>
19  </head>
20
21  <body>
22  <!-- Comments in HTML have their own special format
23  These also can span more than one line. -->
24  <div id="mainContent">
25    <img alt="" src="ogre.jpg" />  <!-- Or go at the end of a line -->
26  </div>
27
28  <script>
29    // Script comments can look like this
30    window.alert ("Presenting the ogre!"); // One line only
31    /* Or they can be multiple-line
32    comments like this, similar to STYLE comments */
33  </script>
```

 When viewed in a code editor like Atom, comments appear in a different shade to set them apart from the rest of the page script. In Atom, the default text style for comments is a light gray, helping you to easily identify them.

Create your first working game in Chapter 3.

WRITING YOUR FIRST GAME

When I was a kid, I invented a complex board game that had so many rules, even I couldn't remember them all.

It's no surprise nobody, including me, wanted to play it! Sometimes the best games are the simplest, particularly when you're just starting out.

In this chapter, you learn how to craft *Number Guess*, a rudimentary number-guessing game—you know, "I'm thinking of a number between 1 and 100. . . ." The rules of the game are simple, as is the coding. It's a good place to begin, so let's get to it.

The tutorial is broken into two playground scripts, which I've identified as Lesson 1 and Lesson 2. Each script develops from the previous one. This building-block approach makes it easier for you to learn coding by breaking down the concepts into separate stages. You can experiment with each stage of development, graduating to the next level when you're ready to discover more.

As always, the completed code for each *Number Guess* lesson is available online; see the Online Support Site for details (Appendix A, page 310). Download all the files for this chapter, unzip them to a convenient place on your computer and dig in.

By necessity, some concepts introduced in this discussion leap forward a tiny bit, referencing ideas and techniques borrowed from chapters to come. This is unavoidable when talking about coding with HTML, CSS, and JavaScript—all three are intensely intertwined.

Don't worry if you don't nail all of the concepts in the first reading. There's a lot to cover here. When practical, I provide cross-references to future chapters should you be interested in flipping ahead. It's not necessary that you do this, however—the chapters in this book are meant to be read sequentially. Give the new ideas time to soak in; there's plenty of opportunity to absorb it all.

▶ Basic Number Guessing—Plain, No Dressing, Low Calories

The first *Number Guess* game is *numberguess-lesson1.html*. This playground script is no frills, but it demonstrates several components that are key to many games. These include:

- Building a user interface for the player to interact with

- Creating a randomness factor

- Storing the player's response and testing it against the random number

- Providing feedback to the player

    To try the game, open it in both the Atom editor and the Chrome browser.

1. If you haven't done so already, fetch the files for this chapter from the Online Support Site. Open *numberguess-lesson1.html* in the Atom text editor.

2. Start Chrome and open the *numberguess-lesson1.html* file (Ctrl+O or Cmd+O; remember, that's the letter *O*, not the number zero).

The *user interface* of the game—the part the player interacts with—is composed of some explanatory text, an input box for entering a number, and a push button labeled *Guess* (see Figure 3-1).

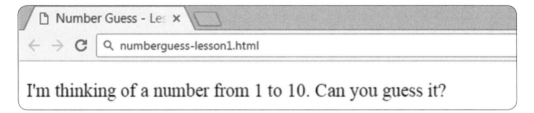

Figure 3-1. The user interface of the basic *Number Guess* game.

---

numberguess-lesson1.html

```
1   <!DOCTYPE html>
2   <html lang="en-us">
3
4   <head>
5   <meta charset="utf-8" />
6   <title>Number Guess - Lesson 1</title>
8   <meta name="author" content="The Gamer's Guide to Coding" />
9   <meta name="dcterms.rights" content=". . .
```

```
10  </head>
11
12  <!-- start of visible page -->
13  <body>
14
15  <p id="prompt">I'm thinking of a number from 1 to 10. Can . . .
16  <input id="guess" type="text" value="" />
17  <input type="button" value="Guess" onclick="numberGuess();" />
18
19  <!-- JavaScript code placed at end of <body> element -->
20  <script>
21
22  function numberGuess() {
23    var randomNumber = Math.floor((Math.random() * 10) + 1);
24    var yourGuess = document.getElementById("guess");
25
26    if (yourGuess.value == randomNumber) {
27      document.getElementById("prompt").innerHTML = "That is . . .
28    } else {
29      document.getElementById("prompt").innerHTML = "Sorry, . . .
30    }
31
32  }
33
34  </script>
35
36  </body>
37  </html>
```

In the preceding code, the ellipses (. . .) at the end of some lines means I've chopped off the code because it's too long to fit on the page. All of the code is provided in the *numberguess-lesson1.html* playground file.

Let's analyze what's in this script and how it works. In subsequent playground scripts, you build on this basic starter game by adding additional features.

HEAD Element

Lines 4 through 10 comprise the HEAD portion of the page. The content is solely informational (example: copyright terms) and for the benefit of the browser displaying the page. (Just as a by-the-way, all playground scripts and bonus games that accompany this book are open-source and may be freely copied, reused, altered, and distributed in accordance to the Creative Commons license.)

BODY Element

Lines 13 through 36 are the BODY element, containing both the visible elements of the page—explanatory text, input box, and button—as well as all JavaScript code.

The visible page elements are defined on lines 15 through 17. There are two types of tags but three distinct types of elements (Figure 3-2):

```
<p id="prompt">I'm thinking...p>
```
I'm thinking of a number from 1 to 10. Can you guess it?

```
<input id="guess" type="text" value="">
```
```
<input type="button" value="Guess"
   onclick="numberGuess();">
```
Guess

Figure 3-2. How the three elements appear.

- The P element displays paragraph text: an instruction to enter a number from 1 to 10.

- The INPUT elements display parts of a form. The script uses two `<input>` tags: one for an input *box* and another for a *push button*. The *type attribute* in each tag (attributes provide additional info about the element) tells the browser the kind of INPUT to display.

- Notice also the `onclick` attribute for the push button INPUT element. This attribute tells the browser to execute specific JavaScript code when the button is clicked with the mouse, or tapped on if using a touch screen.

SCRIPT Element

The JavaScript code is on lines 20 through 34. It primarily consists of a user-defined function, a block of code that is executed only when initiated from someplace else in the script.

- The function has a name: `numberGuess`. It's a name I came up with; user-defined functions can have any name you wish, as long as the name conforms to certain standards, as detailed in Chapter 5: Getting Started with JavaScript: Part 1 (page 67). This function is triggered—"called," in programmer-speak—when the input button is clicked.

- Line 23 produces a random number from 1 to 10. It uses math functionality built into JavaScript. This functionality is quite extensive and is covered more fully in Chapter 18: Using Numbers and Math in Games (page 273).

- Line 24 fetches your guess from the INPUT box. The code does this by asking JavaScript to locate the INPUT element that is identified by the ID name "guess" (it's the INPUT box on line 16). The result of this query is stored in a *variable*, a temporary holding area that stores data. The variable is given a descriptive name—yourGuess—so it can be accessed later in the script.

- Lines 26 through 30 form an if-else test, which performs one of two different actions, depending on the result of the test.

- If the guess and random number match, the script displays congratulatory text.

- If the numbers don't match, the script sends its condolences and tells you the number it had in mind.

▶ Getting a Closer Look at the Code

There's a lot of interesting stuff going on in this script that's common in JavaScript code, so it deserves closer examination. There's a lot to cover here; don't worry, you'll grok all of it soon enough.

Line 15: P Element

Let's begin the detailed look with the P element, which is used to display paragraph text. The format of a P element is pretty simple: `<p>` tags enclose the text you want to print on the screen.

```
<p>This is text to display</p>
```

Numberguess-lesson1.html adds a slight variation to the P element by giving it a unique name, which is prompt. This name allows this P element, apart from any other element on the page, to be uniquely identified later on in the JavaScript code. You'll see how this works in a bit.

Line 16: INPUT Box

The INPUT element is something of a chameleon: It's one tag, but it takes many forms. The *numberguess-lesson1* script uses two of these forms: input box and push button. The type of INPUT element to display is specified in the type attribute.

- When you use a type="text" INPUT element, it creates a box that your player can type into.

- When you use a type="button" INPUT element, it creates a push button that can be pressed in order to invoke some action.

Another attribute of this element, value, specifies any text you want to display in the INPUT box when the page is loaded. There isn't any, so it's left blank. When your player enters a number, that number is stored in the value attribute. Later in the script, JavaScript code checks the value to see what the player typed in.

Line 17: INPUT Button

Line 17 displays a push button. It is a common "action" element that's used on web pages to submit filled-out forms to the server. Although you're not connecting to a server or filling out a form, you can still use INPUT buttons as a way to interact with the player.

The INPUT button element sports two other attributes, value and onclick. Value is the text to display on the button and onclick is an *event listener* that tells the browser what you want to happen when the button is pressed.

The onclick event listener for the INPUT button responds when the push button is clicked. The listener is told to trigger the code in the numberGuess user-defined function as the click response; see Figure 3-3.

Event listeners are *enormously* important. JavaScript can "listen" for various types of signals and respond to those signals when they occur. There's much more to event listeners than discussed here—read about them in Chapters 8 and 12 (pages 127 and 183, respectively).

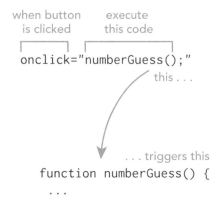

Figure 3-3. How an event listener can trigger JavaScript code.

Line 23: Obtaining a Random Number

Many games are part skill, part chance. The *Number Guess* game is all chance. The game generates a random number from 1 to 10, so you have just a 10 percent chance of making the right guess.

You can read more about random number generation in Chapter 18: Using Numbers and Math in Games (page 273), but for now I want to mention other aspects of this code, because it follows a commonly used pattern. Specifically, the code creates a new variable (recall that variables are temporary holding areas), and that variable is used to store the random number in another part of the code.

To better understand the job of variables, consider this simplistic example:

```
var myNumber = 4;
```

This code creates a new variable named myNumber and assigns it (stores into it) a value of 4. Elsewhere in your script, you can use the myNumber variable as a substitute for the number 4.

You might perform a little bit of arithmetic with the variable and display it in the browser's console window:

```
console.log (2 + myNumber);
```

The result is 6, the sum of adding 2 + 4.

Similarly, the code on line 23

```
var randomNumber = Math.floor((Math.random() * 10) + 1);
```

creates a variable named randomNumber, then stores (assigns) the random number to the variable; see Figure 3-4.

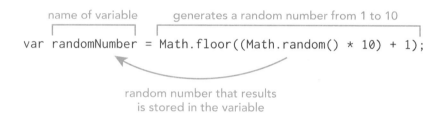

Figure 3-4. How the random number is stored in a variable.

After it's created, the variable is ready for use anywhere else in the script. In the *numberguess-lesson1. html* game, you use the variable twice: Once when comparing the random number to the player's guess, and again to tell the player what the number was should she guess wrong.

Line 24: Grabbing the Player's Response

JavaScript variables can hold much more than just numbers. In fact, a variable can hold an entire HTML element, along with all its associated attributes and other values.

That's exactly what happens on line 24. This line obtains a *reference* to the INPUT box. The box has been given a special name: guess. This name serves as an identifier, and the identifier is used to uniquely locate this element among all the others on the page.

The reference to the entire INPUT box element is socked away inside the yourGuess variable. This reference contains *everything* about the INPUT box.

A *reference* is like the street address to your house. The address isn't the real house, just a method of finding the house in physical space. In JavaScript, references are much the same—they represent things like HTML elements, but they aren't the elements themselves.

When a reference to an element has been stored in a variable, you can use various JavaScript code to ask about and even change things about the actual element—its size, color, position, and much more. This is mighty-cool stuff and something you'll do throughout the examples in this book.

Line 26: Accessing the Value Entered into the Box

As you read, the `yourGuess` variable is filled with a reference to the entire INPUT box element. You're only interested in one small piece: the value that's been entered into the box. This value can be extracted using

```
yourGuess.value
```

This way of formatting is extremely common in JavaScript (as well as many other programming languages).

- `yourGuess is an object`—*objects* are collections of various kinds of data stored as a complete unit. Recall that `yourGuess` contains a reference to the entire INPUT box element. To JavaScript, this element is an object, and if there's one thing JavaScript is terrific at, it's working with objects.

- `value is a property`—*properties* are the separate traits that the object stores about itself (refer to Figure 3-5). Properties are similar to how your physical traits—hair color, eye color, height, and so on—are a part of your makeup.

To obtain a property value from an object, use the name of the object and the name of the property, and connect them with a period:

```
object.propertyName
```

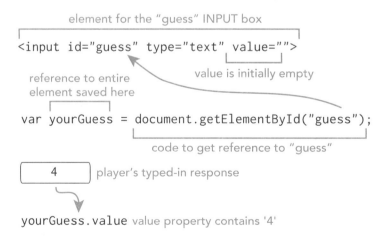

Figure 3-5. Obtaining the value from the INPUT box.

The number entered into the INPUT box is stored in the value property, so to access it, you use yourGuess.value.

Line 26: if Expression

Completing the process is using the yourGuess.value property in an *if-else* test. The test is a good old-fashioned logic problem, also called an *expression*. Expressions can result in either one of two possibilities: true or false. The expression

```
yourGuess.value == randomNumber
```

tests whether the yourGuess.value is equal to the random number stored in the randomNumber variable. Depending on the outcome, the script forks off two different ways; refer to Figure 3-6.

Line 27: if Expression is True

Should the numbers in yourGuess.value and randomNumber match, resulting in the if expression being *true*, then the code on line 27 is executed. This code changes the content of the P element at the top of the page with a congratulatory message.

Line 29: if Expression is False

But should the numbers in yourGuess.value and randomNumber *not* match, the result of the if expression is *false*. In this case, the code changes the content of the P element to tell the player his guess was wrong.

Lines 27 and 29: Change the P Element Contents

Here's where things get interesting and show off some nifty JavaScript magic.

Match or no match, the code on these lines literally reach into the P element and replace the original text there with something else. The wizardry is this piece of code:

```
document.getElementById("prompt").innerHTML
```

You've already seen how JavaScript can obtain a reference to a particular element when that element has been given a unique name. For the P element, that unique name is prompt; the code

```
document.getElementById("prompt")
```

obtains the reference to the P element by this name (see Figure 3-6).

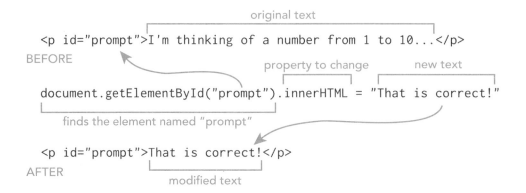

Figure 3-6. Using the innerHTML property.

From there, the code accesses a property of this element, innerHTML. As its name suggests, the innerHTML property defines the HTML text of an element. For a P element, this is the text that goes between the <p> and </p> tags.

The game starts out with

```
<p>I'm thinking of a number from 1 to 10. Can you guess it?</p>
```

and, using JavaScript, the text is programmatically changed to something else, depending on the player's correct (or incorrect) number guess.

HTML text is somewhat different than plain text. You can manipulate both with JavaScript. HTML text can contain other HTML tags, whereas plain text can't.

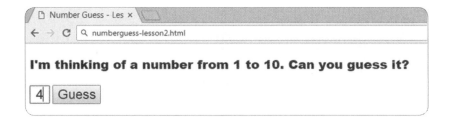

Figure 3-7. The *Number Guess* game with a new style.

▶ Enhancing the Number Guess Game with Styling

The visual look of the basic *Number Guess* game is pretty boring. With only a few alterations, however, you can achieve a brand-new look—a different font, a larger push button, a refined input box. See the example in Figure 3-7.

The *numberguess-lesson2.html* playground example uses the same HTML tags and JavaScript as the first lesson. The only changes are additions to the CSS portion of the page. The style sheet is inserted right before the </head> tag. Because this is the only code that changes, I show just a snip of the script below.

snipped from: numberguess-lesson2.html

```
11 <style>
12
13 p {
14   font-family: "Arial Black", Gadget, sans-serif;
15 }
16
17 input {
18   font-family: Arial, Helvetica, sans-serif;
19   font-size: 1.1em;
20 }
21
22 #guess {
23   border: 1px solid red;
24   width: 30px;
25   text-align: center;
26 }
27
28 </style>
```

STYLE elements contain one or more *selectors* that pair with the HTML elements used in the page. Each selector comprises a set of style *rules*. The rules are contained inside { and } brace characters, as noted in Figure 3-8.

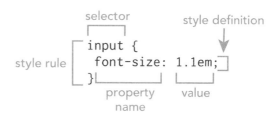

Figure 3-8. The makeup of styles and style rules.

The P Tag Rule

Let's start with the style rules for the P tag:

```
p {
  font-family: "Arial Black", Gadget, sans-serif;
}
```

This rule tells the browser that, when it comes to fonts, any P tags in the document are to be styled in Arial Black (for Windows), or Gadget (for Macintosh), or generic sans-serif for machines that don't recognize these fonts, or don't have the fonts installed.

The INPUT Box Rule

```
input {
  font-family: Arial, Helvetica, sans-serif;
  font-size: 1.1em;
}
```

The INPUT box element contains a rule with two properties: font and font size. For the box the font is regular—not extra-heavy—Arial (common in Windows) or Helvetica (common on Macintosh).

The font size is specified in ems—an *em* is a relative-size unit based on the default or normal font size for that element. A size of 1.1em is 10 percent larger than the default font for that element.

The #guess ID Rule

```
#guess {
  border: 1px solid red;
  width: 30px;
  text-align: center;
}
```

The #guess rule applies only to the element that matches id="guess", which is the INPUT box. The box gets its style from *two* rules: from the generic input selector and also from the #guess selector. The styles are combined:

- Specific font (Arial for Windows, Helvetica for Mac, sans-serif for other)
- Font size of 1.1em
- Thin red border around the box
- A controlled width of 30 pixels
- Horizontally centered text alignment

The rules themselves are composed of a *property name* followed by a *value* for that property. For example: `width: 30px;` specifies a width of 30 pixels. There can be more than one value for a property: `border: 1px solid red;` sets three properties at one time: a 1-pixel solid border, colored red.

There are three main types of selectors, as shown in Figure 3-9:

```
img { width: 30px; }
                              tag selector
<img alt="" src="dog.jpg"/>


#cat { width: 40px; }
                              id selector
<img id="cat" alt="" src="cat.jpg"/>


.mouse { width: 40px; }
                              class selector
<img class="mouse" alt="" src="mouse.jpg"/>
```

Figure 3-9. Three main types of style selectors.

- *Tag* (or type) selectors match specific tags used on the HTML page. These are specified simply by their name—p for the `<p>` tag and input for the `<input>` tag, for example.

- *ID* selectors match an element with the same ID. Only one element on the page can have that ID, but you can have as many different IDs on a page as you want. ID selectors start with the # (hash) symbol.

- *Class* selectors match elements with that style name. Unlike IDs, which must be unique for each element, you can use the same classes for multiple elements on the page. Class selectors start with the . (period) symbol.

There are more types of rules than just these, such as *keyframe* rules used in animation. These are covered throughout the book as they are introduced.

Be sure to play with the playground code to see how changes affect the look and operation of the script.

COMMON HTML ELEMENTS AND WHAT THEY DO

HTML elements are the things you can see on-screen when you play a JavaScript game on a browser. Despite all the action and adventure in your game, it takes only a very small assortment of HTML elements to get the job done.

The past several chapters introduced HTML elements and the way they are used to display things on-screen. In this chapter, you'll learn more about the common HTML elements you're most likely to use and how they work. The discussion of HTML elements isn't long or complex; I don't need to talk about all the elements that HTML has to offer, because you don't need all that many to create a good JavaScript game.

Note: A certain amount of coverage in this chapter is review. Some information is repeated here as reinforcement because it's so important for an understanding of coding in HTML and JavaScript.

▶ Core Elements

There are just four principal elements that define a basic HTML page. The elements are indented to show the hierarchy, the way the elements are subordinate to their neighbors. See Figure 4-1 for a structural view of how these elements relate to one another.

Note: These four elements aren't the only ones you'll encounter in a typical HTML page, but they're the ones that form a kind of backbone for everything that follows.

```
<html>
 <head>
  <title></title>
 </head>
 <body>
 </body>
</html>
```

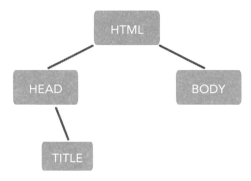

Figure 4-1. Basic structural view of the core HTML elements.

Although HTML elements provide the means to specify *what* to show on the screen, there's much more involved in controlling *how* these elements appear.

A web browser follows built-in rules regarding the way elements are meant to arrange text and graphics (referred to simply as the *content*) on the screen. You can override these rules and specify your own appearance should you not like the browser's built-in default display. In fact, you'll do this quite a bit in games you develop. As you discovered in Chapter 1: Starting at Square One (page 13), this is why game coding using web page technology involves three interconnected parts:

- HTML elements to define the components on the page

- CSS styles to redefine how those elements present the content

- JavaScript to give the games interactivity and smarts

▶ Structure of an Element

As noted in Chapter 2: A Closer Look at HTML Script Pages (page 25), HTML is composed of *tags*. There are paired tags and unpaired tags (see Figure 4-2).

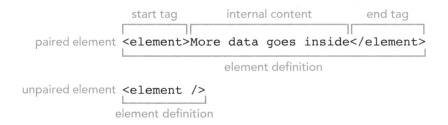

Figure 4-2. Paired and unpaired HTML tags.

For *paired* tags:

- `<name>` is called a start tag. The name part defines the function of the tag, such as head or body.

- `</name>` is called an end tag. It closes up the tag structure. For every start tag, there must be a matching end tag.

- Everything between `<name>` and `</name>` is considered an element. The `<body></body>` tag pair is referred to as the BODY element. (All caps are used merely as a convention to help you quickly identify the purpose of the element.)

For *unpaired* tags, there is only

```
<name>
```

The browser understands the tag as being self-contained. In this book, I explicitly denote the tag as unpaired by including a / character before the closing > angle bracket:

```
<name />
```

Modern browsers, and even many HTML code validators, will not complain if you use > instead of />. However, I include the closing slash for all unpaired tags as a matter of consistency.

There are actually only a few unpaired tags. Just four are used in this book:

- `<img />` ▶ Displays an image
- `<br />` ▶ Inserts a line break into text or an extra space between elements
- `<input />` ▶ Inserts one of many types of "objects" used to create fill-in forms
- `<meta />` ▶ Provides metadata of the page for use by search engines and other tools

If you review HTML code, including the examples accompanying this book, you will also see the following at the top of each page:

```
<!DOCTYPE html>
```

As noted in earlier chapters, technically this is a *directive*, also known as a "declaration," and not an element. It specifies the page as conforming to the HTML5 specification. All of the example scripts and games in this book are designated as HTML5-compliant.

▶ Elements Combined to Make a Page

The elements you use and their order (the *markup*), combine to make the HTML page. Better to show than just tell; Figure 4-3 demonstrates such a page containing the more common HTML elements you'll use in most any game. It's all actually pretty simple—check out the *basicstructure.html* playground page:

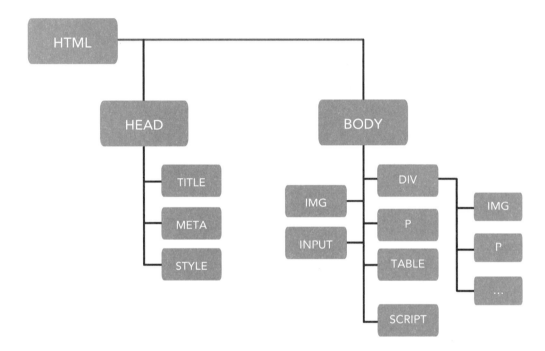

Figure 4-3. Plan-o-matic version of the most common HTML elements you'll likely use, and how they relate to one another.

- A set of HTML elements inside the BODY specify the content of the page

- Some STYLE rules indicate how many of those elements are to appear

Note: For this demonstration, there's no SCRIPT element. I've added a couple of inline HTML comments to provide some additional info.

HTML Element

The HTML element is the root of the page. Except for the <!DOCTYPE html> directive noted above, all content goes inside the <html></html> tags. The element is used as a "parent container" for everything else.

HEAD Element

The HEAD element contains *metadata* about the page. This metadata is conveyed using three principal tags:

- TITLE: <title></title>

  Gives the page a name. The name appears in the browser's top bar, or in a tab.

- META: <meta />

  Provides additional information about the page for search engines and other cataloging purposes.

- STYLE: <style></style>

  Describes "rules" that change the appearance of other elements on the page. What goes into the STYLE element is pretty important stuff, so it gets its own chapter. See Chapter 7: Controlling the Look of Your Games with Styles (page 107) for more details.

BODY Element

None of the previous elements display anything in the browser's window (well, okay, the TITLE element shows the title of the page at the top of the browser). It's the job of the BODY element to serve as a container for other elements that place things inside the browser's main document window.

▶ Visual Elements

As noted above, browsers are designed to display—or *render*—HTML elements that are enclosed between the <body> and </body> tags. The browser renders the elements in the order they appear in the page markup, starting at the top of the window and moving down.

Use the *basicstructure.html* playground page to experiment and see what happens. Open the file in the Atom editor (which you installed on your computer in Chapter 1), and switch around the order of the elements. Feel free to change the wording of the text and make other alterations to see what they do.

```
<div>

<img alt="" src="image3.jpg" /><img alt="" src="image4.jpg" /></div>
```

▶ HTML Comments (Not Elements You See in the Browser)

If you look at many HTML pages, you'll likely come across a funny-looking element that looks like this:

```
<!-- this is actually a comment -->
```

Although comments use the < and > brackets and are elements to the browser, their purpose isn't to display anything on the screen. Instead, they're notes that you can write to yourself and others who review your code.

- Start the comment with <!-- (no spaces)
- End the comment with --> (again, no spaces)

Text between the markup symbols is treated as a comment and is not processed by the browser. Comments can span many lines.

▶ Elements for Displaying Text

The P element is the standard container of text. (In truth, other types of tags can also serve as holders of text, but the P element is considered the go-to solution.) Between the <p> and </p> tags go the text you want to display:

```
<p>This is an example of a P tag.</p>
```

P stands for paragraph, so when multiple P elements are strung together, the browser formats them as separate paragraphs with slight spacing between.

```
<p>This is the first paragraph of text.</p>
<p>This is the second paragraph of text.</p>
```

The BR element supplements text display by inserting a line break—a line break continues the text on the next line but doesn't start a new paragraph the way that the `<p></p>` tags do.

```
<p>This is an example<br />of a BR tag.</p>
```

The BR element can also be used outside of text, serving as a line break to add more space between any elements above and below it.

▶ IMG Element for Displaying Images

The IMG element is designed to explicitly show an image. In HTML, images aren't embedded into the page; the pictures are always separate files. The HTML provides only a *reference* to the image file, and it's the job of the browser to combine the picture with the text and other content on the page.

```
<img alt="" src="image.jpg" />
```

The IMG element uses two required *attributes*. These attributes provide additional important information that the browser needs to display the image.

src Attribute

The `src` attribute specifies the *source* of the image. In this example, the location of the source is relative to the HTML page, so it's referred to as a *relative file reference*. The term *relative* means the browser will look for the picture starting from wherever the HTML file currently resides.

If the image file is not located with the HTML file, you must to provide enough information to the browser so that the file can be located. For example:

```
src="./assets/image.jpg"
```

fetches the image from a subfolder named *assets*. This subfolder is under the *current folder*, the one that contains the HTML file being processed. This is also a relative file reference because the indicated location is relative (starts from) the HTML page.

Compare with:

```
src="http://www.example.com/pictures/image.jpg"
```

which fetches the image from a site on the web. This is an example of an *absolute file reference*. The source points to a very specific place.

alt Attribute

The alt attribute provides text as an alternative to displaying the graphic image. The attribute is primarily intended for use with screen-reader software for the visually impaired. The alt attribute describes the image for those who may not be able to see it.

For graphical games, it makes little sense to use the alt attribute to describe a picture—its size, shape, location, and other aspects are critical to the playing of the game. However, you must still include the alt attribute or else your HTML page will not pass validation muster—the page will not be considered to be fully HTML5-compliant.

You may leave the attribute empty, as in

```
alt=""
```

Or use it as a way to hold transient data during game play:

```
alt="50"
```

where the "50" might mean the current point value for the character depicted in the image.

▶ DIV Container Element

If there's a workhorse in the HTML library of elements, it's DIV. Its primary role: a generic container for other elements and content. But you can also use it to define "zones" where the player can interact with the game. One such zone is an invisible button that sits on top of a picture, like an image of a skull or a rock. The player thinks that she's clicking on the skull or rock, but instead, she's really clicking on an invisible DIV.

Specifying an empty DIV element

```
<div></div>
```

displays nothing. To have the DIV itself actually show—for example, with a colored background or a border—you must add styling rules that define how the DIV is to appear. With a style, you can also give width and height to the DIV, position it precisely in the game where you want it, or even display an image inside it.

You can read about how to use styling in Chapter 7: Controlling the Look of Your Games with Styles (page 107) and in many examples throughout this book.

To use a DIV as a container of other elements, you merely place those elements between the <div> and </div> tags:

```
<div>
 <img alt="" src="image.jpg" />
</div>
```

The IMG element is now nestled inside an otherwise invisible DIV contain element.

- When an element is placed between the tags of another, it becomes a child of that element.

- And conversely, when an element contains other elements, it is considered a *parent* of those other elements.

The advantage of using a container element: You can manipulate the container and its children go for the ride. For example, using JavaScript or a style, you can change the left property (X or horizontal) and the top property (Y or vertical) position of the DIV container. This moves the container, as well as all its children.

▶ INPUT Element

The INPUT element displays a number of different visual *objects* used to build fill-in forms for web pages. These forms may include text boxes, push buttons, checkboxes, color pickers, and images.

For game design, the INPUT push button object has the most universal appeal. It creates a clickable button that you can place anywhere on the page. When the button is clicked, JavaScript code that performs some meaningful task can run.

The HTML markup to define a button using INPUT is

```
<input type="button" value="Click Me" />
```

which creates a basic gray button with the phrase "Click Me" on it. Or to define a button with an image in it (see Figure 4-4).

```
<input type="image" src="image.jpg" alt="" />
```

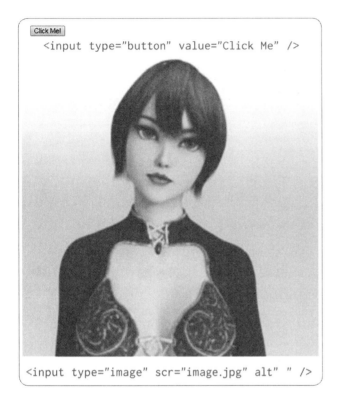

```
  ┌─────────┐
  │ Click Me! │
  └─────────┘
    <input type="button" value="Click Me" />
```

`<input type="image" scr="image.jpg" alt" " />`

The INPUT element has three required attributes, depending on the object type:

- The `type` attribute specifies the INPUT object (e.g. "button").

- A secondary attribute, either `value=` or `src=`, provides ancillary information that supplements the object type.

- And an INPUT image, a third required attribute specifying the `alt` (alternative) text for screen-reader software.

Figure 4-4. The INPUT element can create both text and image buttons.

type Attribute

The `type` attribute specifies the object type you wish to create with the INPUT element. I only talk about INPUT buttons and images here, but if you're interested in the other types, visit the Online Support Site (Appendix A, page 310) for reference guides that list all of the available INPUT element objects.

`type="button"`

produces a gray button. Specify the text in the `value` attribute.

`type="image"`

produces a button filled with an image. Specify the image file in the `src` attribute.

value Attribute (for type="button")

The `value` attribute specifies the text to display on top of an INPUT button.

src Attribute (for type="image")

The `src` attribute specifies the image file you wish to display inside the button.

alt Attribute (for type="image")

The alt attribute specifies alternative text to display in place of the graphic. For INPUT images, the alt attribute should contain printable text, even if it's an X or a space.

INPUT elements were originally intended to be used to build fill-in forms, like "Contact Us" pages, in which you provide your name and email address and then get a lifetime supply of spam. The form connects to software running on the web server, which receives the data when the user clicks "Submit." The server digests the user's input, storing it in a database.

In JavaScript game design—at least the kind described in this book—there's no web server on the other end to collect information. Everything is done using JavaScript code. As you'll discover in future chapters, clicking an INPUT button or image can trigger JavaScript code that causes some response in the game, such as to start or pause play, to fire a missile, or to perform some other action.

▶ SCRIPT Element

Use the SCRIPT element to embed JavaScript code in a page. The element can contain the actual JavaScript code, or it can contain a link to an external file that contains JavaScript.

To include *inline* JavaScript code using a SCRIPT element:

```
<script>
 // JavaScript code goes here . . .
</script>
```

To link to an external file that contains JavaScript code:

```
<script src="myjavascript.js"></script>
```

Before HTML5, good coding practice suggested that you include a type attribute for inline script tags, like so:

```
<script type="text/javascript">
```

In HTML5, using the attribute in the <script> tag is optional. I leave out the attribute in keeping with the current trend.

Your page can have multiple SCRIPT elements, and it can use a mixture of inline and external references. Be careful about the order and placement of SCRIPT elements. You may get an error if your JavaScript references an HTML element that comes after the code.

▶ Block or Inline Elements

HTML elements that are used to render content are defined as either *block* or *inline*. The difference comes into play when a browser renders the element using its built-in style rules.

- *Block elements* start on a new line and span the full width of the content window. They don't allow other elements on the same line. DIV is an example of a block element.

- *Inline elements* start on whatever line is current and only occupy as much width as they need to. IMG is an example of an inline element.

These behaviors apply to the default render styles for any given element. You can override these styles and take full control over either size and position, just by themselves or in relation to other elements on the screen.

You can learn more about these techniques in Chapter 7: Controlling the Look of Your Games with Styles (page 107), but here is a preview (see Figure 4-5 for how these look in the browser):

DIVs on Separate Lines (default behavior)

```
<div>This is a line of text</div>
<div>This is a separate line of text</div>
```

DIVs on the Same Line

```
<div style="display:inline;">This is a line of text</div>
<div style="display:inline;">This is now on the same line</div>
```

DIVs Precisely Positioned

```
<div style="position:absolute; left:10px">This is a line of text</div>
<div style="position:absolute; left:250px">More text here</div>
```

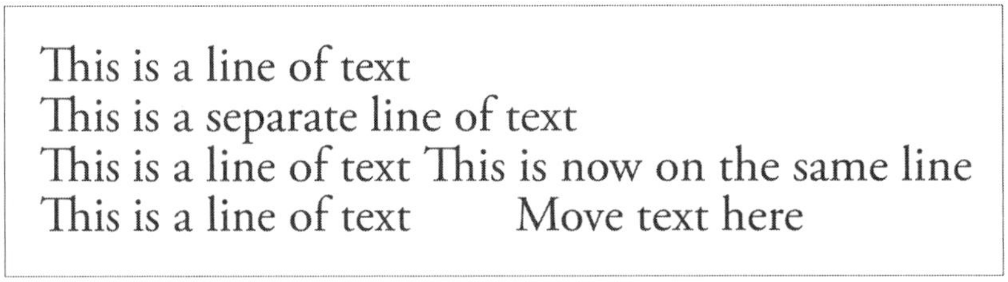

This is a line of text
This is a separate line of text
This is a line of text This is now on the same line
This is a line of text   Move text here

Figure 4-5. Effects of changing the display property.

The net result: Regardless of the default rendering of an element, you can make it behave just the way you want by applying styles.

▶ Global Attributes for All Elements

In addition to the required element-specific attributes listed above, HTML elements can also accept so-called *global attributes*. These attributes provide a way to uniquely identify the elements used on the page and to specify styling rules that change the appearance of the element when rendered in a browser. Of primary importance are the id, class, and style attributes (Figure 4-6).

Figure 4-6. Global attributes are common to all elements.

id Attribute

The id attribute gives the element a name that uniquely identifies it among all the other elements on the page. The attribute is used both in applying CSS styles and for manipulating the element using JavaScript.

The format of the attribute is

```
<element id="name" . . . >
```

where name is the unique identifier you want to use for that element. The name should be just one word (no spaces) and, to avoid confusion, should not be the same as an HTML tag. No other element on the page should use the same ID.

class Attribute

The class attribute lets you categorize elements into groups for use in CSS styling and JavaScript coding. You saw an example of it in the preceding discussion of inline versus block elements.

The format of the attribute is

```
<element class="name" . . . >
```

where name is the class name you want to use. As with the id attribute, the class name should be a just one word (no spaces) and should not be the same as an HTML tag. Other elements on the page can share the same class name.

style Attribute

The `style` attribute lets you specify inline styles for the element. As you've already discovered, styles are used to modify the appearance of the element beyond how they are normally rendered by the browser. These styles can be applied using the STYLE element, as demonstrated in the *basicstructure.html* playground script, or by using the `style=` inline style attribute.

The format of the attribute is:

```
<element style="property:value; property:value. . .;" . . . >
```

Each `property:value` pair specifies a style definition. You can string together many `property:value` pairs by separating each with a ; (semi-colon) character. (However, if there are more than two or three `property:value` pairs in a `style` attribute, it's better to put them in a separate STYLE element. Read Chapter 7: Controlling the Look of Your Games with Styles [page 107] for more details.)

▶ Global Event Attributes

Nearly all HTML elements support *events*—things that happen to the element that can trigger a piece of JavaScript code. Perhaps the most common event is for the mouse-click: Click on an element, and something is made to happen.

Element event attributes all start with the word *on*—as in `onclick` or `onmouseover`—the event name is emblematic of what the event is for and is referred to as the *event listener*. The JavaScript code that is executed when the event occurs is called the *event handler*.

The format of an event attribute takes several forms. One of the more commonly used is:

```
<element onsomething="eventHandler();" . . . >
```

- `onsomething` is the actual event listener, such as `onclick`.

- `eventHandler` is a JavaScript function you've defined elsewhere on the page that is executed when the event occurs.

There are other forms of event attributes; see Chapter 8: Responding to Events: Part 1 (page 127) for more details.

▶ Attribute Order

HTML does not impose any rules regarding the order of the attributes. Both of these elements produce identical results:

```
<img id="dracula" class="vampire" alt="Scary Monster" src="dracula.jpg" />
<img alt="Scary Monster" src="dracula.jpg" class="vampire" id="dracula" />
```

With that said, you'll probably want to develop a general scheme for the order of attributes in the elements you use. Being consistent makes coding easier and helps to avoid mistakes. *In general,* I try to place global attributes in the following order:

- id
- class
- style

and then follow up with element-specific attributes, also in a consistent order:

- for images: follow with alt, src
- for input buttons: follow with type, value (or src)

and then finally, any event attributes.

▶ Other Tags of Merit

There are more HTML elements, of course, and many of these are designed for use in general web pages. A few have specific or limited use in game design, so they're not covered here.

If you want to learn more about all the HTML elements,
check out the Online Support Site (Appendix A, page 310)
for a list of additional reference sources.

PART TWO

LEARNING THE ROPES

GETTING STARTED WITH JAVASCRIPT: PART 1

JavaScript is a programming language that has become the standard way to manipulate the appearance and content of browser-based script pages.

As with any language, the way you use JavaScript determines whether the browser understands what you're trying to say. To program with JavaScript, you need to learn how to "speak" it.

In this chapter, you begin a fast-paced tour of JavaScript fundamentals: What JavaScript code is; how it is structured; the purpose and use of variables; how to use expressions to make "thinking" code; the art and science of functions; and more. Because there's too much to discover about JavaScript in a single sitting, you'll continue your expedition in Chapter 6, aptly titled, "Getting Starting with JavaScript: Part 2" (page 91).

For this book, I concentrate on browser-based scripting using Google Chrome. It's not that Chrome understands JavaScript better than other browsers—it's that by settling on a standard, your learning experience can be both simplified and enhanced. JavaScript can behave a little differently in various browsers. For this book, you are encouraged to use the latest version of Google Chrome for all your JavaScript game development.

▶ Syntax

Syntax is the grammar of coding; it's the rules that dictate how the various parts of code are placed and formatted in the script. If you fail to follow the rules of syntax, your script may not work, or it may work in ways you don't expect. You have to fix the error and try again.

Programming Statements

Think of *programming statements* as any of the words you see in a script. Statements are the road signs that make JavaScript do things and behave in certain ways.

The family of statements can be broken down into individual types, such as "keywords" or "methods," but it's not important to understand the nuances of these variations just to use the language. I may use certain terms throughout the book to specifically refer to a particular type of programming statement, but when you're just starting out, you don't have to memorize all these different types.

Statement lines (see Figure 5-1) are created when one or more individual parts of code are coupled together to form a kind of "complete thought" for JavaScript. A statement line ends with the ; line-termination character. JavaScript runs this code as a complete unit.

```
programming
  statement
    ┌──┐
    var title = "Awesome Guide to Coding";
    └──────────────────────────────────────┘
            statement line
```

Figure 5-1. A JavaScript programming statement.

Case Sensitivity

JavaScript is a *case-sensitive* language. The names of things in JavaScript code must use consistent capitalization. If you name something *MyMonster* at the beginning of the script but later refer to it as *mymonster*, the code will fail because these two names do not match.

Punctuation and White Space

In English and many other languages, punctuation serves as a way to break up words into finite parts to make the text easier to understand. Commas separate phrases, periods separate sentences, and new lines separate paragraphs.

In JavaScript, spaces, tabs, and hard returns (made by pressing the Enter key) are all treated as *white space* (Figure 5-2); to JavaScript, these all look the same. This is unlike some other languages, such as Python, where specific whitespace like spaces and tabs are important to the way the program runs.

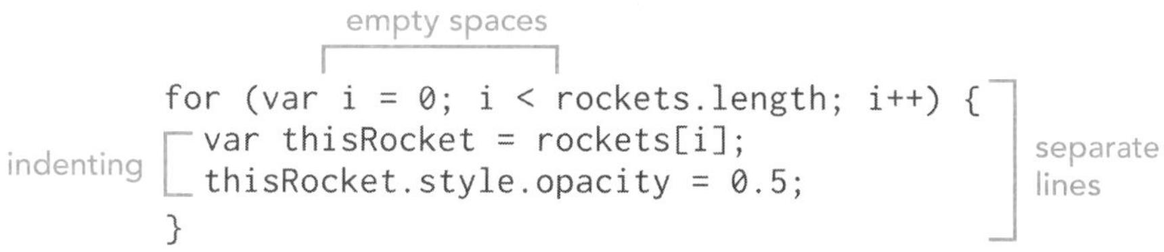

empty spaces

```
for (var i = 0; i < rockets.length; i++) {
    var thisRocket = rockets[i];
    thisRocket.style.opacity = 0.5;
}
```

indenting

separate lines

Figure 5-2. JavaScript ignores white space when running code.

In JavaScript, spaces, tabs, and hard returns (made by pressing the Enter key) are all treated as *white space* (Figure 5-2); to JavaScript, these all look the same. This is unlike some other languages, such as Python, where specific whitespace like spaces and tabs are important to the way the program runs.

Instead of whitespace, punctuation characters are used to help JavaScript sort things out, to help it understand the message you're trying to get across.

- The ; (semi-colon) character denotes a new line and is how JavaScript can understand the separate steps of the code.

- The { and } brace characters define a *block*, a grouping of JavaScript code elements that are meant to be treated as a unit. There can be—and often are—blocks within blocks; the basic rule is that for every { character, you must have a matching }.

- The (and) parentheses work as a lasso to group integral parts of code together. Parentheses might contain an *expression* (see "Expressions and Operators" later in this chapter), which is a math or logic problem that the code must resolve before going on, or the parentheses might contain a list of numbers that are to be added or subtracted.

Comments

Not everything in a script is meant to be processed by the computer. *Comments* are human-readable notes inserted into the code and are used as notes or reminders for your benefit.

There a two forms of comments in JavaScript—single-line and multiple-line:

- Single-line comments begin with two slash // characters. Any text after these characters, up to the next hard return, is a comment and is not part of executable code.

- *Multiple-line comments* begin with the character sequence /* and end with */. Any text within these markings, regardless of hard returns, is construed as a comment.

Examples:

```
// This is a single line comment
/* This is a multiple line comment
and it can span one or more lines */
```

Tokens

Token is a generic term for any valid symbol or word in JavaScript code. A token might be the + character, used when adding things together, for instance. An important part of tokens is their order in the code: When tokens *out place of are*, JavaScript has no clue what you're trying to say—just as you have difficulty understanding the phrase *are out of place* when the words are jumbled up.

Consider this bit of arithmetic:

```
+ 5 1
```

when you really meant to write

```
5 + 1
```

The term *token* is something you see a lot of when reviewing ill-behaving code in the browser's console window (for more about the console window, refer to Chapter 2: A Closer Look at HTML Script Pages [page 25]). If JavaScript encounters syntax it doesn't understand, it may reference *Unexpected token* and specify the errant symbol or other element that's causing confusion.

Keywords

Keywords are a type of JavaScript statement that has been reserved for exclusive use by the language. Because of their importance to the underlying functionality of the language, keywords are often referred to as *reserved words*. JavaScript keywords include `if`, `while`, `var`, `this`, `let`, `for`, and many others. I won't list them all here; many are detailed in context through this chapter and the ones that follow; see also the Online Support Site (Appendix A, page 310) for a reference guide to the current list of JavaScript keywords/reserved words.

▶ Viewing Syntax Errors

JavaScript will nearly always tell you when your code contains a syntax error (I say "nearly always" because the odd exception can occur). To see if your code is not following the rules of syntax, open the console window in a desktop version of the Chrome browser (Shift+Ctrl+J in Windows; Shift+Cmd+J in OS X), then:

1. Click the Console tab if it's not already selected.

2. Reload the page and watch for any errors in the console. Errors are clearly indicated.

Figure 5-3. An error in the console window.

▶ Data Types

Computer programs deal with data. At its lowest level, all data is just a set of binary digits—0s and 1s. Coding in only binary is an extraordinarily difficult task, so languages such as JavaScript define many kinds of higher-order data and give them names so their purpose can be better understood.

JavaScript works with many kinds of data, but these four stand out as central to using the language:

Number

Number data holds a numeric value that can be used in an arithmetic calculation: 2 is a number that, when added to 3, results in 5. Internally, JavaScript stores all numbers the same way, but outwardly, in your scripts, these numbers can represent

- Whole values (called integers)
- Floating-point values (a number with a decimal point)
- Positive and negative values

String

String data is text, either one character or many—the term *string* comes from the analogy of adding text characters together like beads on a string. String data cannot be used in an arithmetic calculation (at least, not without additional manipulation).

String data has many unique features. Read more about them in Chapter 6: Getting Started with JavaScript: Part 2 (page 91).

Boolean

Boolean data has only two possible values: true or false. The name comes from George Boole, a mathematician who first promoted an algebraic system of logic during the nineteenth century.

Undefined/Null

In JavaScript, as in many coding languages, "nothing" has a specific value and is distinct from the numeral zero. JavaScript uses the concept of "nothing" to denote the existence, or non-existence, of data. JavaScript supports two "nothing" data types:

- undefined ▶ the reference to the data does not exist (it's like giving a bogus street address— 123 Main Street, when there is no such house)

- null ▶ the reference to the data exists but the value of the data has not yet been set

Some resources refer to JavaScript as an *untyped* programming language. The term can be confusing when talking about the "different kinds of data" JavaScript can work with—if JavaScript is "untyped," how can it discern between things like numbers and text strings?

JavaScript does indeed deal with different types of data, but it does so in an automatic, or *dynamic*, way. In some programming languages, you must first specify the kind of data you wish to use before creating that data. JavaScript does not require this. You merely define the data you want, and JavaScript will infer what it is by its attributes. More about this concept in "No Defined Types for Variables" later in this chapter.

▶ Variables

Variables are holding areas for data. When placed in a variable, the contents of that variable can be retrieved and used later in the script. Any of the data types listed on the previous pages can be stored in a variable (plus many other kinds of data, as we'll see throughout this book).

Variables are given names so that they can be referenced later. Imagine a variable as an envelope, like that in Figure 5-4. Inside the envelope goes the data you want to keep; on the outside of the envelope you write a name so you can identify what's inside and use it when you want.

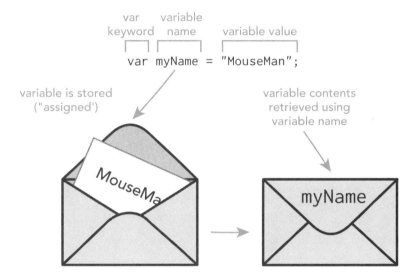

Figure 5-4. Variables hold data for later use.

 Variable names are a form of *identifier*, and the naming restrictions are the same for the other types of identifiers used in JavaScript. These identifiers include things like user-defined functions and objects. You'll learn about these in this chapter and in the one that follows.

The names of variables are up to you. There are a couple of rules when giving variables their names:

- The name must start with a letter, _ (underscore), or $.

- Numbers are okay if the name doesn't start with one. A valid name is `MyVar1`, but not `1MyVar`.

- Variable names are case sensitive. A variable named `MyVariable` is treated as distinct from `myVariable` and any other variation.

- No spaces. Variable names must be one word, without any spaces.

Adapting a Consistent Variable-Naming System

Every JavaScript coder has his or her favorite method for naming variables (and other identifiers). Some like to preference everything with `my` or `My`, as I often do in introductory examples—`MyVariable`, `MyStuff`, `MyNumber`. For these simple examples, I use it to remind you that the name is user-derived; you get to choose it.

However, for actual code, I prefer to give variables a name that describes its use or function in the script. A variable used to hold the score of the game might simply be called `score`.

For variables created out of multiple words strung together, I like to use a naming convention common with many JavaScript coders, so-called *camelCase* capitalization—"low at the ends, high in the middle." The initial word starts with a lowercase letter, and each of the remaining compound words start with an uppercase letter. Examples:

- `gameOver`
- `shipInterior`
- `playerPenalty`

Assigning and Referencing Variables

To use a variable, you must first define it. This is done with

```
var myVariable;
```

which defines (creates) the variable but doesn't fill it with a value. You can later supply that value, or you can both define and assign the variable all in one go.

```
var myVariable;
myVariable = 5;
```

does the same as

```
var myVariable = 5;
```

Both processes are forms of variable assignment. The second method is the most straightforward and the one you'll likely use most. It tells JavaScript you want to both define a variable named myVariable, and assign it a value of 5.

The var keyword informs JavaScript that you wish to create a new variable. You use it only when preparing a new variable.

Later in the code you may refer to the variable (this is called a *variable reference*), and the value of 5 is substituted for the variable:

```
myVariable + 1
```

results in 6, the sum of 5 plus 1.

No Defined Types for Variables

Briefly mentioned above, but here it is again: JavaScript variables do not use defined data types. That means, unlike some other coding languages, you don't have to first specify what kind of data the variable will contain—number or string or whatever. You just assign the value to the variable, and you're done.

Depending on your point of view, this either makes coding easier, or it introduces the potential for errors. I won't debate the merits of JavaScript *typeless* variables other than to note a few potential issues you need to be aware of.

First and foremost is JavaScript's use of *type coercion*, a fancy phrase for the automatic process of converting (or "promoting") one type of data into another. This is most-commonly done in expressions (see "Expressions and Operators," later in this chapter) and when adding number values.

Consider:

```
var MyNumber = 5;
var MyString = "5";
```

Add these two together with

```
MyNumber + MyString
```

and the result may be surprising! Instead of the value of 10—5 + 5—you get 55. JavaScript has coerced (converted) MyNumber to be a string, combining it with the textual contents of MyString.

You can largely avoid these problems by being careful in the way you assign values to variables. If you intend to add two numbers together, be sure only actual numbers are assigned to those variables. Don't use strings that look like numbers—the two are different.

You can also force JavaScript to either not perform the automatic coercion, or you can provide your own conversion to ensure that the data is the type you intend. Examples of both methods are described throughout this book.

Changing the Contents of Variables

After a variable has been defined and assigned a value, you can change its value as much as you like later on in code.

```
var myVariable = 1;                    // Start out with value of 1
// Some other code here
myVariable = 5;                        // Updated with value of 5
```

Note that you don't use the var keyword when updating the value of a variable. The var keyword is only used when first defining the variable.

▶ Expressions and Operators

An *expression* is a number or logic problem that JavaScript must resolve before it can continue. *Operators* are symbols used in expressions. Operators define what to do with the numbers and other data that are part of the equation. For example, the * character is an operator that means to multiply two numbers:

```
2 * 5
```

There are two broad, commonly used types of operators:

- Mathematical Operators ▶ used to calculate some result using numbers
- Logical Operators ▶ used to determine if something is true or false

▶ Conditional Testing

A *conditional test* uses Boolean logic to determine whether an outcome is either true or false. The most common form of conditional test is the JavaScript if statement

```
if (expression) {
 // do this if the expression is true
} else {
 // do this is the expression is false
}
```

An example expression is testing whether the value in a variable is equal to, less than, or greater than some known value. Suppose a variable named MyVal contains the number 7. You use logical operators to determine whether the value in MyVal is equal to, greater than, or less than some other value:

```
if (MyVal == 7)          // result is true; 7 equals 7
if (MyVal > 8)           // result is false; 7 is not greater than 8
if (MyVal < 10)          // result is true; 7 is less than 10
```

Notice the equality operator is ==, and not =.

= ▶ assigns a value to a variable.

== ▶ tests for equality.

A common newbie mistake is to write the conditional test as

```
if (MyVal = 7)
```

which always results in the same thing: *True*. This may seem odd, but here's why: The expression MyVal = 7 *returns* (results in) 7. In JavaScript, the number 0 means false; any other number means true. You can avoid this problem in either of two ways:

- Just be careful about using the == equality operator in expressions. The habit is not a difficult one to develop, and as you learn JavaScript, you can remind yourself to be aware of it.

- When practical, reverse the order of the expression; 7 == MyVal is allowed by JavaScript and yields the result you want, but 7 = MyVal is flagged as a syntax error that you can see in the browser's console window.

▶ Order of Progression

JavaScript starts at the beginning of a script and progresses one statement line at a time until it reaches the end of the code. This requires that the script be organized so that the code follows a logical *progression*. The sequence has to be correct, or errors can result.

Consider this script, which results in "undefined" in the browser's console window:

```
console.log (MyVal);
var MyVal = "hello";
```

The error occurs because the `MyVal` variable has been referenced before it has been assigned. The execution progression is in the wrong order. To fix the mistake, you must flip the statements:

```
var MyVal = "hello";
console.log (MyVal);
```

The console window now says "hello," as you intended. Of course there are some exceptions to this rule, with user-defined named functions topping the list. Functions are described later in this chapter.

▶ Looping Code

JavaScript lets you repeat the same code two or more times in what's called a *loop*. Looping is a way to save code space and simplify your scripts.

The most common loop is made with the JavaScript `for` statement—see Figure 5-5 for an example. You specify the number of times you want the loop to repeat. Code you wish to repeat is placed inside the block defined by the { and } characters.

A quick example of the `for` loop is:

```
for (var i = 0; i < 5; i++) {
 console.log ("Number is: " + i);
}
```

This code counts between 0 to 4 and prints out a series of five lines in the browser's console window:

```
Number is: 0
Number is: 1
Number is: 2
Number is: 3
Number is: 4
```

Note: The control parts of the `for` loop are separated by semicolons—not commas as you might expect. There's a reason for this: Each of the control parts is really a separate statement line. They are often traditionally combined in one line, as shown here, to save space.

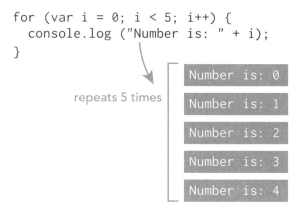

```
for (var i = 0; i < 5; i++) {
  console.log ("Number is: " + i);
}
```

repeats 5 times

```
Number is: 0
Number is: 1
Number is: 2
Number is: 3
Number is: 4
```

Figure 5–5. Loops repeat code.

Understanding the Control Parts

Let's take a closer look at the three control parts of the `for` loop.

```
var i = 0;
```

creates a new variable named `i` and assigns the initial value of 0 to it.

```
i < 5
```

is an expression that controls the end of the loop. The loop continues as long as `i` is less than 5.

```
i++
```

increments the value in the `i` variable by one each time the loop goes through. The first time through the loop, `i=0`, the second time `i=1`, and so on.

Counting by Other Values (Step By)

The above is a good example of counting by 1s. You can count by other values as well: by 2s, 5s, 10s, 100s, whatever. For this, change the *iterator control* to increment by another value. For example:

```
for (var i = 0; i < 25; i += 5) {
 console.log ("Number is: " + i);
}
```

The iterator is

```
i += 5
```

which is shorthand for "add 5 to whatever is already in the i variable."

▶ A Common Use of the for Loop

One of the most common uses of the for loop is to iterate through a collection of HTML elements based either on their class name or their tag name. For example, in the following playground script (*loops.html*), three P tags are inserted into the HTML of the page.

snipped from: loops.html

```
16 <p>Some text goes here.</p>
17 <p>More text goes here.</p>
18 <p>And even more text goes here.</p>
```

Using a for loop, you can round up all those P's and do something to them. This script merely pulls out the text of each P element and displays it in the console.

```
35  var paras = document.getElementsByTagName("p");
36  for (var i = 0; i < paras.length; i++) {
37    console.log (paras[i].innerHTML);
38  }
```

Line 35 produces a collection of P tags stored in the paras variable. It does this using a feature that queries the HTML document to round up all the P elements that are on the page.

What's inside the paras is formally known as an *array*. It contains three separate variables, one for each P element in the document. You'll read more about arrays in the next chapter, but for now, just make note that each value in an array is numbered, and the numbering starts at 0.

Lines 36 through 38 comprise the for loop. The loop iterates through each component in the paras array, printing out its contents.

Note the code paras[i] on line 37. Each time through the for loop, the i variable is incremented by 1. The numbering starts at 0, so the first time through, i = 0. The code references the first part (called an *element*) in the paras array—this is paras[0]. The second time through, the code references the next element in the paras array, paras[1], and so on.

Another example is to make those three P elements disappear, which you might do in your game code when you set up the game before first play:

```
42  var paras = document.getElementsByTagName("p");
43  for (var i = 0; i < paras.length; i++) {
44    paras[i].style.visibility = "hidden";
45  }
```

Using the while Loop

The while loop is another way to repeat a series of code. The control method of a while loop is simpler than the for loop, and it is also easier to mess up. The structure of the while loop is

```
while (expression) {
  // repeat this part
}
```

where as long as expression results in a *true* condition, the while loop continues. When the expression results in a *false* condition, the loop ends.

Here's a trivial example that counts from 0 to 4.

```
var i = 0;
while (i < 5) {
  console.log (i);
  i++;
}
```

Here's how it works:

The first line sets up the control variable, named i.

The while loop is formed by creating a block of code using the { and } braces, which spans the remaining lines. Code inside this block is to be repeated.

The control expression is i < 5, meaning the loop is repeated as long as i is less than 5.

The i control variable is incremented by 1 each time through the loop using i++.

Some Important Points About while Loops:

It's *entirely too easy* to construct a while loop that never ends. The code finds itself in an infinite loop, which is probably not what you intended. You often have to exit the browser to regain control.

Unlike the for loop, where the control method is part of the loop, with while you have to create all the aspects of the control yourself. In the above example, variable i is used to control the iterations of the loop. It's first set to 0, and each time through the loop, its value is incremented by 1. The expression i < 5 evaluates to *true* as long as i is less than 5.

If you accidentally leave out a mechanism to increment the control variable, *the loop will never stop!* So be careful. If you do ever accidentally do this, you may have to force-quit your browser in order to return things to normal.

Using the do/while Loop

A variation of while is the do/while loop. The structure of do/while is hauntingly familiar:

```
do {
 // repeat this part
}
while (expression)
```

The do/while loop differs in that the control expression comes at the end; because of this, the code inside the loop is guaranteed to be processed at least once. This contrasts with the while loop, where the loop is skipped over and never executed if the control expression evaluates to *false* first time around.

Example:

```
var i = 0;
do {
 console.log (i);
 i++;
} while (i < 5);
```

The control mechanism for the do/while block is the same as the while example above, except that the control expression comes at the end of the loop.

- **Which loop to choose ▸** The three types of loops—for, while, and do/while—perform similar tasks, but how they go about it is different, and so are the possibilities.

- **Stick with a for loop for most jobs ▸** They're less likely to result in endless loops.

- **If you want to manage when the control variable is incremented, use while or do/while ▸** In a for loop, the control variable is always incremented at the start of the loop. With while and do/while, you can increment the control value at the start of the loop, at the end, or anywhere between. You can even increment the control value more than once. This flexibility can come in handy for more esoteric forms of coding.

▸ Functions

Functions are self-contained bits of JavaScript code. Among their many uses, functions allow you to:

- Organize code so you can keep better track of it

- Reuse the same code any number of times, from different parts of the script

- Develop common code bits that you can insert into different games

JavaScript supports several types of functions, each with subtle and not-so-subtle differences from one another. In this book, I limit the use of functions to two main types: *named function declarations* and *anonymous functions*. In this chapter, I introduce only named function declarations. Anonymous functions are described in numerous examples throughout the book.

There are two steps in creating and using a named function declaration (Figure 5-6):

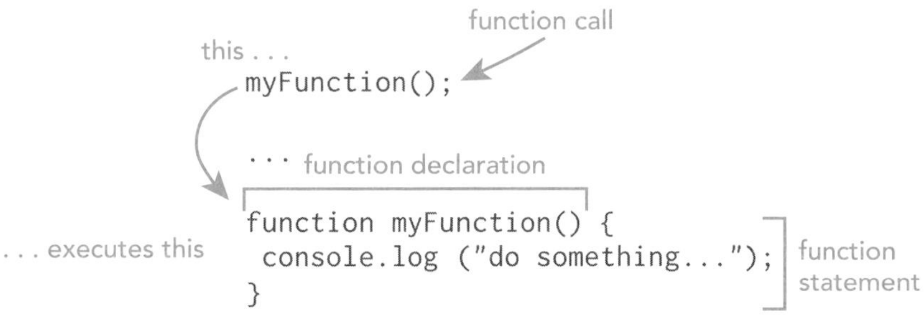

Figure 5-6. The parts of a named function.

Declare the Named Function and the Code That Goes in It

Functions are created—or *declared*—using a specific but easy-to-use syntax:

```
function myFunction() {
 // Stuff in here is the function body
}
```

To declare a named function, you use the function keyword, a function name you make up followed by () characters, and a set of braces that form the function body. Code within the braces is what gets executed. This entire piece of code is known as the *function statement.*

Call the Function Somewhere Else in Your Code

With the function defined, you can now *call* it using a calling statement. This is what actually executes the code inside the function. To call a function you just reference it by name—don't forget the parentheses:

```
myFunction();
```

You can repeat this call at any place in your script where you want to execute the code in the function. This means you can readily reuse the same function many times in a script. This saves space by not repeating its code each time.

Where Named Functions Go in the Script

As you read in "Order of Progression" earlier in this chapter, JavaScript code should be arranged in the order you want the script to be executed. For the most part, the script begins at the top and runs down to the end, where it finally stops. An exception to this rule is the named function declaration, which acts as a kind of code island. Named functions do not need to be organized in order of execution. The definition of the named function can appear anywhere. It's the placement of the calling statement that matters.

All this is made possible because of the way JavaScript "hoists" the function definition to the top of the code when the script is loaded into the computer's memory. You can't see this hoisting—it's all done internally.

What this means is that you're free to place function definitions where you like in your script. Still, for the sake of consistency, you should pick the top or bottom and stick with it. (I like to place named functions toward the bottom of the code.)

Hoisting rules vary depending on the type of function, and the results can sometimes be confusing, even to more-experienced programmers. This is why, especially for a beginner's book like this one, I limit the type of functions used in the examples to just the two types I mentioned above.

Other types of JavaScript functions work in different ways. If you go poking around the Internet and find examples of other types of function, don't automatically assume they'll all behave the same way. My comments above pertain to named function declarations.

Using Function Parameters

Parameters are variables that you can *pass* into a function. You might create a function that adds two numbers together. Those numbers are *passed* to the function as parameters, like so:

```
function addMe (number1, number2) {
 console.log (number1 + number2);
}
```

The values number1 and number2 are parameters. A function can have up to 255 parameters, though it's more common to have far fewer than that, or even none at all. Inside the function, the parameters act as variables. You can use them just as you would any variable.

When you call the function, you provide *arguments* that match the parameters expected by the function. For the addMe function, you might call the shebang like this:

```
addMe (1, 2);
```

When the function is executed, it prints the answer 3 in the browser's console window.

Returning Values from Functions

Sometimes you want a function to execute its code and send back a value. You can then use that value in another part of your code. This process is referred to as *returning* a value from a function. An example is a random-number generator, which supplies a random number—say, from 1 to 10.

In JavaScript, all functions return a value. That value is *undefined* unless you explicitly tell JavaScript you want to return something else. Use the return statement to have JavaScript return a specific value from a function:

```
function addMe (number1, number2) {
 return number1 + number2;
}
```

To call such a function, you might do this:

```
var result = addMe(1, 2);
console.log (result);
```

or more succinctly, without defining the middleman `result` variable:

```
console.log (addMe(1, 2));
```

Both print 3 in the browser's console window.

Sharing Variables Inside and Outside of Functions

In JavaScript, variables follow strict rules of *scope*—no, not mouthwash; it's a system that dictates how variables may be shared in different parts of the code. Scope has the most meaning in relation to functions. Here are the basic rules:

- A variable defined inside a function is *visible* (can be used) only within that function. Any code outside that function—including other functions—is not able to access the variable. This is referred to as *local scope*, or because it relates specifically to functions, as *function scope*.

- A variable defined in the main body of the script—that is, outside any functions—is visible anywhere in the script, including inside any functions. This is referred to as *global scope*.

If you need to access a variable both inside and outside functions, simply declare it at the top of your code in the main body of the script:

```
var myGlobalVariable;              // Declaration only
```

or

```
var myGlobalVariable = "abc";      // Declaration and assignment
```

It's best to avoid creating too many global variables. Use function parameters if you need to share specific values with a function (refer to Figure 5-7).

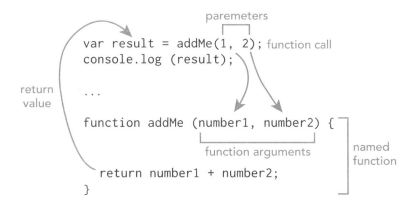

Figure 5-7. Use function parameters for cleaner code.

This:

```
addMe(1, 2);
function addMe (number1, number2) {
 console.log (number1 + number2);
}
```

is better than this:

```
var number1 = 1;
var number2 = 2;
addMe();
function addMe () {
 console.log (number1 + number2);
}
```

USING let INSTEAD OF var

You already know about the var keyword, used to define a variable. Many newer browsers support an updated version of JavaScript that provides a second way of defining variables: the let keyword. The let and var keywords do much the same basic job of defining a variable, but they do it in somewhat different ways.

Declaring variables with var produces either global- (entire script) or function-level variables, where the variable declaration is "hoisted" to the beginning of the script or function.

Consider this code:

snipped from: var-or-let.html

```
console.log (dog);
var dog = "dalmation";
```

When JavaScript runs this script, it internally modifies it to be

```
var dog;

console.log (dog);
dog = "dalmation";
```

where the declaration and assignment are functionally separated. This is why, when you run the code, you get "undefined" in the browser console rather than a complaint that the dog variable doesn't exist.

Conversely, variable declarations are not hoisted when using let. The following code displays a bona fide error message in the console window because cat is referenced before it's been defined:

```
console.log (cat);
let cat = "maine coon";
```

Another main difference: The **let** keyword operates in what's known as block-level scope. Recall that blocks are created in JavaScript using the { and } brace characters. Only code inside the particular block can see a **let** block-level variable:

```
for (var i = 0; i < 5; i++) {
 console.log ("Number: %s", i);          // Prints 0 through 4
}
console.log ("Last number: %s", i);      // Prints 5
for (let j = 0; j < 5; j++) {
 console.log ("Number: %s", j);          // Prints 0 through 4
}
console.log ("Last number: %s", j);      // Error: j is not defined
```

You can use this feature to effectively insulate variables from trampling over one another.

All of this begs the question: **let,** or **var**—which is better? In their proper contexts, both are fine. I (somewhat reluctantly) elected to use only the **var** keyword in examples in this book, because it's far more common in code you'll find on the web. I didn't want the use of **let** to be a source of unnecessary confusion. You are free to set your own rules for your JavaScript code. Just be aware that the **let** keyword isn't supported in older browsers, so use care to avoid broken code if your games are played on antiquated systems.

We'll continue the JavaScript conversation in Chapter 6,
Getting Started with JavaScript: Part 2 (page 91).

GETTING STARTED WITH JAVASCRIPT: PART 2

This chapter picks up where the last one left off and continues your excursion into JavaScript.

If you haven't read Chapter 5 yet, you'll want to do so now before carrying on with this one (page 67).

▶ Strings

In Chapter 5, you learned that *strings* are collections of one or more characters, like beads on a string—hence the term. Strings are commonly used to communicate with your player. You'd use a string to display a "Game Over!" sign, for instance.

Making a String

The most direct way of creating string data is to simply specify it as part of the script's output:

```
console.log ("This is a string of characters.");
```

A value entered by typing it directly into the script is called a *literal*. The same technique can be used with numbers, Boolean values, and other JavaScript data types.

More often than not, you'll want to assign a literal string value to a variable.

```
var myString = "This is a string of characters.";
```

The variable myString now contains the text, *This is a string of characters*. You can use the variable in place of the literal string.

```
var myString = "This is a string of characters.";
console.log (myString);
```

You can also make a string by using new String. This method explicitly produces a *String object*. The previous method produces what's known as a *primitive string type*. Read more about how they differ in "Differences Between Primitive Strings and String Objects" later in this chapter. You can also read more about JavaScript objects in the section "Objects" later in this chapter.

```
var myStringObject = new String("This is a string of characters.");
```

Using Single or Double Quotes for Strings

JavaScript lets you define a string using either single-quote or double-quote characters. Both of these do the same thing:

```
var stringA = "this is a string";
var stringB = 'and so is this';
console.log (stringA + stringB);
```

Neither method is better as far as JavaScript is concerned. All that matters is that you use the same type of quote characters to both begin and end the string.

You can use this feature to your advantage to display ' and " quote marks as part of the string. For example, if you want to show "double quotes" in the string, surround the whole string with single quotes, and simply type in the double quotes:

```
var stringB = 'this "is" a string';
```

You'll probably want to develop a habit of using one form of quote mark over the other. I prefer to use double quotes because I find it easier to see the marks when the code is printed. But you can, and should, develop your own methods based on your personal preferences.

Combining Strings

Sometimes you have two (or more) strings and you want to combine them together. JavaScript provides a couple of methods for doing this, but the easiest is to simply use the + (plus) operator, like so (see Figure 6-1):

Figure 6-1. Use the + (plus) symbol to add strings together.

```
var text1 = "this is ";
var text2 = "a test";
console.log (text1 + text2);                    // Prints 'this is a test'
```

Making Long Strings

You can also use the + operator to build up very long strings that span many lines of code. The trick is to append a + character at the end of each line except the last one. Like this:

```
var myLongText = "Four score and " +
  "seven years ago our fathers " +
  "brought forth on this continent a " +
  "new nation, conceived in liberty, " +
  "and dedicated to the proposition " +
  "that all men are created equal."
console.log (myLongText);
```

Using String Properties and Methods

Data assigned to a variable carries with it information that tells JavaScript how to manage and work with that data. This information is called *properties*. For a string of text, an important property is *length*, which—as its name implies—tells you how many characters are in that string.

To use a string property, you use *dot notation* to specify both the variable you wish to work with and the name of the property, like so:

```
var myString = "this is a string";
console.log (myString.length);                    // Result is 16
```

    myString ▶ the name of the variable.

    length ▶ the name of the property.

    The . (period or dot) ▶ separates the two pieces.

In a similar vein are *methods*. These are "actions" that can be performed on the data in the variable. There are a gaggle of string methods, some more commonly used than others. I'll describe just a few here.

toUpperCase method—Making the Text ALL CAPS

Use the toUpperCase method to capitalize all the characters in the string:

```
var myString = "this is a string";
console.log (myString.toUpperCase());             // Result: THIS IS A STRING
```

As you'd imagine, there's a companion toLowerCase method that makes all the characters lowercase.

substr method—Get Just the First (or Last) Characters

Use the substr ("sub string") method to extract just a portion of the string:

```
var myString = "this is a string";
console.log (myString.substr(0, 7));              // Gets first 7 characters
```

indexOf method—Get Location of Specified Text

Use the indexOf method to get the starting location of a character or text fragment. The method returns −1 if the text/fragment can't be found.

```
var myString = "this is a string";
console.log (myString.indexOf("a"));              // Result: 8
console.log (myString.indexOf("Alfred"));         // Result: -1
```

In the first example, the result is 8: The letter *a* is found at character position 8. In the second example, the result is −1: The text fragment *Alfred* is not in the string.

Notice something here: All methods use parentheses. For some methods, one (or more) *parameters* specify additional details the method needs to complete its task. Example: For indexOf, you need to specify the text you wish to find within the string.

Several methods have optional parameters that can be omitted. When they are, JavaScript applies a default value. There are *waaaay* too many methods, parameters, and options to cover here. I provide several handy references for this stuff on the Online Support Site; see Appendix A (page 310) for details.

Strings Start at Zero

In JavaScript, strings are stored in memory one character at a time. Each character occupies a numbered space, like in a parking lot. As shown in Figure 6-2, these spaces are numbered starting at 0, not 1. Bear this in mind whenever working with strings. You witnessed this in the previous example:

```
var myString = "this is a string";
console.log (myString.indexOf("a"));          // Result: 8
```

JavaScript tells you the *a* is at position 8. But if you count the characters starting at 1, you'll get 9 instead. To effectively use strings in your coding, you need to get into the habit of counting from 0.

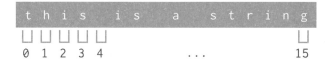

Figure 6-2. Strings characters start at position 0.

Differences Between Primitive Strings and String Objects

As noted earlier in the chapter, JavaScript supports creating two kinds of strings:

```
var myString = "string";                  // Creates a primitive string
var myString = new String ("string");     // Creates a String object
```

Being simpler creatures, primitive strings are often computationally faster, so many JavaScript coders prefer them. But there's a potential snag: Primitive strings don't have any properties or methods associated with them.

Not to worry—if you use a property of method on a primitive string, JavaScript automatically "promotes" the string to a full String object. This process is called *auto boxing*, and is completely transparent to you. In the end, you can create a primitive string type and still enjoy all the benefits of String objects.

You can always explicitly create a String object using the `new String` statement, but be prepared for subtle differences. Rather than recount the differences here, I provide several online references you can review on the subject of String objects. Refer to the Online Support Site (Appendix A, page 310) for more details.

▶ Arrays

An *array* is a collection of variables stitched together to make a single unit. Each individual variable is placed into a separate *element* of the array. Elements are numbered, starting at 0. An array with a total of five elements will have five variables, numbered 0 through 4 (see Figure 6-3). As you go through this section, be sure to experiment with arrays by fiddling with the *arrays.html* playground script.

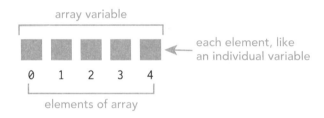

Figure 6-3. The concept of an array variable.

Creating an Array

You can create an array and fill it using the following simple syntax:

```
var myArray = ["Element 1", "Element 2"];
```

`myArray` is the name of the array. The elements you wish to pack into the array are placed within [and] bracket characters. The value of each variable element is separated by a comma; this example shows two elements, each containing a string. Therefore, the `myArray` array contains two elements.

This is an example of defining an array using literal data—you type it directly into the code editor. The literal method requires you to know ahead of time what elements to fill into the array. You can also create an empty array and then "push" new elements into it.

```
var myArray = [];
myArray.push("Element 1");
myArray.push("Element 2");
```

There are many other ways to create and fill an array. I'm not going to iterate all of them, but simply note that there are alternatives.

Getting a Value from an Array

To get a value from an array, you use its name followed by the element number you wish to access, enclosed inside [ ] bracket characters. The following code retrieves the contents of element 1 (the second element) of the myArray array (see Figure 6-4):

```
console.log (myArray[1]);                        // Prints 'Element 2'
```

Remember: element numbering is zero-based. If you want the very first element of the array, use myArray[0].

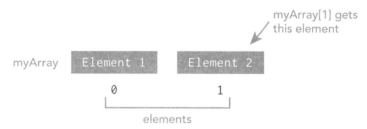

Figure 6-4. Specify the array element you want by referencing its number.

Changing the Value of an Array Element

By specifying an element of the array, you can update the value of just that element. Simply use:

```
myArray[1] = "Replacement Element";
```

Using Array Properties and Methods

Just as with strings, JavaScript supports several useful properties and methods for arrays. You've already seen one method in action: push, which "pushes" a new element onto the end of an existing array.

As with strings, arrays also have a length property. But in this case, length tells you how many elements are in the array:

```
var myArray = ["Element 1", "Element 2", "Element 3"];
console.log (myArray.length);                          // Result: 3
```

Several methods for arrays are indispensable, and you're likely to use them quite a bit in your code. Here's the short list:

push Method: Add a New Element to the End of an Array

You've already seen the push method in action, but here it is again. Simply specify the contents of the new element, and JavaScript does the rest.

```
myArray.push("Element 4");
```

Most methods—for arrays or otherwise—return a result value when you use them. You can capture that result and use it in other parts of your code. In the case of the push method, the result of the action is the new length of the array.

```
var myArray = ["Element 1", "Element 2"];
var newLength = myArray.push("Element 3");
console.log ("The array now has %s elements", newLength);
```

pop Method: Remove an Element from the End of an Array

Inverse to push is the pop method, which grabs the last element in the array and removes it. The resulting return value of the method is the removed element. When you pop an element, the array is truncated accordingly and its length is reduced by 1.

```
var myArray = ["Element 1", "Element 2"];
var removed = myArray.pop();
console.log (removed);                          // Prints 'Element 2'
console.log (myArray.length);                   // Prints 1
```

fill Method: Create an Array and Pre-fill All Elements with the Same Value

Use the fill method as a quick way to fill each element of an existing array with the same value.

```
var myArray = new Array(10);          // Make an array with 10 elements
myArray.fill(0);                      // Fill each element with a zero
console.log (myArray);
```

This example also demonstrates an alternative method for creating an array, using the new Array statement. After the Array keyword, specify the number of elements in the array.

The new Array statement builds the array with the specified number of elements; each element is empty and undefined. The fill method populates each element of the array with an initial value. The idea is that elsewhere in your code, you can then update an element by writing a new value to it:

```
myArray[5] = 100;  // Changes element 5 to 100
```

indexOf Method: Find an Element in an Array

Use the indexOf method to determine if the array contains a certain unique value, such as a name or number. The value returned from the indexOf method is the array element where the first match is found. If the value is not in the array, the method returns −1.

```
var myArray = ["red", "green", "blue"];
var element = myArray.indexOf ("blue");
console.log ("'Blue' found at index: %s", element);
```

Difference between Declaring an Array and Defining Its Elements

The method you use to declare an array determines how its elements are initially defined. Some methods of declaring arrays build the array, but the array has no elements. This can cause errors if you try to access elements that don't yet exist. For example,

```
var myArray = [];
```

only declares the myArray array. The array has no elements, as demonstrated with

```
console.log (myArray.length);                 // Result: 0
```

Conversely,

```
var myArray = ["red", "green", "blue"];
console.log (myArray.length);                    // Result: 3
```

not only declares the array, but fills it with elements at the same time.

The steps of declaring an array and defining the elements of the array can be separated. This is a highly useful feature, but it can also cause confusion to new coders. Adopting a standardized practice helps reduce possible errors.

■ If you don't know the elements ahead of time, use the first method:
  ▶ Declare an empty array, and, in code, use the push method to add the elements you want.

■ If you know the elements of the array ahead of time, use the second method:
  ▶ Define the elements along with the array declaration.

▶ Objects

If you thought arrays were fun (and they are!) you're going to love JavaScript objects!

Like arrays, JavaScript *objects* are containers for data. Objects are a further refinement of the array concept. With objects, data is naturally stored as *key/value* properties, like that in Figure 6-5. Provide the name of a key, and JavaScript goes into the object to pull out the property associated with that key.

You've actually already seen JavaScript objects at work: Arrays are objects, as are strings created with the new String statement. To access the data in an object, use dot notation to reference the object name and its property:

```
objectName.propertyName
```

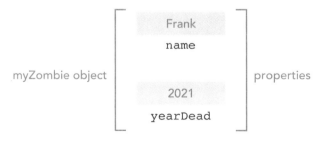

Figure 6-5. The idea behind the object key/value data pair.

As with arrays, objects also have methods, and these methods are referenced using the same dot notation. Recall that methods are actions that the object can perform on the data it contains.

JavaScript supports a number of built-in objects, such as the Date and Math objects. Discover more about these in the handy JavaScript language reference links I provide on the Online Support Site (Appendix A, page 310). For now, let's concentrate on how to create your own objects.

Creating Your Own Objects

You can quickly and easily create new objects in JavaScript and stuff them with various bits and pieces of information (properties), and you can even create clever functions that manipulate this data (methods). There are many ways to make objects in JavaScript. I'll cover a few of the more common ones and give examples. You can try out many of these techniques in the *objects.html* playground script.

Using new Object

Build a brand-new object by using new Object:

```
var myZombie = new Object();
```

You can then add properties and methods simply by coming up with suitable names and filling in their values.

```
myZombie.name = "Frank";
myZombie.gender = "male";
myZombie.food = "brains";
myZombie.yearDead = 2021;
```

Here, you've created four properties and given those properties names and values. Later in your JavaScript code, you can retrieve this data by specifying the object name and the property you want.

```
console.log (myZombie.yearDead);                    // Result: 2021
```

To create a method for the object, define a *function* to the property name (See Chapter 5: Getting Started with JavaScript: Part 1 [page 67] for more details about functions).

```
myZombie.intro = function() {
 return this.name + " likes to eat " + this.food;
}
```

Then, when you want to access this method,

```
console.log (myZombie.intro() );
 // Result: Frank likes to eat brains
```

Notice the parentheses after the intro method name. The parens are necessary to tell JavaScript that you wish to call and execute the function itself, rather than just return the definition of the function— yeah, it's weird, but that's how it works. If you forget the () parentheses, JavaScript dutifully returns the function definition, instead of the function result.

So you may be asking, "What's with the this in the object function?" As used here, this is a special keyword that basically ties the name and food properties to the current object. If you were to leave out the this and write only name or food, then you'd get an error when the script is run. JavaScript needs a specific *context* to know how to apply these properties. The this keyword does precisely—umm—this.

Creating an Object Implicitly

You can also define an object implicitly, using {} brace characters. The new Object statement is not required.

```
var myZombie = {name:"Frank", gender:"male", food:"brains", yearDead:2021};
console.log (myZombie.yearDead);
```

This method looks similar to the one you use to define an array. But instead of [] brackets when making an array, for an object you enclose the property definitions in {} brace characters.

In many ways, arrays and objects are quite similar—in fact, in JavaScript, arrays are a type of object with specific properties and methods attached to them. Trimmed to their basics, the main differences are that

- Objects ▶ containers for named values

- Arrays ▶ containers for numbered values

Defining an object all on one line saves coding space but makes the object definition harder to read. So feel free to use the classic, indented formatting, where each property is placed on its own line:

```
var myZombie = {
 name: "Frank",
 gender: "male",
 food: "brains",
 yearDead:2021
};
```

This is the same object as before, but now it's more readable. Make note of the commas: There should be a comma after each property name/value except for the last one.

Using a Constructor Function

And yet another method is to create a *constructor function*. This is a preferred method when you have many objects you'd like to create from a single "template" that defines the structure of the object.

First, define the constructor function:

```
function Zombie(name, gender, food, yearDead) {
 this.name = name;
 this.gender = gender;
 this.food = food;
 this.yearDead = yearDead;
}
```

And then, elsewhere in the code, call that function to create a new object:

```
var myZombie = new Zombie("Frank", "male", "brains", 2021);
console.log (myZombie.yearDead);                                // Result: 2021
```

To define more zombies, just add more new Zombie statements, each with their own properties.

By convention, constructor functions use names that start with a capital letter. Zombie is the *object constructor type*; myZombie is a new object based on the Zombie constructor type.

▶ Events

Events are things that happen on the web page that can in turn trigger JavaScript code. Events are part of a push model that frees JavaScript from having to constantly check whether some condition is met—did the player click on that button yet? No, okay, check again in another tenth of a second. . . . That's not very efficient.

Besides clicking on things, common events include moving the mouse, pressing a key, or when the complete page finishes loading.

There are two parts to dealing with an event (see Figure 6-6):

▪ Indicating which event to listen for

▪ Specifying how the event is to be handled

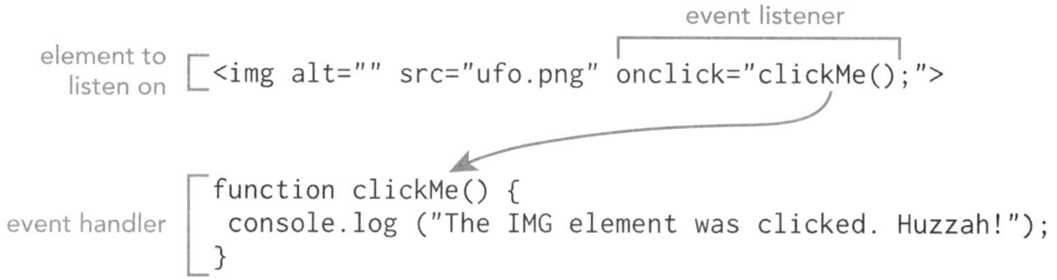

```
                                                    event listener
                                              ┌─────────────────────┐
 element to   ┌<img alt="" src="ufo.png" onclick="clickMe();">
  listen on   └


 event handler  ┌ function clickMe() {
                │   console.log ("The IMG element was clicked. Huzzah!");
                └ }
```

Figure 6-6. JavaScript events components: listener and handler.

Any HTML element can have an *event listener*. There are several ways to attach a listener to an element. Here's one:

```
<img alt="" src="ufo.png" onclick="clickMe();">
```

The code onclick="clickMe();" is an attribute, and adds an onclick *event listener* to the IMG element. The attribute specifies a JavaScript function, clickMe, elsewhere on the page to execute when the mouseclick occurs. The clickMe function is the *event-handler*. Its code runs when the image is clicked on.

```
function clickMe() {
  console.log ("The IMG element was clicked. Huzzah!");
}
```

Another common way to add an event listener is using the addEventListener method. When using this technique, there's nothing added to the element to be listened on:

```
<img alt="" id="myImage" src="ufo.png">
```

Instead, everything is done in the JavaScript code itself:

```
myImage.addEventListener("click", clickMe);
function clickMe() {
 console.log ("The IMG element was clicked. Huzzah!");
}
```

For more information on using the **addEventListener** method, go to Chapter 8: Responding to Events: Part 1 (page 127) and Chapter 12: Responding to Events: Part 2 (page 183).

CONTROLLING THE LOOK OF YOUR GAMES WITH STYLES

Games that have an attractive appearance are more likely to be played, and the player is more likely to enjoy the experience. Using styles, you can alter and control every aspect of your game's look.

Styles are part of the triumvirate of web page scripting: HTML, JavaScript, and (CSS), and as such are an essential part of your game development. Although you don't *have* to use styles to modify the appearance of your games, you'd be missing out on a lot of potential.

Styles in general, and CSS in particular, are heady concepts when taken as a whole, but you don't need to learn every last detail in order to enjoy their benefits. In this chapter, I present just the front-line concepts you need to whip your games into shape, and in doing so, you'll learn what you really need to know about styles.

▶ Basic, No Style, No Frills

Let's start with a basic page without style. It consists of a single P element for a line of text, and a 600-by-600 pixel image of Earth from several miles in space.

Because styles are not used, the appearance of the page background, text, and picture are interpreted by the browser using *default*, or standardized, rules. These *rules* include the font and size of the text, the color of the background, and the placement of the text and image. See Figure 7-1 for how this page looks in the browser.

snipped from: styles-basic.html

```
12 <body>
13  <p>This is a page with no style at all.</p>
14  <img alt="" src="earthview.jpg" />
15 </body>
```

Figure 7-1. When no styles are used, the browser applies default appearance rules.

▶ Page with Basic Styles Added

By adding a few very basic styles to the background, text, and image elements, you can dramatically change and improve the look of the page, as shown in Figure 7-2.

You see the difference much better in full color, so be sure to open the *styles-styled-background.html* playground file in your browser to get the full effect.

---

snipped from: styles-styled-background.html

```
12 <body style="background-color: cadetblue;">
13  <p style="font-size: 1.2em; font-weight: bold;">
    This is a page with basic styles</p>
14  <img style="border: 2px solid white;" alt="" src="earthview.jpg" />
15 </body>
```

Line 12 ▶ sets a style for the BODY element, which creates a colored background. I've chosen one of the several dozen named colors supported by modern browsers—cadetblue is an appealing aqua that can be used with either black or white text.

Line 13 ▶ sets a style for the P element. The font size is increased, and the text is made bold to help it stand out.

Line 14 ▶ sets a border around the picture to help separate it from the cadetblue background. The style provided is fairly self-explanatory: The border is 2px (pixels) wide, a solid line, and painted white.

Figure 7-2. With styles applied, the appearance of the page can be dramatically altered.

▶ Page with Basic Styles Using a STYLE Element

Placing styles within the HTML elements is called *inline styling*. For each element, you add a style= attribute, and then specify one or more styles that you want to apply to that element.

Inline styling is a perfectly acceptable method, but for greater flexibility, you'll want to place the styles within a set of <style></style> tags. This makes your pages easier to read and review, especially when elements use a half dozen, a dozen, or even more styles.

snipped from: styles-styled-background-css.html

```
11 <style>
12 body {
13   background-color: cadetblue;
14 }
15 p {
16   font-size: 1.2em;
17   font-weight: bold;
18 }
19 img{
20   border: 2px solid white;
21 }
22 </style>
23 </head>
24
25 <body>
26   <p>This is a page with basic styles</p>
27   <img alt="" src="earthview.jpg" />
28 </body>
```

STYLE Element

Lines 11 through 22 comprise a complete STYLE element. Inside this element you add one or more *rules* for how your page is to be styled (refer to Figure 7-3).

▨   Selectors ▶ specify what part of the page to apply the style to. As you'll discover in this chapter, there are several ways to define style selectors. In the *styles-styled-background-css.html* playground script, I use the names of elements to denote that the BODY, P, and IMG elements are to be styled in a particular way.

▨   Properties ▶ specify what part of the element you want to style. For an IMG tag, you can set styles for size, position, border (as shown), and more.

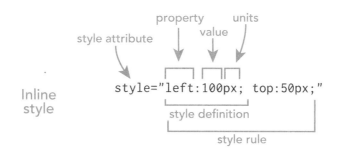

Figure 7-3. Styles affect the appearance of the page.

The style definition ▶ the actual setting for that property. For the IMG element, its border property is set to 2 pixels, solid line, white. If you wanted to make the border 5 pixels and yellow, as an example, you'd change the property and value to

```
border: 5px solid yellow;
```

Displayed Page Elements

With the style definitions moved to inside the `<style>` tag, the HTML elements have been returned to their simplified form. This is generally the easier way of working with HTML and CSS.

▶ Anatomy of a Style

A style is composed of two parts—see Figure 7-3 again:

Property name ▶ This is the aspect of the element to be styled.

Value ▶ This is the value of the property. A value may be a number, descriptive text, or a selection from a list of possible choices.

For styles related to position and size, the value may or may not include *units of measure*. The three most common units of measure are:

UNIT	WHAT IT MEANS
px	Value is specified in screen *pixels*.
em	Value is specified in *em units*; an em is a relative size based on the height of the default font for that element.
%	Value is specified as a percentage of the normal or default size of the element.

One complete *property:value* pair is a *style definition*. One or more style definitions make up a *style rule*. As demonstrated in the previous two examples, style rules may be:

▨ `Inline` ▶ The style is defined inline with the element and specified as a `style=` attribute of the element.

▨ `STYLE element` ▶ The style definition is placed inside the `<style></style>` tags.

Additionally, styles may be defined *externally* to the page. The style definition (same format as used in the STYLE element) is placed in a separate file, and that file is linked to from the HTML page. See "Using External Style Sheets" later in this chapter.

▶ Moving Elements on the Page

Unless you instruct otherwise, the browser makes all decisions regarding how elements are positioned on a page. As shown in Figure 7-4, the appearance is governed by a set of rules that depend, among other things, the type of elements used, their size, and their order in the HTML.

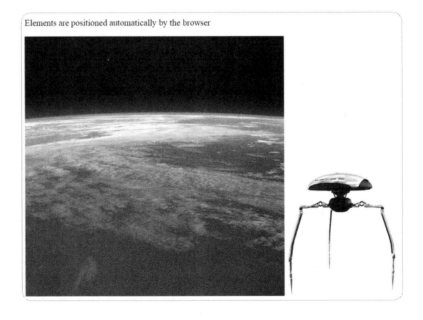

Elements are positioned automatically by the browser

Figure 7-4. Without styles, all elements are automatically positioned by the browser using its own internal rules.

```
<body>
 <p> Elements are positioned automatically by the browser </p>
 <img alt="" src="earthview.jpg" />
 <img alt="" src="martian-machine.png" />
</body>
```

Adding more text or graphic elements causes them to be positioned around one another. This may work fine for general web pages, but it's common in games to overlap elements to create more sophisticated layouts. With styles, you can indicate that you wish to take control over position by using the position: absolute property, and then specifying a left and top location for the element.

snipped from: styles-styled-background-moving.html

```
19 img{
20   position: absolute;
21   border: 2px solid white;
22 }
. . .
29   <img alt="" style="left: 50px; top: 200px;" src="martian-machine.png" />
```

⬚ The position: absolute property is added to the IMG rule on line 20. Now, all IMG elements can be manually positioned.

⬚ A specified positon of left: 50px (pixels) and top: 200px is applied directly (inline) to the IMG element for the newly added *martian-machine. png* graphic. Because these style properties are only applied to the martian IMG element, they don't affect anything else on the page.

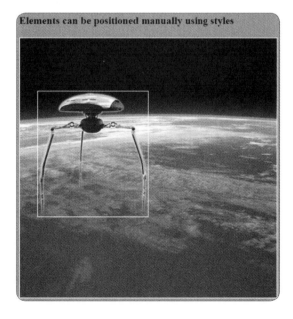

Figure 7–5. Use styles to supersede the built-in defaults.

▶ Using ID and Class Selectors in Styles

Specifying element types as selectors—BODY, P, and IMG, for example—is only one way to apply styles using the STYLE element. Two other methods are using ID names and classes:

ID Names

An ID *name* uniquely identifies one element in the entire page. You can have as many different ID names as you'd like on the page, but only one element can have that name. Using IDs and ID selectors let you target a specific element.

▪ In the style definition, ID selectors are specified by starting their names with a # (hash) character.

Class Names

A *class name* identifies a group of elements. Any number of elements can share the same class. Using class and class selectors lets you target one or more elements that match that class.

▪ In the style definition, class selectors are specified by starting their names with a . (period or dot) character.

Naming Conventions for IDs and Classes

Apart from the # and . characters used to indicate the type of selector, ID and class names should contain only alphabetical and numeric characters. Spaces are not allowed.

▪ Selector names in CSS are case sensitive. The selector `myClass` is distinct from `myclass`. You can avoid mistakes by adopting a consistent capitalization scheme for IDs and classes. One approach: For names with just one word, use only lowercase characters. Examples: *cat*, *dog*, *mouse*. For names that are made up of several words, use camelCase—low at the ends, high in the middle. Instead of `mybigclass`, use `myBigClass`.

▶ Applying ID and Class Selectors to Elements

With ID and class selectors established, you must "connect" them to the elements you want to use them with.

▪ For ID names ▶ insert an `id="name"` attribute to the element, where `name` is the ID selector you've defined.

▪ For style names ▶ insert a `class="name"` attribute to the element, where `name` is the class selector you've defined.

Here's an example showing ID and class names assigned for the P and IMG elements. Note that elements can have both an id= and class= attribute, and that these attributes do not require a matching style selector. This permits future expansion and allows for flexibility when coding with JavaScript. See Chapter 11: Working with the Document Object Model (DOM) (page 169) for more information about this topic.

```
snipped from: styles-selectors.html

12 body {
13   background-color: cadetblue;
14 }
15 #text {
16   position: absolute;
17   left: 20px;
18   top: 50px;
19   font-size: 1.2em;
20   font-weight: bold;
21   color: cornsilk;
22 }
23 .image {
24   position: absolute;
25   border: 2px solid white;
26 }
27 #martian {
28   left: 50px;
29   top: 200px;
30   border: none;
31 }
32 </style>
33 </head>
34
35 <body>
36   <img id="earth" class="image" alt="" src="earthview.jpg">
37   <img id="martian" class="image" alt="" src="martian-machine.png">
38   <p id="text">Elements are moved using styles</p>
```

ID Selectors

The p tag style selector has been removed and replaced by a specific ID selector, #text, on lines 15 through 22. The P element itself has been updated to include an id= attribute, to match the element with this selector (line 38). The revised style rule moves the element to left:20px and top:50px.

The #martian ID selector (lines 27 through 31) applies specific style rules to the IMG element with id="martian" (line 37). All of the inline styles (those with the style= attribute) from the previous example have been moved to the #martian rule to keep everything together. This is simply for housekeeping and not a strict requirement.

◼ Note line 36: It defines the id="earth" IMG element. There is no #earth style rule, so the id="earth" is included only for future development, or for possible manipulation with JavaScript. It's perfectly acceptable to give elements ID (or style) names but not to connect them with rules in the STYLE element.

.image Class Selector

Rather than use an img tag selector, which applies to any and all IMG elements in the pages, images are now identified by the class .image. This approach allows you to include other IMG elements that have different styling. Simply use a different class name for those IMG elements.

◼ Lines 36 and 37 define these two IMG elements as belonging to the image class. Notice that the martian IMG element inherits its styles from two places: the .image class rule, and its own #martian ID rule. This is very common, and I wanted to demonstrate it here.

◼ The .image class rule first sets the border to 2px solid white. But this rule is then countermanded in the #martian rule by setting the border property to border:none. Style rules follow an order of precedence, detailed later in this chapter.

◼ Notice a curious thing: I moved the P element to come after the two IMG elements. Why? The P element now contains positioning properties to move it into the same space occupied by the main graphic. If I didn't do this, the text would be covered up by the image of Earth. The browser "stacks" images in the order they appear in the HTML markup. The last element goes on top. Read more about this and how to take advantage of this feature in Chapter 9: Using Graphics (page 139).

▶ Using External Style sheets

A page can contain style rules in a STYLE element, rules contained in an external style sheet file, or a combination of both. External style sheets are referenced like this:

```
<head>
  . . .
  <link rel="stylesheet" type="text/css" href="my-stylesheet.css">
</head>
```

The style sheet takes the place of, or adds additional style rules to, any STYLE element that's in your page. In this book, none of the examples use external style sheet files. All of the examples use only a STYLE element.

There are several reasons for this:

1. External style sheets are recommended when there are many dozens, or even hundreds, of style rules. It's easier to maintain your pages if large chunks are separated into individual files. Most of the examples and games in this book use a relatively small assortment of styles, so they don't take up much space when combined with the rest of the page. It's just simpler to keep things together.

2. Most of the full game examples rely on an add-in JavaScript library called *PrefixFree*. This library performs certain housekeeping chores related to making style definitions cross-browser compatible. When used with Google Chrome to access pages on your local computer, PrefixFree fails if the styles are located in an external file. (There is no such problem when your pages are on a web server.) More about PrefixFree later in this chapter.

As your scripting skills evolve and you develop your own robust games for publishing on a website, you are free to use external style sheets rather than embed everything in a STYLE element.

▶ Adding Comments to Style Definitions

Comments are notes you write to yourself (or others reading your code) and are ignored by the browser when processing your script pages. To add a comment within the STYLE element, use the /* and */ characters. Anything between these on/off blocks is treated as a comment.

```
/* this is a comment */
.image {
 position: absolute;
 border: 2px solid white; /* so is this */
}
```

When viewing pages in the Atom editor, commented text is shown in light gray. Most code editors use similar color cues when displaying commented text. This feature helps you avoid mistakes. Without it, it's surprisingly easy to miss that a comment isn't closed with a matching /* */ set, making *all* of the remaining code in your script is one big comment!

▶ Style Order of Precedence

You can apply styles from many separate rules. When the styles don't conflict—different properties are set in each style—the rules are merely added together; you get the combination of all of them.

But in the case of conflicting rules, where the same properties are set in different styles, CSS applies an order of precedence; it gives higher weight to rules depending on the type of selector and on their order in the STYLE element. You can try out many of these techniques in the *styles-selectors-class-order.html* playground script.

```
left starts        img {
at 100px             left:100px; TAG
                   }

left is now        .image {
200px                left:200px; CLASS          increasing specificity
                   }

left is updated    #myImage {
to 300px             left:300px; ID
                   }
                                   INLINE
finally, left is   <img id="myImage" class="image" style="left:400px;... />
now 400px
```

Figure 7-6. Conflicting styles are applied in increasing order of specificity.

Specificity

Styles can be set using tag, class, or ID selectors, as well as inline styles applied directly to the element itself. As shown in Figure 7-6, CSS applies greater weight to selectors that are more specific.

In order of increasing specificity:

1. Tag
2. Class
3. ID
4. Inline

CSS overrides a tag style if a conflicting rule is found in a class, ID, or inline rule. Similarly, CSS overrides an ID rule if a conflicting rule is found in an inline style setting.

Class Order (Cascade)

Similarly, elements can be styled using more than one class. In the case of conflicting class rules among classes, CSS applies the style found in the last class as it appears in the STYLE element.

Trumping these rules of precedence is the !important qualifier, which can be appended to a style definition to give it more weight. Given these three style rules:

```
.imageA {border: 2px solid yellow;}
.imageB {border: 2px solid red !important;}
.imageC {border: 2px solid blue;}
```

The .imageB style will win out, regardless of its order in the STYLE element, because it has been marked as !important.

▶ Common Style Properties

There are hundreds of style properties; so many that there are books devoted entirely to teaching about CSS styles and how to use them. Fortunately, there is a core group of the most-commonly used style properties. Here they are:

Sizing Properties

height	Specifies the height of the element. Commonly used with the px and % units of measure. If height is not specified, the browser will render the element at its default size. Note that some elements, such as DIV, do not have a default size; their size is either derived from the elements they contain, or from style sizing properties.
width	Specifies the width of the element. The same conditions as height apply.

Positioning Properties

left	Specifies the position of the left edge of the element. Commonly used with the px unit of measure.
top	Specifies the position of the top edge of the element. Commonly used with the px unit of measure.
position	Specifies positional control of the element. When set to relative, the position is relative to other elements and is largely determined by the browser; when set to absolute, the position is an absolute location in the browser window and may be determined via style rules.

Text Properties

color	Specifies the color of text. Color may be one of several dozen predefined colors (e.g., white, black, blue, yellow, etc.), or an RGB hexadecimal value where the red, green, and yellow components are individually specified. Examples:
	`color: white;   color: #ffb900;`
	Note: There are online tools for determining the RGB hexadecimal values of colors. See the Online Support Site (Appendix A, page 310) for a list of these sites.
font-size	Specifies the size of the font. Commonly used with the em, %, and px units of measure.
font-weight	Specifies the "heaviness" of a font. Commonly indicated as a preset value, such as normal or bold; or as a value from 100 (light) to 900 (heavy). 400=normal, 700=bold.
font-family	Specifies a family of fonts for reproducing the text. Routinely specified in sets of three: *Primary Font, Fallback Font, Generic Substitute*
	In common usage, a Windows font is often given for the primary font and a Macintosh font for the fallback. It is acceptable to append more than one fallback font, each separated by a comma. The browser applies the first font that it can. Example:
	`font-family: "Times New Roman", Georgia, Serif;`
	`Serif` is not a font but a generic substitute should the other fonts be unavailable.

Border Properties

border	Specifies the width, style, and color of a border drawn around the element. Border values may be given in one line, as follows:
	`border: width style color;`
	Example: `border: 2px solid blue;`
	Border values may also be specified by using individual properties:
	▸ `border-width` Usually specified as a px value.
	▸ `border-style` Specified as a preset value. Options include solid, dotted, dashed.
	▸ `border-color` Specified as a named color or RGB hexadecimal value. See the `color` entry under "Text Properties" for details on valid color values.
	In addition you may set each of the four sides of the border individually by specifying the edge (top, right, bottom, left) and the border element to change (e.g. width, style, color). Examples:
	▸ `border-top-style:`
	▸ `border-right-style:`
	▸ `border-bottom-style:`
	▸ `border-left-style:`
border-radius	Specifies the radius, typically given in px, for the border corners. The higher the value, the more rounded off the corners.

Miscellaneous Common Properties

animation	Specifies values to use for CSS animation. See Chapter 15: Creating Motion with CSS Animations (page 225).
background-color	Sets the background color of an element. See the color entry under "Text Properties" for details on valid color values.
background-image	Sets a graphic image as the background of an element. The syntax is: `background-image: url('mypicture.png');`
background-repeat	Specifies whether the background-image repeats, should the image be smaller than the element. Common values are: `background-repeat: repeat;` ▸ repeat both vertically and horizontally `background-repeat: repeat-x;` ▸ repeat only horizontally `background-repeat: repeat-y;` ▸ repeat only vertically `background-repeat: no-repeat;` ▸ no repeat
cursor	Specifies the pointer shape when the mouse is over the image. Common preset values are (actual shape depends on the computer platform): ▸ default: standard titled arrow ▸ grab: grabbing fingers ▸ pointer: pointing finger ▸ non-allowed: x in circle ▸ none: no cursor shown
opacity	Sets the opacity of the element. An opacity of 0 means totally transparent (cannot be seen). An opacity of 1 means totally opaque.
overflow	Specifies how content larger than the element is shown. Common preset values are: ▸ hidden: overflow is clipped, and is not visible ▸ scroll: overflow is clipped, but scroll bars are added to manually view more ▸ visible: overflow is not clipped
transition	Specifies values to use for CSS transitions. See Chapter 14: Creating Motion with CSS Transitions (page 209).
visibility	Sets the visibility of the element, either hidden or visible.

Margins and Spacing Properties

margin	Specifies the outside space between the element and other elements. Commonly used with the px unit of measure. Settings apply to the top, right, bottom, and left. ▸ `margin: 5px` ▸ 5px margins all around ▸ `margin: 10px 5px` ▸ 10px margin top/bottom, 5px left/right ▸ `margin: 1px 2px 3px 4px` ▸ Individual settings: top, right, bottom, left Properties for individual margins are also provided: ▸ `margin-top:` ▸ `margin-right:` ▸ `margin-bottom:` ▸ `margin-left:`
padding	Specifies the inside space of an element and elements contained inside it. Commonly used with the px unit of measure. Settings apply in a similar manner to margin to the top, right, bottom, and left. Properties for individual margins are also provided: ▸ `padding-top:` ▸ `padding-right:` ▸ `padding-bottom:` ▸ `padding-left:`

As noted, this list is not exhaustive, but it does represent a lion's share of properties you will encounter in most web pages, including the game examples and demos in this book. Check out the Online Support Site (Appendix A, page 310) for more complete style-property listings.

▸ Using PrefixFree

Many of the full, working game demos that accompany this book use an open-source add-in library, PrefixFree. The actual filename of this add-in is *prefixfree.min.js*. The job of this utility script is to automatically add browser-specific prefixes to any CSS properties that need them.

The "min" in the *prefixfree.min.js* filename means that it's been "minified," a process to reduce its file size. The advantage of minification: Smaller files download faster when they're on a website, and faster downloads mean more nimble web pages.

Without PrefixFree, your CSS style definitions can become outrageously convoluted when using the newer and more "experimental" style properties. As it turns out, games often use the cutting-edge techniques for image display and animation, so auto-prefixing is a handy tool.

Consider the `transition` style property, which is used to create basic transitional animations (see Chapter 14: Creating Motion with CSS Transitions [page 209]). A typical transition style looks like this:

```
transition: top 2s;
```

which tells the browser that you want a two-second transition whenever an element's `top` style is changed.

Unfortunately, some browsers—particularly older ones, or those used on mobile devices—don't understand this property name. They instead require a *prefixed* version of the property:

```
-webkit-transition: top 2s;        /* certain versions of Safari */
```

Other browsers, depending on age, use different prefixes. These prefixes are more or less standardized:

PREFIX	UNDERSTOOD BY
-webkit-	Chrome, Safari, newer versions of Opera
-moz-	Firefox
-o-	Older versions of Opera
-ms-	Internet Explorer

Having to add separate prefixed versions of style properties, or even knowing when they are and aren't required, can be a real drag. PrefixFree fills this gap by providing the required prefix when it's needed. This makes your coding a lot simpler.

For this book, the browser of choice for development is an up-to-date desktop version of Google Chrome. This browser doesn't require a ton of prefixed properties, so if you only use Chrome to play your games, PrefixFree probably isn't necessary.

But every once in a while, there's a new style property that throws Chrome a curveball. You can either add the required prefix yourself, such as:

```
-webkit-text-stroke: 4px red;          /* webkit-specific prefix */
```

or use just the unprefixed property with PrefixFree.

```
text-stroke: 4px red;                  /* unprefixed version as backup */
```

For those games and examples in this book that use PrefixFree, a reference to the PrefixFree library script is already included. For your own pages, you can add a reference to the PrefixFree library by inserting the following right before the </head> tag:

```
<script src="prefixfree.min.js"></script>
```

If the PrefixFree library is contained in a subfolder, such as *assets*, include the path to that subfolder as well:

```
<script src="./assets/prefixfree.min.js"></script>
```

or

```
<script src="assets/prefixfree.min.js"></script>
```

I prefer the former method: The ./ (dot-slash) notation simply means to start from the folder that contains the current script page.

▶ Bonus Examples

Tic-Tac-Toe
(Lessons 1 through 3)

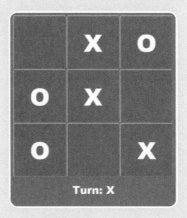

See how styles are used to define the look and feel of a traditional tic-tac-toe game.

- **TicTacToeLesson1**
  Rudimentary game example with click events for placing X and O in a 3-by-3 table grid. No scoring.

- **TicTacToeLesson2**
  Enhanced version of the basic game, with styles used to format the table. Game keeps track of score and announces whether X or O is the winner.

- **TicTacToeLesson3**
  As above, but with styled INPUT buttons. The table structure is not used; the placement of the buttons is dependent on style position properties.

For all Bonus Game-related materials in this chapter and chapters hereafter refer to Appendix **A** (page 310).

RESPONDING TO EVENTS: PART 1

Events are things that happen that JavaScript can react to.

Pressing a key on the keyboard produces an event; clicking the mouse produces an event; even the act of loading the page produces an event.

JavaScript can respond to these events and perform some action. The action is up to you. That key press might cause your game character to move forward; that mouse-click might fire a missile; that page load might display a splash image announcing the start of the game.

In this chapter, you learn the basics about events and how to set things up so that your JavaScript code can respond to them. As this is a fairly involved topic, I've split the discussion into two parts. Read the second part in Chapter 12: Responding to Events: Part 2 (page 183).

▶ Common Events

Events are another way of activating JavaScript code. Without events, all the JavaScript on the page would execute all at one time. Events give interactivity to your games by responding to the player.

There are three basic types of events used in creating JavaScript games.

▦ Mouse-click (or tablet taps) ▸ Click on an element (doesn't have to be INPUT buttons), and something happens.

▦ Mouse moves ▸ Just the act of moving the mouse over an area can trigger an event.

▦ Page load ▸ When the page has loaded, an event can signal that everything is ready.

These are just the most-commonly used events. There are many others, including listening for keyboard presses, waiting for animations and transitions to end, and more. Look for additional information in Chapter 12: Responding to Events: Part 2 (page 183).

▶ Events Playground Script

The short examples in the first half of this chapter are demonstrated in the *events-playground.html* playground script. Be sure to follow along by opening this page in your browser and code editor.

▶ Setting Up an Event

The first step in using events in JavaScript is setting up, or *listening*, for them. This requires indicating that you want to capture an event and specifying what you want to have happen when the event occurs (see Figure 8-1).

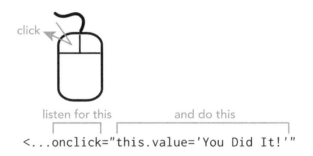

Figure 8-1. Events allow your code to react to the player.

JavaScript supports several methods for setting up events. One of the more-commonly used is the onEvent attribute added directly to the HTML element on which you want to listen. For instance, to add a mouse-click event to an INPUT button, you use the onclick attribute. For the value of the attribute, you tell JavaScript what you want your code to do when that event occurs.

For example:

snipped from: events-playground.html

```
<input type="button" value="Click Me" onclick="this.value='You Did It!'" />
```

This code displays a button with the text *Click Me*. The onclick handler tells the browser to change the button text to *You Did It!* when the button is clicked, as demonstrated in Figure 8-2.

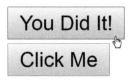

Figure 8-2. Changing a button using a JavaScript event.

- onclick ▸ the name of the event to listen for. It literally means "when clicked on, take this action."

- Though there are no <script> tags involved, what goes into the onclick attribute is indeed JavaScript. Executable code is assumed.

- this ▸ a special keyword that (in this instance) means "this current element." Because this is used inside the body of the element, JavaScript doesn't need any additional help in figuring out what you're referring to.

- value ▸ the name of the property you're changing. The this.value property refers to the button text, which was initially set to *Click Me*.

▶ Calling a Function Rather Than Using Inline Code

Specifying the action to perform right inside the element is referred to as *inline code*. It works as long as the code is minimal. Things get messy-looking when you want to add more than a single action.

One method is to separate each separate action with a semicolon:

```
<input type="button" value="Click Me"
 onclick="this.value='You Did It!'; this.style.backgroundColor='red'" />
```

This example modifies both the button text and its background color. Yep—starting to get messy. A better way is to call a named JavaScript function

```
<input type="button" value="Click Me" onclick="buttonClick(this);" />
```

along with the JavaScript code, typically at or near the bottom of the page:

```
<script>
 function buttonClick(button) {
  button.value="You Did It!";
  button.style.backgroundColor="red";
 }
</script>
```

Notice some differences:

1. The onclick attribute specifies a separate function named buttonClick. The this keyword —remember, it means the current element containing the event-handler—is passed as an *argument* to this function. This allows you to reference the button from within the function.

2. The responding function, buttonClick, is contained in a SCRIPT element.

3. The this keyword has no meaning inside the function, so you can't use it there. Instead, the button parameter acts as its substitute. The parameter holds the this value passed by the onclick event (see Figure 8-3).

4. The line button.value="You Did It!"; changes the text of the button.

5. The line button.style.backgroundColor="red"; changes the background color of the button.

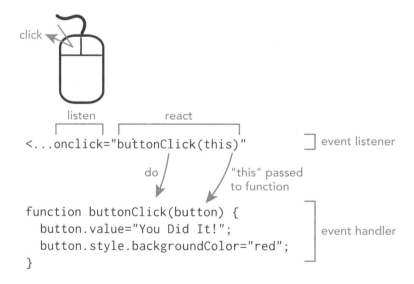

Figure 8-3. Code for changing a button using a JavaScript event.

How to Get this to There

You've read that the **this** keyword, when used inside an HTML element like an INPUT button, means that current element. You can see this in action with the following bit of code:

```
<input type="button" value="See Console" onclick="console.log(this)" />
```

Click the button and look at the browser's console window. You'll see the framework of the INPUT button echoed right back at you. What you're seeing is an *object* that represents the INPUT button. Recall from Chapter 6 that an object is a collection of data that represents something.

The object contains everything about the button, including things you don't see in the console window. For instance, change the line to

```
<input type="button" value="See Console" onclick="console.log(this.style)" />
```

and now you see a much more complex listing of values. Click the pointer arrow beside the result to expand this listing in the console window. Quite a bunch of stuff. And all that just for the style properties of the button!

By including the **this** keyword in the function call for the event, you are really passing a reference to the entire object of the INPUT button to the function. Inside the function, you give the object a distinct name—since it's a button, I just used the name **button**.

If you tried using **this** inside the function, you'd get an error. This is because, inside the function, **this** has no contextual meaning. Try modifying the function to:

```
function buttonClick(button) {
 console.log (this);
 button.value="You Did It!";
 button.style.backgroundColor="red";
}
```

and look in the console window. It'll show *undefined* for the **this** value.

▶ Listening for Other Mouse Events

Clicks are probably the most common events you'll use in JavaScript. Click events work with the mouse, as well as taps on tablets and other devices that have touchscreens.

JavaScript supports a rich variety of other mouse-specific events that can be quite useful in creating games. For example, instead of responding to a click, you could wait for when the mouse simply passes over an HTML element.

```
<input type="button" value="Click Me" onmouseover="this.value='You Did It!'" />
```

The only difference between this example and onclick is the name of the event you're looking to capture. The onmouseover event watches for any time the mouse pointer passes over the button. When it does, the event is triggered.

There's nothing stopping you from defining more than one event for an element. Various mouse events are typically used together so that different things happen, depending on whether the mouse is over the element, or has left it.

In this example, an onmouseover event changes the button text to *Mouse Over*, whereas onmouseleave changes it back to *Click*.

```
<input type="button" value="Click"
  onmouseover="this.value='Mouse Over'"
  onmouseleave="this.value='Click'" />
```

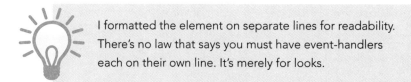

I formatted the element on separate lines for readability. There's no law that says you must have event-handlers each on their own line. It's merely for looks.

The following mouse events are supported by *most* browsers. There are some others that are specific to Internet Explorer and are considered outdated (*deprecated* in programmer-speak).

MOUSE EVENT	LISTENS FOR
onclick	Single mouse-clicks or finger taps on an element
ondblclick	Double mouse-clicks or finger taps on an element
onmousedown	Mouse button is pressed while over an element
onmousemove	Moving the mouse over the area of the element
onmouseover	Mouse entering the area of the element
onmouseout	Mouse leaving the area of the element
onmouseup	Releasing the mouse button over an element
onwheel	Mouse wheel is moved

For each of these events, you can determine the location of the mouse pointer in relation to its position on the element, or in the browser window. This is most useful for events like onmousemove, where you can track the X and Y coordinates of the pointer as it moves over the element. See the section "Tracking Mouse Position" on the next page for more information.

If you're only changing the style attributes of an element—background color or border, for example—it's better to use CSS styling than JavaScript events. This is particularly handy for the onmouseover/ onmouseout events. Use the CSS :hover or :active pseudo-classes to make these on-the-fly changes. No events or JavaScript code necessary.

Here's an example: This style-sheet definition changes the background color of any INPUT element whenever the mouse passes over it. The normal color is returned when the mouse moves away from the element.

```
<style>
input:hover {
 background-color: blue;
}
</style>
```

▶ Tracking Mouse Position

Events carry information about themselves. For mouse events, among the more useful is the X (horizontal) and Y (vertical) position of the mouse pointer. The X/Y location is helpful for such tasks as using the mouse as an aiming device and firing light-cannon rounds at an ugly alien.

To get the mouse-pointer position, you need to slightly alter the event attribute in the element, like so:

```
<input type="button" value="Roll Over Me" onmousemove="mouseMove(event);" />
```

You also need to make a corresponding change in the JavaScript:

```
function mouseMove(event) {
 console.log (event.x + "," + event.y);
}
```

Rather than use the this keyword, you replace it with event. This allows you to pass the event information to the JavaScript function. Inside the function, you can extract the X and Y coordination information. In the above example, the mouse X/Y position is printed out in the browser's console every time the mouse moves over the button. The X and Y coordinates you see are relative to the upper-left corner of the document area (the body) of the browser window.

▶ Obtaining the Element Reference from the event Keyword

The event keyword carries all the event information for the element, including the identity of the element that produced the event. This comes in handy if two or more elements share the same event-handler function. Suppose you have:

```
<input type="button" value="Click On Me" onclick="mouseClick(event);" />
<input type="button" value="Me Too" onclick="mouseClick(event);" />
<input type="button" value="And Me!" onclick="mouseClick(event);" />
```

Inside the JavaScript you ask for the *target* name of the element that produced the event. What you get is a reference to the element that made the event, and in most cases it's the same as the this keyword.

```
function mouseClick(event) {
 console.log (event.target);
}
```

Click on a button, and you'll see the clicked-on element printed in the browser's console.

What you do with this information is up to you. How about a turkey shoot where the buttons disappear when you click on them?

```
function mouseClick(event) {
 event.target.style.visibility = "hidden";
}
```

Okay, so far it's not much of a game, but it shows what you can do! You can always spruce it up by adding sound and maybe buttons that pop up at random in different parts of the window.

▶ Using Events on Non-Button Elements

Just because the examples so far have used INPUT buttons, doesn't mean they are the only kinds of elements you can use with events. You're free to use events with other elements, too, like IMG images, P text, DIV containers, and more. Simply add an onEvent attribute to the element.

Let's see an example using a DIV element as a "hot spot" for a game board. A hot spot is an otherwise invisible area that responds to the event. The player thinks she's clicking on a skull (or something) in the game, when it's really the invisible DIV element that is positioned over the skull. By using multiple pictures, each with a separate DIV, you can determine where the player clicks. Each DIV is given a unique name, letting you easily differentiate between them.

Open the *skulls.html* playground game in both Chrome browser and the Atom code editor.

The HTML portion of the *skulls.html* is straight forward. It starts with a background image of three skulls, and then overlaid on top of that, three invisible DIV elements.

snipped from: skulls.html

```
<p>Open the browser console window to see the result!</p>
<img alt="" src="skulls.jpg" />
<div id=yellow style="left:15px;" onclick="divClick(this);"></div>
<div id="red" style="left:145px;" onclick="divClick(this);"></div>
<div id="green" style="left:275px;" onclick="divClick(this);"></div>
<p id="text">Click the Red Skull</p>
```

All three types of elements—IMG, DIV, and P—need styles to work. In each case, the position of the element is defined as absolute to give control of its placement on the page. For each DIV, its left position is uniquely specified using a style attribute. All the other styles for the element are defined in the CSS of the page.

```
<style>
img {

...
div {
   ...
#text {
      ...
</style>
```

The IMG element is placed in the default upper-left corner of the window with no margins defined. All three DIVs are given the same width, height, and top properties. The P element named text is forced toward the bottom of the image, and its font, font size, and color are changed. (Note that the other P element, which reminds you to open the console window to see the result, is not styled.)

The position of each DIV is specified as left and top style properties; as with width and height, left and top are specified in pixels. In this example, all of the DIVs share the same top location, leaving only the left property to be individually set. Finally, the JavaScript is just a few lines:

```
<script>
 function divClick(div) {
  if (div.id == "red") {
   console.log ("Correct choice!");
  } else {
   console.log ("That skull isn't red.");
  }
 }
</script>
```

Whenever the player clicks over an invisible DIV, the element's onclick event is triggered (see Figure 8-5). That event is handled by the divClick function. Passed into the function is the this keyword, so that the specific DIV can be identified.

The code if (div.id == "red") checks to see whether the ID of the element matches "red." If it does, the correct DIV was clicked, and a corresponding message is displayed in the browser's console window. If a DIV other than "red" is clicked, a different message appears.

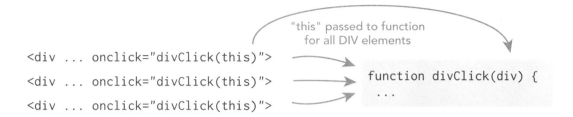

Figure 8-4. Clicking on a DIV hot spot triggers the divClick function.

Note the code `div.id`. The `.id` property lets you examine the ID name of the element that triggered the event. For this script, that ID will be either `yellow`, `red`, or `green`. These names correspond with the `id=". . ."` attributes specified for each DIV element.

Being that DIVs are by their nature invisible, how do you see them in order to overlay them on the graphic? Just add these two temporary lines of code to the *div* selector in the STYLE tag:

```
background-color: red;
opacity: .5;
```

This fills the DIV with a semi-transparent red background. You can now edit the code to adjust the `left`, `top`, `width`, and `height` properties of the DIVs so that they overlay the background image precisely where you want them. Remove the `background-color` and `opacity` styles when you're done.

▶ Bonus Examples

Check out the following bonus game examples for more clues on building JavaScript code that responds to events.

15 of 16 Tile Puzzle, Lesson 1

Click on the tiles to move them into the proper order. Game play is with numbered buttons. No graphics are used.

Tic-Tac-Toe, Lesson 4

Classic tic-tac-toe game to be played between two human players. Uses INPUT buttons as clickable tiles.

USING GRAPHICS

By their nature, most games are graphics-intensive.

Backgrounds, pictures, human and alien beings, guns, bombs, explosions, spaceships, galaxies, you name it—graphics add fun and interest to all kinds of games.

In this chapter, learn how to add 2-D graphic images and then manipulate these images using styles and JavaScript. You can precisely position any image, overlap images, hide and show them, and much more.

There are two basic ways of adding 2-D graphics to games: procedural, and image-based.

1. *Procedural graphics* use programming commands to build images from building-block shapes —lines, squares, circles, and so on. These blocks are then combined to create recognizable things such as characters, weapons, and settings.

2. *Image-based graphics* use picture files to produce the art seen in the game. These image files are separate from the game code itself.

Both techniques have their advantages. First, it's easier for scripting newcomers to see how the graphics are made. Programming commands for building artwork from primitive shapes can get complicated, even for a simple graphic. Second, image-based graphics are easier to modify or exchange … just edit or replace the image file, using any graphics program. And third, image-based graphics give your games a more modern look.

For this book, I've settled almost entirely on constructing games using image-based graphics, as they are easier to create, use, and repurpose.

▶ Displaying a Background Image

The basic graphic is a simple background image. On top of that image you can place text, colored rectangles, and other elements to add to the visuals of your game. All it takes is a single IMG element. Here's an example:

snipped from: using-graphics-1.html

```
12 <body>
13  <img alt="" src="./assets/bug1.jpg" />
14  <p>Magnumus Bugus</p>
</body>
```

The background picture is a graphic file named *bug1.jpg*. For organization purposes, the file is stored in a subfolder (*assets*) found under the main folder containing the *using-graphics-1.html* page file.

The *bug1.jpg* image measures about 500-pixels square, and because no additional sizing information is provided in the HTML page, this is the size that the image appears in the browser.

Underneath the image is the text, Magnumus Bugus, a fake, Latin-sounding term for this species of fake bug. The text is contained in a P element.

You can easily spruce up the look of your bug by adding some simple style rules to the text. In this new version, the text is larger, bolder, and colored blue.

snipped from: using-graphics-2.html

```
10 <style>
11 p {
12  font-family: "Arial Black", Gadget, sans-serif;
13  font-size: 1.5em;
14  color: blue;
15 }
16 </style>
```

You're not limited to displaying images and text separately in the window. You can overlap them by making a few more changes to the style rule for the text (Figure 9-1). The technique shown here to position and size text over a graphic image is commonly employed in games, so you'll encounter it quite frequently.

```
snipped from: using-graphics-3.html
10 <style>
11 p {
12   position: absolute;
13   width: 500px;
14   text-align: center;
15   color: yellow;
16   text-shadow: 0.1em 0.25em black;
17   font-family: "Arial Black", Gadget, sans-serif;
18   font-size: 1.5em;
19 }
20 </style>
21 </head>
22
23 <body>
24   <img alt="" src="./assets/bug1.jpg" />
25   <p style="top:180px;">Magnumus Bugus</p>
26   <p style="top:225px;font-size:1.3em;">The common nose mite.</p>
27 </body>
```

Line 12 ▶ sets the position of the P element to absolute, allowing you to control its position.

Lines 13 and 14 ▶ set the width of the P element to 500 pixels, to match the image, and instruct the browser to center the text within its 500-pixel width.

Lines 15 and 16 ▶ the text is further enhanced by changing its color to yellow and adding a black drop shadow.

Lines 25 and 26 ▶ provide inline styling information for the two P elements.

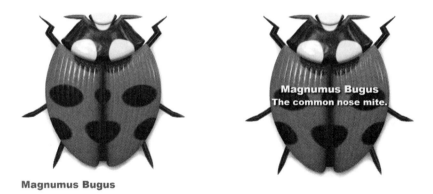

Figure 9-1. In the image on the left, a simple background image is combined with text. On the right, styles are shown applied to overlap the text with the background image.

▶ File Formats for Graphics

Graphics files come in different formats, and the format specifies how the image data is stored. Although Chrome and most other modern browsers support many kinds of images, you are likely to only use a few. The three most common are:

FORMAT	WHAT IT IS AND WHAT IT'S BEST FOR
JPG	JPG is the workhorse on the graphics format farm, favored because of its flexibility in letting you set the amount of image compression when the file is saved. The more compressed the file, the smaller (in bytes) it is. But at higher compression settings, the image can get distorted, so you must weigh file size against quality.
PNG	PNG images are also compressed, but they use a "lossless" compression format which helps them retain better quality. More importantly, PNG files can have transparent backgrounds, meaning you can overlay a PNG on another image, and the two appear to seamlessly merge. This is commonly used in game design.
GIF	GIF files once played the same role as PNG, including support of a transparent background, but now are mostly just for small, icon-size images. Quality isn't as good as with PNG, because the format can only support up to 256 colors and the transparency can leave a colored outline around the edges.

Standard practice is to apply the three-letter graphics format as the filename extension, such as *MyImage.jpg* for a JPG file, or *YourPicture.png* for a PNG file.

▶ The Importance of Transparent Backgrounds

As noted in the table above, both PNG and GIF support *background transparency*, also called an *alpha channel*. In a graphics program such as Adobe Photoshop®, this background appears not in white or some other color, but by a special checkerboard—see Figure 9-2—that denotes the background is see-through.

When saving a GIF file, you most often specify one of the 256 colors to represent the alpha channel. For PNG files, the graphics program automatically creates the alpha channel.

Throughout this chapter, you'll have a chance to experiment with alpha channels and play with images with transparent backgrounds by "stacking them up" one over the other.

▶ Displaying an Image Anywhere in the Browser Window

In the typical web page, you add images and text to the HTML page and let the browser figure out where everything is supposed to go. For games, you probably want more creative control. With just a few CSS style rules, you can take firm command over the layout of the page and precisely dictate—down to the pixel—where each image and letter appears on the screen.

Here's a minimalistic page (*using-graphics-4.html*) that shows this concept in action. It also serves as a springboard for a number of additional examples I show you in this chapter.

This is the working part of the page.

Figure 9-2. How a transparent background is shown in many graphics programs.

snipped from: using-graphics-4.html

```
10 <style>
11 #mainContent {
12   position: absolute;
13   background-image: url("./assets/robot-apocalypse-bg.jpg");
14   left: 150px;
15   top: 150px;
16   width: 800px;
17   height: 500px;
18 }
19 </style>
20 </head>
21
22 <body>
23   <div id="mainContent">
24   </div>
25 </body>
```

DIV Background Image

The page contains one graphic as a background to a DIV container (see line 23/24). I like to use this approach for the backgrounds for games because it provides greater flexibility in resizing and moving stuff around. Notice that the DIV container is given a unique ID: `mainContent`. This allows it to be manipulated by both CSS styles and (later on) JavaScript.

DIV Styling

The look of the `mainContent` DIV container is specified in the STYLE element that begins on line 11. There are a number of important things here:

- `position: absolute` ▸ tells the browser you're taking over the placement of the element.

- `background-image` ▸ specifies the background picture you want to display inside the DIV. Even though a DIV is not an IMG element, it can still contain a picture as its background. Be sure there is not a space between `url` and (`"./assets. . ."`). Some browsers won't display the image otherwise.

- `left and top` ▸ specify the horizontal and vertical position, respectively, of the upper-left corner of the DIV container, as measured in pixels from the upper-left corner of the document area of the browser window. See Figure 9-3.

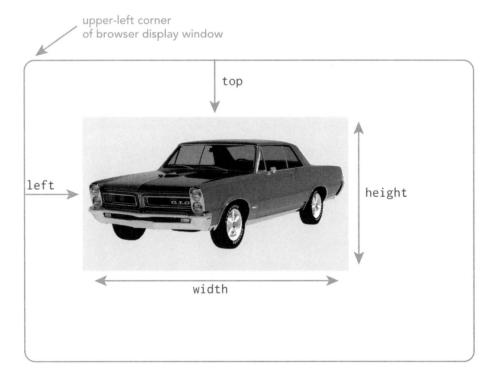

Figure 9-3. Using the left/top and width/height properties.

width and height ▶ specify the size of the DIV container in pixels. *This is very important!* When using position: absolute you must specify the size or you won't see the image.

Play with the size and position of the mainContent DIV. Don't be afraid to go wild—negative numbers for left and top properties are allowed. How about –150px for the left property? As you might have guessed, this causes the image to partially slide off the left side of the window.

What happens when you make the DIV smaller? You'll see that has the effect of cropping the image, not reducing it. Make the DIV bigger? Hmmm . . . that causes the background to repeat itself (called *tiling*). This kind of interactive playing is the best way to learn.

▶ Overlapping Images Onto a Background

If you've ever watched a documentary on how they made "old-school" cartoons, you know they placed *cels* over background drawings and photographed everything together. Well, computer graphics and animation are pretty much the same. Take a plain background, mix in a foreground image, and you've got yourself a pretty picture.

No post-apocalyptic scene would be complete without at least one marauding killer robot, so it's time to add one. This next example makes the following additions:

```
snipped from: using-graphics-5.html

23   <div id="mainContent">
24   <img style="position:absolute;" alt=""
     src="./assets/robot-apocalypse-front.png" />
25   </div>
```

Inside the mainContent DIV is an IMG element: a PNG graphic with an alpha channel. Because the IMG element is nested inside the DIV, it's considered part of the DIV container; it will move with the rest of the DIV. (Try it: Change the left and top properties of the mainContent style). What's more, the PNG graphics will appear to be in front of the background.

Note the style="position:absolute;" property added to the IMG element. This is needed to tell the browser you wish to overlap the image with the background. In later examples, this inline style will be moved to the STYLE element; I put it here for convenience for this demonstration.

▶ Multiple Layers and the Order of Elements

Going back to that old-cartoon example: Each character was commonly drawn on its own transparent cel, and the cels were stacked up to make a full composite. Likewise, you can add more characters to Apocalypse Land simply by adding more IMG tags inside the DIV container.

But be careful: Images are stacked in the order they appear in the HTML markup of the page. That is, elements that appear lower down on the page will appear toward the front of the stack. Here's a working example:

snipped from: using-graphics-6.html

```
. . .
19 img {
20   position: absolute;
21 }
22 </style>
23 </head>
24
25 <body>
26   <div id="mainContent">
27     <img alt="" src="./assets/robot-apocalypse-left.png" />
28     <img alt="" src="./assets/robot-apocalypse-right.png" />
29     <img alt="" src="./assets/robot-apocalypse-front.png" />
30   </div>
. . .
```

Lines 19 through 21 define a new style rule for all IMG elements, specifying that each is to use absolute positioning. Without this property, the images will not stack on top of one another.

All three graphics are added inside the DIV container in their order of stacking, with the objects that are to appear behind any others listed first (see Figure 9-4).

You can experiment with the stacking order by swapping the position of the *robot-apocalypse-front.png* image. Move it to the first element, and reload the page. If you look closely, you'll see parts of the robot on the left actually in front of the big robot, which ruins the illusion of depth.

▶ Moving IMG Elements

The position of the three killer robots is automatically set by way of the size of the images themselves. All the robot graphics measure the same height and width as the background. When each graphic was made, the robots were pre-positioned at the spots you see in the composite picture. If you were to examine the robot on the right, for instance, you'd see that it's inside an 800-by-500 pixel transparent background, positioned toward the right side—check out Figure 9-5.

Figure 9-4. Three PNG images stacked and overlapped.

Lining up overlay images in this way is a matter of convenience. It saves having to specify the left and top coordinates for each picture, but it doesn't prevent our being able to do so.

The *using-graphics-7.html* playground example shows this in action. It first adds these CSS rules to the STYLE element.

Figure 9-5. Robots are are pre-positioned within the background area.

```
#left   { left:-175px; }
#right  { left:175px;  }
#front  { top:100px;   }
```

The ID names (#left, #right, and #front) match those added to the IMG elements.

```
<img id="left" alt="" src="./assets/robot-apocalypse-left.png" />
<img id="right" alt="" src="./assets/robot-apocalypse-right.png" />
<img id="front" alt="" src="./assets/robot-apocalypse-front.png" />
```

With these changes, the right and left robots are moved off to the edges, and their images actually trail off the background. The front robot is similarly moved down, so it appears to be stepping out of the picture.

Always remember that the position values are relative to the parent container of the IMG elements, in this case the mainContent DIV. That's why you can move the DIV itself, and the positions of the IMG follow that of their main DIV.

▶ Specifying the Placement of IMG Elements

By using left and top CSS style properties, you have full control over the placement of IMG element and the images in these elements.

As with the previous examples, you must first demand supreme power over the layout engine of the browser with the position: absolute property.

Then, for each IMG element on the page, use the left and/or top property to indicate placement. (Remember: The left and top values are relative to the parent container of the IMG elements—for these examples, that's the mainContent DIV.)

The position properties accept a number of unit values. The two you'll use the most are pixels and percentage. To set a value in pixels, append px after the number. To set a value in percentage, append %.

In each of the following, the property affects the position of the IMG element within its parent container.

PROPERTY	WHAT IT DOES
left: 100px;	Sets the left side of the IMG element 100 pixels to the right
top: -50px	Sets the top of the IMG element 50 pixels up
left: 50%	Sets the left side of the IMG element 50 percent of the width of its parent container

▶ Specifying the Size of IMG Elements

The same process is used for setting the size of IMG elements: specify the width and/or height of the element.

You can keep the proportion of the image if you set just width *or* height. The browser will calculate the other value. However, this is deemed to be less computationally efficient than providing explicit values for both width *and* height, so use it judiciously.

Here again you can use pixel or percentage units. Example: A percentage value of 50 percent shrinks the IMG to half-size. Check out the *using-graphics-8.html* playground script in the Atom editor and Chrome. It shows a set of three buildings nestled next to each other. Try modifying the example with explicit width and/or height properties, like so:

```
29 #center {
30   left: 130px;
31   top: 20px;
32   width: 90px;
33 }
```

This sets the width of the center building to 90 pixels. This results in a size reduction, because the graphic is normally 240 pixels wide. Because you've only specified the width, the browser automatically adjusts the height in equal proportion.

You can provide non-proportional sizes to images, which makes them look squeezed or stretched out. Try width: 90% and height: 400px, for instance.

Careful when resizing a graphic. If you enlarge an image too much, you risk making it look fuzzy or pixelated. You've seen this effect if you try to enlarge a small photo from your smartphone. If you make it too big, it loses quality.

If you want a bigger image, it's best to prepare it at the desired size in your graphics app. The better programs, like Adobe Photoshop® or GIMP (which stands for GNU Image Manipulation Program), have built-in features that help maintain quality when an image is enlarged or reduced.

▶ Hiding and Displaying Images

It's easy to show and hide images by using the visibility style property. You can control the visibility with a simple bit of JavaScript code. This short example hides the center building when you click on it.

snipped from: using-graphics-9.html

```
40 <img id="center" alt="" src="./assets/buildings-center.png"
   onclick="this.style.visibility='hidden';" />
```

You can also do the inverse, as shown in this example. The visibility property of the center building is initially set to hidden. Clicking anywhere in the mainContent DIV shows the building by setting visibility='visible'.

snipped from: using-graphics-10.html

```
29 #center {
30  left: 130px;
31  top: 20px;
32  visibility: hidden;
33 }
. . .
38 <div id="mainContent"
   onclick="document.getElementById('center').style.visibility='visible'";>
```

▶ Setting the Opacity of Images

Another common technique with graphics is to set their *opacity*, or the amount of the background that shows through them. Opacity is set with the opacity style property, using a value from 1 (100 percent) to 0 (0 percent). The lower the number, the less opaque (more transparent) the image.

In this example, clicking the center building changes its opacity from the default 1 (100 percent) to .4 (40 percent). See Figure 9-6.

snipped from: using-graphics-11.html

```
40 <img id="center" alt="" src="./assets/buildings-center.png"
   onclick="this.style.opacity=.4;" />
```

Figure 9-6. Opacity varies
the transparency of elements.

▶ Finding and Creating Graphics Assets

Graphical games need graphics. If you're also an artist, you can create the art for your game. Drawn art can be scanned into your computer, or you can produce it using a graphics program.

Pixel-Based Images

Pixel-based images, where the picture is made of up separate dots, can be created and edited using *bitmap* software such as Adobe Photoshop®, Corel Photo-Paint, and Paint Shop Pro. These are popular paid programs; on the free side there's the open-source GIMP, among others. There are even some free online drawing tools; see the Resources pages on the Online Support Site (Appendix A, page 310).

Vector-Based Images

Vector-based images, where the picture is made up of geometric shapes, can be created and edited using *vector* software: Adobe Illustrator® and Corel Draw are well-regarded vector image tools. I prefer Inkscape, which is open-source freeware. Again, see the Online Support Site for more leads on popular vector-based graphics applications.

Not everyone is good at creating art from scratch. Fortunately, you may be able to find what you want by using free and paid *clipart*. With clipart, someone else has drawn the base artwork, and you can use it as-is or combine it with text and other art to build the graphics for your game.

▶ Where to Keep Images

The typical game may contain a dozen or more image files. Throughout the playground scripts in this chapter—and in the examples throughout the book—I've shown image files kept in a separate subfolder named *assets*. My choice of the subfolder, and its name, is merely a convention I've developed. You're free to place your image files any place you'd like. Regardless of your method, you'll want to keep the following in mind:

Only a Few Images

If the game has just a couple of image files, you can probably just toss them in with the script file itself. Reference the image filename without a folder:

```
src="image.jpg"
```

More Than a Few Images

If the game has more files, for the sake of housekeeping, it's best to contain them into a subfolder so they don't clutter up things:

```
src="./subfolder/image.jpg"
```

Use the ./ Dot Notation (or Not)

You don't have to use the ./ style of indicating the folder. The following works, too (although, because it's not as specific, it can be more prone to mistakes):

```
src="subfolder/image.jpg"
```

Keep Everything Together

You can keep all of the external files in the same subfolder as the images. Although it's common in larger websites to separate the different types of files into different folders—separate folders for scripts, images, sounds, or whatever—for games it's usually best to have things as self-contained as possible. I often use the *assets* folder as a generic repository for all external files.

Stay Within the Same Folder as the HTML Script File

Avoid linking to graphics files outside the current folder (or its subfolders). Putting your images into arbitrary folders on your computer just makes it harder to keep track of where everything is. Your pages won't load correctly if you change the folders on your PC, because your browser won't be able to find all the necessary files.

▶ Bonus Examples

These bonus game examples provide more insight on using graphics in your JavaScript games.

Tic-Tac-Toe, Lesson 5

Classic tic-tac-toe game, to be played between two human players. Uses the HTML5 canvas feature to draw lines across the winning squares.

15 of 16 Tile Puzzle, Lesson 2

Click on the tiles to move them into the proper order. Game play is with graphics. The game selects one of several image backgrounds at random.

Ghoul's Blackjack

Simplified blackjack card game makes extended use of graphics. Of note: All of the playing cards are derived from a single graphics file.

Zombie Girl Dressup, Lessons 1 and 2

Click on articles of clothing to add and remove them from the image. There are two lessons to look at:

- **ZombieGirl–Lesson1**
  Basic game version with simple buttons to show or hide clothes, hair, and shoes demonstrates how graphic images may be overlaid by the browser to create a composite.

- **ZombieGirl–Lesson2**
  Refined version of above, with stylized buttons and internal logic to prevent overlaying two of the same kind of clothing articles (two tops, for example).

WRITING CODE
THAT THINKS

Your games don't need sophisticated artificial intelligence to appear smart. All they need is some basic decision-making that steers things along.

Those decisions are typically based on very simple logic problems—"if this happens, then do that." This kind of program logic is often referred to as the *if-then* test, and it forms the basis of writing programs that think.

In this chapter, discover how to make your games and other scripts do this thinking on their own. Using external results—from the player or from the computer itself—your code will make split-second decisions that alter its course of action. You'll also learn JavaScript's language of logic and how to use its special symbols to construct all kinds of thought problems.

▶ How Programs Make Decisions

Programming code is simplistic when it comes to making decisions. There are no gut reactions— just logical comparisons that would make Mr. Spock proud. Decisions begin with an *expression*, which *evaluates* to either true or false. There are no other possible outcomes.

The most common way to stipulate the expression is to use an `if` statement. The basic JavaScript `if` statement goes like this:

```
if (expression) {
  // true: do this code
}
```

Expression is what's being evaluated—the question being posed. If expression resolves to *true*, then the code underneath is executed. If expression resolves to not true (*false*), then the code is skipped.

It's not uncommon to also provide a specific alternative, should the `if` expression resolve to *false*:

```
if (expression) {
  // true: do this code
} else {
  // false: otherwise to this code
}
```

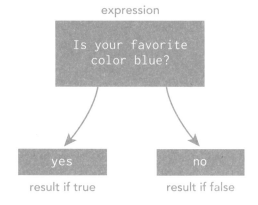

Figure 10-1. Expressions pose a question.

The { and } characters form a *block* so that multiple lines of code can be grouped together for either the *true* or the *false* condition.

If there's just one line of code to perform after the `if` or `else` statement, then JavaScript allows you to leave off the { and } block characters.

```
if (expression)
  // true: do this code
// Any code that follows is not part of the if test
```

However, although this makes for slightly more tidy code, there is a greater potential of introducing errors in the code if it's later modified with additional lines. At least while you're learning to code, it's best to always use the { and } braces for all your `if` statements.

▶ Inside an Expression

The most common expression tests a variable against some unchanging, or literal, value. The data in a variable can change each time the program is run, but the literal value is always the same.

```
if (x == 5)
```

is an example of an expression that tests whether the value in the variable named x is equal to the literal number 5. (Presumably, the contents of the x variable have been filled in some time prior to this if test. If that's not the case, the expression results in an error because there's nothing inside x to compare against.)

You can test text strings the same way. In the following example, the expression evaluates to true if x contains the text "cat":

```
if (x == "cat")
```

- x ▶ contains the value you wish to check
- "cat" ▶ the value you wish to compare against
- == ▶ the *comparison operator*; it means "equal to"

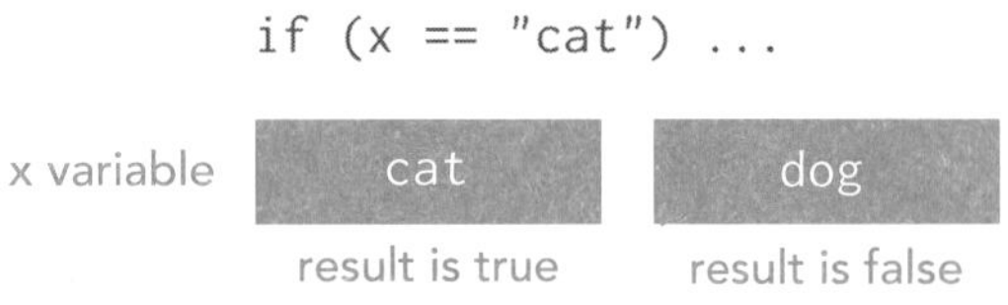

```
if (x == "cat") ...
```

	cat	dog
x variable	result is true	result is false

Figure 10-2. The basic if expression.

Although == is the most-commonly used comparison operator, you have others at your disposal. These include:

OPERATOR	MEANS
!=	Not equal to
<	Less than
>	Greater than
<=	Less than or equal to
>=	Greater than or equal to
===	Equal to, in both value and **type***
!==	Not equal to, in value or **type***

* *Type* means the kind of values being compared, not just the values themselves. JavaScript knows the difference between the number 5 and a string with the text "5" in it. Depending on the comparison you use, the result could be *true* or *false*.

▶ What's True, What's False

As in most any programming language, the meaning of true and false in JavaScript can be a source of confusion. Let's dispel some of that confusion right here.

True and False Can Be the Result of an Expression of Equality

As you've seen, comparing two values results in *true* if the values are the same, or *false* if they are different. The expression if (5 == 5) results in *true*, whereas if (5 == 4) results in *false*.

Negative Logic Inverts the Finding of True and False

Using an expression like if (5 == 5) is an example of *positive logic*: You're testing whether 5 is equal to 5 (and of course it is). You can also test when something is *not* equal by appending the ! (logical NOT) operator to the expression. This introduces *negative logic,* and the result of the expression is the inverse to what you get with positive logic.

The expression if (5 != 5) results in *false*, whereas if (5 != 4) results in *true*. Negative logic has the potential of adding confusion, but when used appropriately it can help create more concise code.

Simple Numbers Can Be Treated as True and False

A comparison that results in a value of 0 is considered false. Any other number—1, 476, –5, anything— is considered true. For example, the expression if (3 - 2) is considered true because the result of the subtraction is 1. Conversely, if (3 - 3) is false because the result of the subtraction is 0.

True and False Can Be Boolean Values That Specifically Denote True or False

Variables can contain the JavaScript values *true* and *false*. When they do, they are called *Boolean values,* named after the nineteenth-century mathematician George Boole, who first defined the algebraic system of logic in common use today. There are only two Boolean values: *true* and *false*. They are self-resolving, meaning they already express themselves as either *true* or *false*. Example: The expression if (true) most appropriately evaluates to *true*.

▶ The Difference between the = and == Operators

You've probably noticed that sets of equals signs are used to denote equality in `if` expressions. Hmm. . . . Why not just something like:

```
if (x = "cat")
```

The reason: As with many languages, the developers of JavaScript decided to use different operators for assigning a variable and for testing equality.

The single = operator is used to assign a value to a variable:

```
var myVar = 5
```

The double == operator is used to test values for equality:

```
if (myVar == 5)
```

It's a common newbie mistake to use a single equals sign in an `if` expression. The following won't cause an error, because it is technically valid (and, sometimes, it's what you want to do):

```
if (myVar = 5)
```

Rather than compare the values against each other, this code quite happily assigns the number 5 to myVar. The result of the expression is the number 5; recall that any value other than 0 is treated as *true*, so the `if` expression evaluates this line of code to *true*. Probably not what you intended.

Some programmers use a different coding pattern to avoid this mistake. Although

```
if (myVar = 5)
```

is not flagged as an error, the following *is* flagged (in the browser's console window):

```
if (5 = myVar)
```

JavaScript complains it is an "*Invalid left-hand side in assignment,*" because it can't assign something to a literal value. Whether you wish to adopt this programming practice is up to you. Some don't mind it; others consider it counterintuitive and don't like to use it.

For this book, I opted to use the more traditional comparison pattern of myVar == 5 (it's what you'll see in 98 percent of the code examples out there), while encouraging the practice of double-checking that the comparison syntax is correct.

▶ Example: Single-Condition Expression

The *condition* is the result of a comparison. Scripts may contain one comparison (condition), or several, all intertwined to create an elaborate logic problem.

The best way to learn about using if-then conditional expressions is to try one in action. Open the *conditional1.html* playground script in both browser and code editor. In the browser, open the console window in order to see the script output. This playground script demonstrates resolving a single decision-making condition.

snipped from: conditional1.html

```
51    function divClick(div) {
52     if (div.id == "yellow") {
53      console.log ("Correct, that skull is yellow.");
54     } else {
55      console.log ("Wrong, that skull isn't yellow.");
56     }
57    }
```

The script displays a set of three skulls, each in a different color. As shown in Figure 10-3, you're asked to click on the yellow skull. To run the code through its paces, click on a colored skull.

▤ Invisible DIVs ▸ sized to overlay onto each skull, serve as click "hot spots." Clicking on any DIV triggers its onclick event listener, which calls the divClick function (line 51).

▤ Line 52 comprises the if expression if(div.id == "yellow") ▸ for each clicked DIV, the code examines its ID property, which is either yellow, red, or green

▤ If div.id equals yellow ▸ the script displays its *Correct* text (line 53)

▤ If div.id does not equal yellow ▸ the script displays its *Wrong* text (line 55)

Click the Yellow Skull

Figure 10-3. Using OR and AND logic.

▶ Evaluating More Than One Thing at a Time

From time to time, your code might need to perform more elaborate tests in which you must check for multiple simultaneous conditions. Your code can check whether *any* of the tests are true or false, or *all* of the tests are true or false.

▶ Testing for Any Result

Multiple expressions may be combined to test whether any one of them is *true* or *false* by using what's known as *OR logic*. It goes like this:

```
if condition1 == 1 OR condition2 == 2
```

Should either condition1 or condition2 be true, the entire if test evaluates to *true*.

In JavaScript, OR logic is accomplished using the || double-pipe characters. (The pipe character is the one produced by pressing Shift+\ [backslash] on your keyboard.)

```
if (condition1 == 1 || condition2 == 2)
```

This results in *true* if either condition1 equals 1, or if condition2 equals 2 (see Figure 10-4).

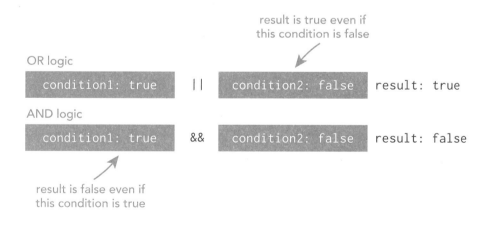

Figure 10-4. Using OR and AND logic.

Testing for All Results

You can also combine expressions and test if they are all *true* or *false* by using *AND logic*, like this:

```
if condition1 == 1 AND condition2 == 2
```

Should both condition1 and condition2 be *true*, the entire if test evaluates to *true*. In JavaScript, AND logic is accomplished using the && double-ampersand characters.

```
if (condition1 == 1 && condition2 == 2)
```

This example results in *true* only if both condition1 equals 1 and condition2 equals 2 (see Figure 10-4).

Handy-Dandy Logic Tables

The below logic tables help visualize the result of multiple-condition expressions. *Condition1* and *Condition2* are the two tests.

OR Truth Table

CONDITION1	CONDITION2	RESULT
false	false	false
true	false	true
false	true	true
true	true	true

AND Truth Table

CONDITION1	CONDITION2	RESULT
false	false	false
true	false	false
false	true	false
true	true	true

▶ Using Nested if Statements

Another—sometimes less confusing—way of testing for multiple conditions is to use multiple if expressions and "nest" them in order to combine their evaluations. The general idea is:

```
if (A == 1) {
 if (B == 1) {
  // do this if both A ·== 1 and B == 1
 }
}
```

This performs the same function as if (A == 1 && B == 1), but in a way that's a little easier to follow. This alternative method is most useful if you need to combine several conditional tests. Rather than creating elaborate single-line expressions, you can break them down:

```
if (A == 1 || B == 1) {
 if (C == 1) {
  // do this if either A == 1 and B == 1, but only if C == 1
 }
}
```

The first test is true if either A or B equal 1. The second test is true only if the previous expression evaluates to true, PLUS C equals 1. This takes a little more code, but it is less likely to confuse and cause coding errors.

▶ Evaluating Both Value and Type

I briefly mentioned this earlier, but it bears repeating with more detail here: Sometimes you need to compare not just the value of two things but the type of these values. Consider this test:

```
var myVar = "5";
if (myVar == 5)
 . . .
```

JavaScript tells you the two are the same because the value of myVar is indeed 5. But there's something sly going on here: During the evaluation, JavaScript takes it upon itself to *coerce* the value in the myVar variable from a string to a numeric. What was the string "5" becomes the number 5. This process is called *automatic type conversion*, and it's one of the features of JavaScript that makes it easier to use.

This isn't always what you want. So JavaScript adds an additional method to test for both the value and the type of data you're comparing. To do this, you use the === *identity comparison operator*.

```
var myVar = "5";
if (myVar === 5)
 . . .
```

Now the result is false, because even though "5" and 5 can represent the number 5, the two types of data are not the same. The "5" is a string data type, and the 5 is a numeric data type. Under the hood, when you use the === operator, it tells JavaScript not to do the automatic type conversion.

The === identity comparison goes a little deeper than what I've described here. The rules outlined above apply if the types of data being compared are simple numbers or strings.

When comparing objects—JavaScript's handy collections of data—the === operator checks if the comparison is made against the same object. This caveat may or may not come up very often in your JavaScripting, but it's something to keep in mind.

▶ Using the switch Statement to Test Multiple Outcomes

Sometimes you need to perform a whole series of tests on a value. If any of the tests match, your code performs a specific task. You could do it with only the if statement:

```
if (A == 1) {
 // A is 1
}
if (A == 2) {
 // A is 2
}
if (A == 3) {
 // A is 3
}
```

It works, but a better method might be to use the switch statement, which is engineered for exactly this sort of thing.

```
switch (A) {
 case (1):
  // A is 1
  break;
 case (2):
  // A is 2
  break;
 case (3):
  // A is 3
  break;
 default:
  // None of the above
}
```

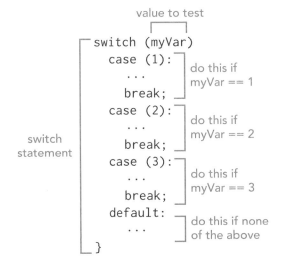

Figure 10-5. The switch statement tests a value against many possibilities.

Okay, you're probably thinking the switch approach doesn't cut down on the lines of code, and it doesn't look all that easier. Both are correct for this trivial example, but it's when the code gets more elaborate that the switch statement shines. Using switch tends to reduce the visual complexity of the code, which makes it easier to write and maintain. The switch statement is composed of the following parts:

Statement block ▶ This is enclosed in those pesky { and } brace characters.

Expression to evaluate ▶ This is most-commonly just a variable whose contents you want to compare against.

One or more case statements ▶ For each case, you provide a value to compare the expression against. The example tests if A contains 1, 2, or 3.

Code to execute for each case ▶

I'm showing just a comment, but you'd use write lines of code here for each case.

A break Statement (optional but typical) ▶ The break statement literally breaks out of the switch block when it's encountered. Without the break, JavaScript would proceed to the next case. This is sometimes useful, but it is often not what you're after.

A default statement (optional) ▶ The default statement provides a "fall through" should none of the previous matches pan out.

▶ Example: switch Statement

I've reworked the pick-the-yellow-skull example to use switch instead of if. Check out the *conditional2 .html* playground script. You'll quickly notice than an advantage of using switch is that you can provide different results for each choice—it's not just either/or as with a simple if-else statement. There's a different printed response for each skull choice.

Try some variations. For example, change the script to accept either yellow or green, but not red. Or add more skulls; you can accommodate an unlimited number of colors simply by adding more case statements.

snipped from: conditional2.html

```
51 function divClick(div) {
52  switch (div.id) {
53   case ("yellow"):
54    console.log ("Correct, the skull you chose is yellow.");
55    break;
56   case ("red"):
57    console.log ("Wrong, the skull you chose is red.");
58    break;
59   case ("green"):
60    console.log ("Wrong, the skull you chose is green.");
61    break;
62  }
63 }
```

Variations on a switch Theme

You're not limited to just comparing the contents of a variable against expected values. You can also do this sort of thing:

```
switch (true) {
  case (A == 1):
    // A is 1
    break;
  case (B == 2):
    // B is 2
    break;
  case (C == 3):
    // C is 3
    break;
}
```

When the **switch** expression is set to true, you get a match if any of the case's evaluate to true. It's the equivalent of stringing a whole bunch of **if** statements one right after the other but in a more compact format.

Here's another: By leaving out the **break** statement, you can combine two or more cases. If any of the case statements match, the subsequent code is executed.

```
switch (A) {
  case (1):
  case (2):
    // A == 1 OR A is 2
    break;
  case (3):
    // A is 3 (Note: break isn't needed for last case)
}
```

This is the perfect approach when setting up *keyboard events* (explained in Chapter 12: Responding to Events: Part 2 (page 183). The **switch** statement responds to various keypresses, and some of the keypresses are doubled-up to mean the same thing. For example, the letter W is the same as the Up Arrow, letter S is the same as the Down Arrow, and so on.

Here's a shortened version of setting up for the keyboard from the bonus game *Kitteh in Space*.

```
switch (keyName)) {
  case "w":
  case "arrowup":
    moveShip(-12);
    break;
  case "s":
  case "arrowdown":
    moveShip(12);
    break;
  case " ":
    fireTargets();
    break;
}
```

▶ Bonus Examples

All of the bonus scripts that accompany this book contain at least one example of self-thinking programming, but here are several notable games you can look over for their explicit treatment of the subject.

Ruins of Ramic, Lessons 1 and 2

Click on any two cards to match them up. You score with each match. There are two lessons to look at: Lesson 1 is a simple shell that demonstrates the overall construction of the game; Lesson 2 shows how to use if-else tests to check when the two cards match.

Zombie Girl Dressup, Lesson 3

More *Zombie Girl Dressup;* in Lesson 3, if-else tests are used to determine whether specific clothing types have already been applied and, if so, to remove them before applying the newly selected apparel.

Pipeworks

In *Pipeworks*, a complex series of if-else tests are used to determine if a segment of pipe can be placed into the game board. The tests calculate the "in" and "out" orifices of the pipe so they can connect together to allow water to flow through. This is a more advanced game, so take your time studying it.

WORKING WITH THE DOCUMENT OBJECT MODEL (DOM)

When the HTML elements on a web page are processed by a browser, each element is converted into an object; these objects form a collection called the *document object model*. The primary use and benefit of the document object model is that it allows for interactive access of the individual objects.

The document object model—or *DOM* for short—is the foundation that makes interactive–web page coding possible. No document object model, no web page games—or at least, no games that are fun enough to play!

As you've read through this book, you've been learning about the document object model all along—I've been using it in various examples from the beginning. But it's time now to turn a serious eye toward the DOM and discover what it is and how it works. The DOM provides the programming links to locate, inspect, and even change in an HTML document.

In the processing of an HTML page, the browser converts elements to something called *nodes*; these nodes are the objects from which the visible page is formatted and rendered on the screen.

The exact architecture of nodes and how they are implemented in browsers is not important to this discussion; it's just important that you are aware of the terminology. The term *node* can crop up from time to time as you use JavaScript to manipulate a web page. Just be aware that a node defines a particular piece of the page.

▶ DOM Starter Playground Script

The DOM is best discovered by playing with it. So let's begin with the *dom-starter.html* playground script. It's very basic and doesn't actually do anything—yet. Don't worry; we'll get there!

Load the *dom-starter.html* document file into the Atom text editor (or whatever editor you're using for the projects in this book). Also load the file in your browser—the page will look like that in Figure 11-1 —and open the console window. In the code below, I'm only showing the main HTML of the script; for space reasons, the STYLE element is omitted. Review the full code in your text editor.

snipped from: dom-starter.html

```
48  <div id="mainContent">
49   <img id="earth" class="image" alt="" src="earthview.jpg">
50   <img id="martian" class="image" alt="" src="martian-machine.png">
51   <p id="text">The Martians Invade</p>
52  </div>
53
54  <script>
55
56   var mainContent = document.getElementById("mainContent");
57   var earth = document.getElementById("earth");
58   var martian = document.getElementById("martian");
59   var text = document.getElementById("text");
60   var images = document.getElementsByClassName("image");
61   var body = document.getElementsByTagName("body")[0];
62
63  </script>
```

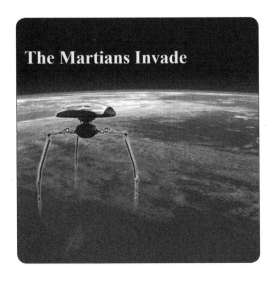

HTML Content

The displayable HTML content is on lines 48 through 52. It consists of a DIV container, two IMG images, and one P text element.

Each of the elements is given an ID name, in order to uniquely differentiate it from the others on the page. For example, the Earth horizon image is named "earth"; the invading Martian warship is called "martian", and so on. In addition, the two IMG elements have class names ("image"), which sorts them into a shared group.

Figure 11-1. The *dom-starter.html* playground script.

Both ID and class names can be used for two different goals:

1. They provide a means to alter the style of a specific element or group of elements.

2. They provide a means for JavaScript to isolate the element (or group of elements) in order to perform additional processing on them.

JavaScript

The JavaScript code uses the power of the DOM to select, and therefore isolate, the individual elements on the page. Each statement line defines a variable that contains an element (or group of elements). I've given these variables descriptive names—in fact, they're the same as the ID/class names given to the elements.

As it stands, nothing is yet done using the elements that have been rustled up, but this starter code readies the stage for further development.

▶ The DOM and the DOM Programming Interface

When an HTML page is ingested by the browser, all of its elements are turned into JavaScript objects. As you've learned in previous chapters, as JavaScript objects, they offer both *properties* and *methods*.

Properties ▶ values of the element objects that you can query or change. In many examples in this book, you've seen how to change the position properties of an element to move it across the screen.

Methods ▶ functions built into the element objects that perform some kind of helpful action. For example, there is a method to ask the DOM to collect all of the elements with a given class name and stick them into an array.

Collectively, the way you access HTML element using properties and methods is through the DOM *application programming interface*, or *API*. The term may connote complexity, but in practice, it's designed to have the opposite benefit: to make it much easier to access the individual elements of a page.

▶ Code for Accessing DOM Elements

In *dom-starter.html,* three different methods are used to fetch references to the HTML elements in the page; refer to Figure 11-2. These three are very commonly used in all kinds of JavaScript code, including games, so it's important that you get to know them.

getElementById

The getElementById method finds the named element on the page and returns a *reference* to that element. (A reference means a finger-pointer to the real McCoy; you don't get the actual element, or even a copy of it.) The syntax for the method is

```
document.getElementById("elementName");
```

where elementName is the name of the element that you want. The name is a text string, so enclose it in quotes. The quotes can be 'single' or "double"—I prefer using double-quotes, but you can adopt any approach you want as long as you're consistent.

Because IDs are assumed to be unique, this method will always return only a single element. If you make a mistake and give two elements the same ID, this method will return the first one it finds on the page.

With the reference to the element now in hand, you can go about fetching information about the element or changing things about it. You'll learn how in the next section.

```
                                         gets element where
                                             id="myId"
        getElementById("myId")   <div id="myId"... ></div>


                                        gets all elements where
                                           class="myClass"

                                      <img class="myClass"... />
getElementsByClassName("myClass")   <img class="myClass"... />
                                      <img class="myClass"... />


                                        gets all elements where
                                              tag="p"

        getElementsByTagName("p")   <p> ... </p>
```

Figure 11-2. Using DOM methods to collect matching elements.

getElementsByClassName

The getElementsByClassName method finds all the elements on the page that match the class you specify and returns an array of references to those elements (remember arrays; they were detailed back in Chapter 6).

An array is used instead of a regular single-value variable because you are likely to get more than one element back. The syntax for the method is

```
document.getElementsByClassName("className");
```

As used in *dom-starter.html*, the references returned by the method are stacked into an array named images.

```
var images = document.getElementsByClassName("image");
```

So to get to the individual images, you need to specify which element of the array you wish to use. Array elements start at 0, so

```
images[0]
```

references the first image element, and

```
images[1]
```

references the second image element.

Using a for loop, which you learned about in Chapter 5: Getting Started with JavaScript: Part 1 (page 67), you can peek into all of the elements in an array without worrying about how many there are. I'll recap that method later in this chapter.

> Be careful about spelling and capitalization — it's named getElements . . . *Elements* with an s. Furthermore, notice that it's ClassName . . . and not Classname. You must type the method name correctly, or JavaScript will report an error.

getElementsByTagName

It should come as no surprise that the getElementsByTagName method collects all the elements that match a particular tag name and returns them to you. The syntax for the method is

```
document.getElementsByTagName("tagName");
```

As with the getElementsByClassName method, getElementsByTagName also returns an array. But notice something strange in the code on line 61:

```
var body = document.getElementsByTagName("body")[0];
```

As noted, `getElementsByTagName` returns an array, but as demonstrated in this code, only a reference to a single element comes back. I know that there's only one BODY on the page, so I include the array element [0] at the end of the method to indicate I want just the one. What goes into the `body` variable, then, is a single reference and not an array. Tricky!

This technique is useful when you know there's only one such tag in the document, or when you know you only want a specific element that matches the criteria. The elements are stacked into the array in the order they are in the page, so [0] gets the first tag, [1] gets the second, and so on.

The code

```
document.getElementsByTagName("body")[0];
```

is functionally equivalent to

```
document.body;
```

I used the former method because it showed off the [0] array element trick when collecting elements by tag name, and I really wanted to show you this technique. In a real (non-demo) script, you'd probably want to use the simpler `document.body` instead.

▶ Changing an Element via the DOM

With a reference to an element in hand, you can now go about changing something about that element. Let's start with the P text element. You'll move the element over to the right a little, change its color, and alter the text itself.

snipped from: dom-starter-changetext.html

```
63 text.style.left = "190px";
64 text.style.color = "#40e0d0";
65 text.style.fontSize = "2.0em";
66 text.innerText = "The Martians Are Here";
```

▪ Line 63 ▶ changes the left style of the text from its original 25px to 190px. This pushes the text toward the right.

▪ Line 64 ▶ modifies the color of the text. The #40e0d0 RGB hexadecimal value produces a turquoise tint.

▫ Line 65 ▸ slightly reduces the size of the text so it can accommodate more characters.

▫ Line 66 ▸ changes the text displayed in the P element to "The Martians Are Here."

Because all the HTML elements on a page are objects, the objects and their individual properties are accessed using the now-familiar

```
objectName.propertyName
```

dot notation. This is what's happening on lines 63 through 66, where text is the objectName, and style or innerText are the propertyNames. In the case of the style property, it has properties of its own, and these are likewise identified using dot notation:

```
text.style.color
```

is the color style property of the text object.

Notice line 65 and the fontSize property, and compare it to the property name in the STYLE element on line 34, where it says font-size. The general rule is that for style properties accessed from JavaScript, you drop the – hyphen character and capitalize the next word: font-size becomes fontSize, and background-color becomes backgroundColor.

If you only plan on accessing an element once or twice in your code, you don't need to first create a variable to hold a reference to the element. Instead, just use the getElement method directly with the property you want to change:

```
document.getElementById("text").style.left = "190px";
```

In these demo scripts, I show assigning element references to variables because it's easier for newcomers to follow this chain of logic. You save some code space and reduce the number of variables in your code by omitting these variable assignments when they're not required.

▸ ## Altering Multiple Groups of Elements at a Time

The getElementsByClassName and getElementsByTagName methods are designed to collect all the matching elements on the page and then stuff their references in an array. (Exception: As demonstrated for the BODY tag on page 174, you can talk JavaScript into giving you back only one item by prespecifying the array element you want.)

Once in an array, you can reference each element. Suppose you want to change the background color of all the DIV elements on the page. After using the getElementsByTagName method to collect all the DIV elements:

```
var divs = document.getElementsByTagName("div");
```

you can then specify each one by indicating which element of the array to use:

```
divs[0].style.backgroundColor = "#87ceeb";
divs[1].style.backgroundColor = "#87ceeb";
divs[2].style.backgroundColor = "#87ceeb";
```

Obviously, if there are lots of DIVs on the page, this code could get quite lengthy, so the better approach is to use a for loop.

Let's see this technique in action. In the *dom-starter-noimages.html* playground script, two IMG elements are collected into the images array, using the getElementsByClassName method—the class name is image. Using a for loop, the elements are then made invisible by changing their visibility style.

snipped from: dom-starter-noimages.html

```
60  var images = document.getElementsByClassName("image");
. . .
63  for (var i = 0; i < images.length; i++) {
64    images[i].style.visibility = "hidden";
65  }
```

The for loop iterates each element in the images array, previously obtained in line 60 of the script. You don't need to know ahead of time how many tags there are that match the image class name; that info is conveniently derived by the images.length property in the loop.

Instead of hard-coding an array element each time, the loop substitutes a variable used for keeping count. First time through, i=0, so images[0] is modified. Second time through, i=1, so images[1] is modified. The more elements to change, the more the for loop saves coding time and space.

The getElement methods are not the only means to fetch objects from the DOM. Two other methods are querySelector and querySelectorAll. These are more generalized methods that do much the same as the getElement but require a more strict attention to the format of the name parameter.

▶ Reading Values via the DOM

You're not just limited to using the DOM to change an element. You can read existing values of an element, too. But there's a catch to getting this to work in all circumstances, so pay particular attention to this section.

To get some value from an element, you use the reference to the element and access one of its properties, like this:

```
console.log (text.innerText);
```

In the browser console, you see the text of the P element. Try it with the original *dom-starter.html* document by adding this code after line 61. The console reads "The Martians Invade"—that's the text inside the P element.

This method works fine for many element properties but not all. Specifically, style properties may not always return a usable value, depending on how the property was originally set:

▨ If the property was only set in a style, or has not been set at all

   ▸ JavaScript will not return a value.

▨ If the property has been previously set in JavaScript

   ▸ JavaScript will return that value.

Try adding this to the *dom-starter.html* playground file:

```
63  console.log ("mainContent left: " + mainContent.style.left);
```

Reload the page and look in the console window. It says only

```
mainContent left:
```

without a value! Obviously that won't do. To fetch a value for a style property, do one of these things.

Use the getComputedStyle Method

Though JavaScript can't directly reach the style value, the browser nevertheless knows what it is. You just have to ask in a different way. This takes using the getComputedStyle method, which queries the browser to get the "live," or computed, value for any style property. The syntax is:

```
window.getComputedStyle(element).property
```

where element is the element you're checking, and property is the style property you want to return.

Note: element is the *reference* to an element, such as what you get with the getElementById method. In the examples throughout this chapter, this reference is contained in a variable, and you can use that variable with the getComputedStyle method.

In modern browsers, you can leave off the window part and the getComputedStyle method will still work. I include it here and in other examples throughout the book for the sake of consistency with most other examples you'll find on the Internet.

Now try adding these two lines to the code:

```
64  var cLeft = window.getComputedStyle(mainContent).left;
65  console.log ("mainContent left: " + cLeft);
```

This code fetches the left style property for the mainContent element. The value for the left property hasn't been set yet, so you get the browser's default.

Set the Value Previously in JavaScript

JavaScript doesn't have a problem getting the property value for a style if previous JavaScript code has set that value. Add this code to see how it works:

```
67  mainContent.style.left = "20px";
68  console.log ("mainContent left: " + mainContent.style.left);
```

The browser console correctly reports 20px as the left style value. See the *dom-starter-fetchleftproperty.html* playground file, which demonstrates both of these techniques.

▶ Reading and Updating Style Values

A primary goal of reading a style value, such as left or top, is so that you can reposition an element relative to its current position This can be accomplished using either of the alternatives provided above and on the previous page. For this next demonstration, I show the getComputedStyle method.

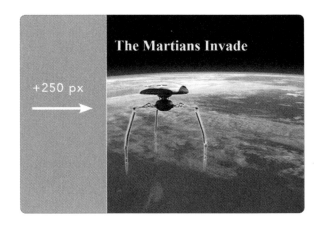

Figure 11-3. Moved text from its previous location.

The *dom-starter-movemain.html* playground page moves the mainContent DIV 250 pixels from wherever it currently is. It does this by first obtaining the current left style property value and then adding 250 to it, as shown in Figure 11-3.

```
snipped from: dom-starter-movemain.html

63  var cLeft = window.getComputedStyle(mainContent).left;
64  mainContent.style.left = parseInt(cLeft) + 250 + "px";
```

Notice some extra code on line 64. The value returned by getComputedStyle for the left style property is the current left position, including a unit of measure. By default, this unit is pixels. So, what you get back from getComputedStyle is some number followed by px, such as 10px. This causes problems when simply adding another number to it. If you were to try adding 250 to this, you'd get

```
10px250
```

which won't work. Instead, you must:

1. Strip off any extraneous text from the value returned from getComputedStyle.

2. Convert it to a number value.

3. Add 250 to that.

4. And then finally append the px unit of measure.

The parseInt function performs steps 1 and 2. For example, assuming an input value of 10px, the result of parseInt is simply the number 10.

From this initial number, an additional 250 pixels is added on and finished by appending px to the value. You can experiment with how this works by making a change to the STYLE rule for the #mainContent element. Add the following:

```
20 left: 100px;
```

and rerun the script. This time, the mainContent DIV moves to the right even farther.

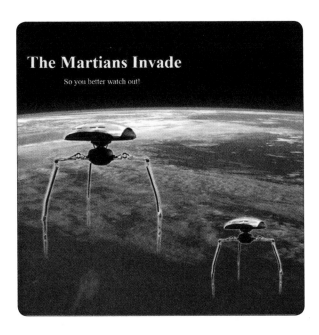

Figure 11-4. New elements can be added when the code is executed.

Adding New Elements to the Document

You've seen that document object models provides a rich assortment of tools for manipulating elements, but you can also add new elements that weren't there when the page first loaded. You might use this feature, for example, to dynamically append new treasures for your game character to locate and collect.

Adding elements to an existing document is best demonstrated starting with a simple example. The *dom-starter-elementappend.html* playground example shows adding a new P tag to the end of the mainContent DIV, as well as a new IMG element. As shown in Figure 11-4, the new text is formatted so that it appears right under the main headline, "The Martians Invade."

snipped from: dom-starter-elementappend.html

```
63  var para = document.createElement("p");
64  var textNode = document.createTextNode("So you better watch out!");
65  para.setAttribute("style",
    "position:absolute;top:100px;left:100px;color:#fff;");
66  para.appendChild(textNode);
67  mainContent.appendChild(para);
```

Line 63 uses the createElement method to specify you want to create a new P element. A reference to the new element is contained in the para variable. Other element types are similarly produced by specifying their tags—div, img, and so on.

The P element contains a *text node* inside the <p> and </p> tags (there's that *node* word I warned you about . . .). This node, and the actual text itself, are created on line 64.

Line 65 sets up an inline style for the new P tag; otherwise, it appears as black and is shuffled behind the other content on the page, making it invisible. The setAttribute method inserts a style= attribute into the P element with a style rule for the position, top, left, and color properties.

Even though the text node has been created, at this point it's floating out in space. Line 66 "attaches" the text node to the new P element.

And finally, the new P element itself is situated into the document tree by appending it to the `mainContent` element.

You can view the updated HTML by opening the browser console, if it's not open already, and clicking on the Elements tab (see Figure 11-5). Click the arrows to expand the tree—you'll see the new P element is nestled right at the bottom of the `mainContent` DIV, just as it should be.

Figure 11-5. Viewing the newly created HTML elements in the console window.

▶ **Bonus Example:**

Color Puzzle displays a set of six colored squares. The colors are randomized across the spectrum. Click on each color, and move that color to the blank squares above, in spectrum order. The game demonstrates using DIV elements and the document object model to move colors between the squares.

RESPONDING TO EVENTS: PART 2

In Chapter 8 (page 127), you learned what events are and how common events like mouse-clicks can trigger JavaScript code of your choosing.

Here we pick up where we left off in that chapter and continue our excursion into JavaScript–event-land, including how to add and remove events strictly from within JavaScript code, how to trigger events when transitions end, and how to watch for certain keypresses on the keyboard.

▶ Using the addEventListener Method

Chapter 8 concentrated on the on... event methods that are added directly to HTML elements. A typical example of an on... event is onclick, which listens for a mouse-click on an element.

The listener goes like this:

```
<img src="ufo.png" onclick="clickMe();">
```

and the JavaScript code handler looks like this:

```
function clickMe() {
 console.log ("Yippee, the IMG element was clicked!");
}
```

Many seasoned JavaScript coders prefer a different listener mechanism: using the addEventListener method. It does the same thing, but it provides more flexibility, including being able to easily add and remove the listener at any time in code, plus allowing you to provide multiple listeners for the same kind of event.

The addEventListener method is used like this. First, add a unique ID name to the element you want to use. This makes the subsequent JavaScript easier to write.

snipped from: events-basic.html

```
<img id="saucer" alt="" src="./assets/ufo.png">
```

Next, set up the event listener and handler (see Figure 12-1).

```
document.getElementById("saucer").addEventListener("click", clickMe);
function clickMe() {
 console.log ("Yippee, the IMG element was clicked!");
}
```

Don't also add the onclick attribute to the HTML tag. The addEventListener method does everything you need. The events to listen for are similarly named to the on... events, except you leave off the "on" part: onclick becomes click, onmousemove becomes mousemove, and so on. As addEventListener is a method of an HTML object, you use dot notation to specify this relationship. The object to add the listener on to is specified by the code document.getElementById("saucer").

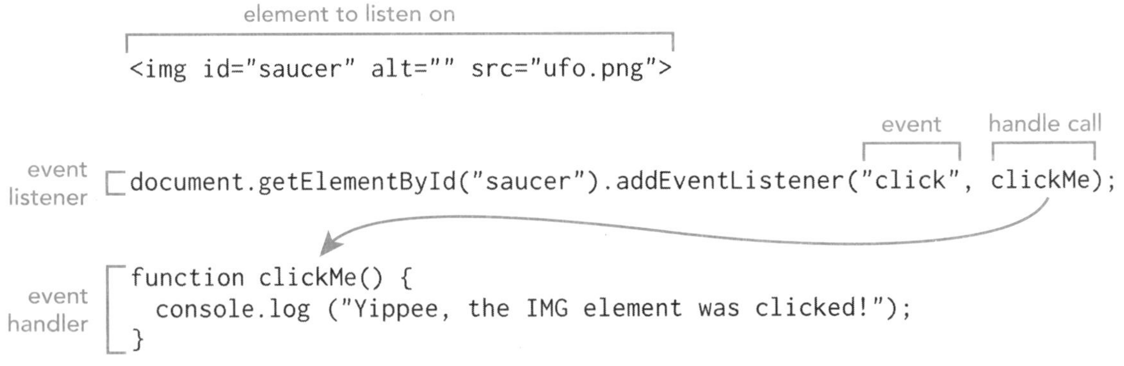

Figure 12-1. The basic structure of the addEventListener listener/handler.

Be sure **NOT** to do this:

```
document.getElementById("saucer").addEventListener("click", clickMe());
```

You might be tempted to add parentheses after the clickMe function name because this is how functions are called in other parts of JavaScript. But not here. Adding the parentheses tells JavaScript to *immediately* execute the clickMe function. You don't want that; clickMe is only supposed to be executed when the event occurs.

You often need to apply multiple pieces of code to the same HTML element. So using

```
document.getElementById("saucer") . . .
```

each time to identify the element you wish to use consumes code space and makes JavaScript slightly less efficient. In these instances, consider assigning the element to a variable, then using the variable with the subsequent code:

```
var saucer = document.getElementById("saucer");
saucer.addEventListener("click", clickMe);
```

Common Mouse Events

These mouse events for the addEventListener method are supported by Chrome and most other modern browsers.

▶ Using Anonymous Functions with addEventListener

The quick demonstration on the previous pages and many of the game examples that come with this book use the addEventListener method with a named function definition. You put the name of the function as the second parameter and then, elsewhere in your JavaScript code, include the named function itself.

However, if the code is short, you can also use an *anonymous function* with addEventListener and thereby save some code space. The listener itself contains the function, which is not given a name—hence the term anonymous function.

```
document.getElementById("saucer").addEventListener("click", function() {
 console.log ("Yippee, the IMG element was clicked!");
});
```

▶ Removing an Event Listener

Sometimes you want to stop an event listener so it no longer triggers on the event. For example, you might do this when the game is over and you don't want the player to keep interacting with the game elements.

Use the removeEventListener method to remove a listener added with addEventListener. Apply the same element and "signature" with the remove... method as you used for the add... method:

```
saucer.addEventListener("click", clickMe);
```

and then when you want to remove the listener:

```
saucer.removeEventListener("click", clickMe);
```

See the *events-addremove.html* playground script for a hands-on example.

▶ Adding Multiple Event Listeners to a Single Element

You can readily use addEventListener to listen for a number of events on a single element. Simply attach the listeners, specifying the event you want to use.

snipped from: events-multiple.html

```
17 var saucer = document.getElementById ("saucer");
18 saucer.addEventListener("click", mouseClick);
19 saucer.addEventListener("mouseover", mouseOver);
20 saucer.addEventListener("mouseout", mouseOut);
```

Try this out with the *events-multiple.html* playground script. Load the script into your browser and open the console window. Click on the saucer and move the mouse over and out of the saucer image. You'll see that each of these three events triggers a response in the console window.

You don't have to define separate functions for each listener that you've attached to the element. When using addEventListener, JavaScript automatically passes the handler function a laundry list of nifty info, including the type of event that got triggered. Just provide an object name as an argument of the handler function, and use that object to query things about the event that was triggered.

Here's an example of three event types attached to the flying saucer image. As shown in the *events-multiple.html* script, all three event types—click, mouseover, and mouseout—use the same handler function, saucerListen.

events-multiple.html continued

```
21 function saucerListen (ev) {
22   console.log (ev.type);
23 }
```

Line 21 defines the handler function, saucerListen. It specifies an object name for the argument passed into the function. I've named this object ev; the object carries numerous properties about the event that occurred. (You can use just about any name for this object; I like ev for *event*.)

Line 22 prints the event type into the browser's console window. It'll be one of the three being listened for: click, mouseover, or mouseout.

ev is the object　　　　　type is the property

The event object carries a lot of properties. Here's a list of some of the most-commonly used properties. Some of these properties are filled in only when used with certain event types. For example, movementX and movementY only apply to an event that captures mouse movement.

EVENT PROPERTY	WHAT IT DOES
button	Mouse button (if any) pressed at the time of the event. The value depends on which button is pressed. 0　　Main button (usually left button) 1　　Auxiliary button (usually middle) 2　　Secondary button (usually right)
clientX clientY	Mouse X and Y coordinates, relative to the so-called client area of the window (the visible part of the browser window minus scroll bars, toolbars, and so on) at the time of the event.
movementX movementY	The change ("delta") of the mouse X or Y coordinates since the last time the same event occurred. (NOTE: This is one of those events that's not supported in all browsers. Be careful when using it.)
target	The target object that originally dispatched the event.
target.className	The class name, if any, of the target.
target.height target.width	The displayable height and width of the target.
target.tagName	The type of HTML element (e.g., IMG for <img>) of the target.
target.id	The ID name of the target.
type	The type of event; e.g., click or mousemove.

To view all the properties of the `ev` object, use

```
console.log (ev);
```

and in the browser's console window, click the arrow beside `MouseEvent`. All of the properties of the event are shown in a list.

▶ Understanding Event Bubbling and Capturing

Bubbling and *capturing* define how events ripple (*propagate*) through the HTML object model. Suppose you have one element nestled inside the other. Both have click events. If you click on the inside object, you will trigger two events, because the click was within each of the elements.

The order in which these events occur is called a *phase*; which phase your code is told to listen for is defined as bubbling and capturing—see Figure 12-2.

- `When events are bubbled (the default)` ▶ they occur "inside-out"; the element on the inside gets triggered first, followed by the outside element. You can think of the events "bubbling up" through the object model.

- `When events are captured` ▶ they occur "outside-in"; the element on the outside gets triggered first. Events are handled at the higher levels first, then filter down to the lower elements.

Here's an example of event bubbling. It consists of our favorite flying saucer IMG contained inside a DIV element. Lines 36 and 39 specifically set the bubble/capture setting to *false*, which means to use bubbling. This is the default setting, so if you simply leave out this setting, you'll get the same result.

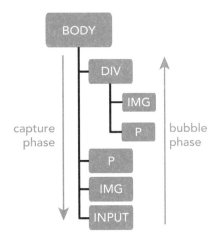

Figure 12-2. Events propagate through the HTML on the page in two phases.

snipped from: events-bubble.html

```
34  saucer.addEventListener("click", function() {
35    console.log ("saucer");
36  }, false);
37  div.addEventListener("click", function() {
38    console.log ("div");
39  }, false);
```

When you click on just the DIV ▶ only the event-handler for the DIV is triggered.

When you click on the saucer ▶ the saucer event is first triggered, followed by the DIV event.

Now try the script with the bubble/capture setting set to *true*.

snipped from: events-capture.html

```
34  saucer.addEventListener("click", function() {
35    console.log ("saucer");
36  }, true);
37  div.addEventListener("click", function() {
38    console.log ("div");
39  }, true);
```

As before, when you click on just the DIV ▶ only the event-handler for the DIV is triggered.

When you click on the saucer ▶ the DIV event is triggered first, followed by the saucer.

Which method you choose depends on what you're doing with the events. It's often easiest to use bubbling, because you can handle the first event and then ignore the rest.

Event propagation can get to be complex and confusing. In cases where clicking on an element causes two or more events to fire, perhaps the simplest approach is to define handler functions for each element and to use the stopPropagation method in each one to prevent bubbling (or capturing) from triggering successive events.

Using the method is simple:

```
ev.stopPropagation();
```

See the *events-capturebubble-simple.html* playground script for a working example.

When you run the code, you'll see only the message for the specific, directly clicked-on elements; either saucer or `mainContent` DIV.

Sometimes you have to use a single event-handler function to take care of all the elements that are clicked on. You can readily accomplish this by adding code that examines which element was the "target" of the event. But there's a catch. . . .

Ordinarily, you can fetch the identity of the element that caused an event with code like this:

```
var saucer = document.getElementById ("saucer");
saucer.addEventListener("click", clicked, false);
function clicked(ev) {
 console.log (ev.target.id);
}
```

This works when there's just one element "bound" to the event-handler. When there's more than one element attached to the handler, you need to step up your game a little and use a slightly different approach:

```
var saucer = document.getElementById ("saucer");
var div = document.getElementById ("mainContent");
saucer.addEventListener("click", clicked, false);
div.addEventListener("click", clicked, false);
function clicked(ev) {
 console.log (ev.currentTarget.id);
}
```

By using the currentTarget.id method instead, JavaScript reports the element that caused that specific event. You can use this information to decide how you want to handle that event. One way is to use the JavaScript switch statement (read more about it in Chapter 10: Writing Code that Thinks (page 155).

snipped from: events-capturebubble.html

```
32 var saucer = document.getElementById ("saucer");
33 var div = document.getElementById ("mainContent");
34 saucer.addEventListener("click", clicked, false);
35 div.addEventListener("click", clicked, false);
36 function clicked(ev) {
37  ev.stopPropagation();
38  switch (ev.currentTarget.id) {
39   case "saucer":
40    console.log ("the saucer was clicked");
41    break;
42   case "mainContent":
43    console.log ("the mainContent DIV was clicked");
44    break;
45  }
46 }
```

Line 37 ► stops event propagation, so only the first event is allowed to pass through. Since the events are set to bubble (inside-out order), clicking on the saucer causes just the saucer event.

Line 38 ► specifies the ev.currentTarger.id value for the switch statement, which contains the ID of the element that caused the event. Lines 39 and 42 match a possible expected result. Code then prints out the corresponding response in the browser's console window.

▶ Responding to Keyboard Events

Key presses from the keyboard are another common event your scripts can watch for. Your code can differentiate which key was pressed and so do different things. For example, the four arrow keys on a standard desktop PC keyboard can be used to navigate a character around the game board. Or the spacebar might fire a rocket or throw a knife.

To listen for any keypress, attach an addEventListener to the document object, like so:

snipped from: events-keyboard-simple.html

```
32  document.addEventListener('keydown', getKey);
33  function getKey(ev) {
34    console.log (ev.key);
35  }
```

Open the browser's console window, click anywhere in the document area of the browser, and press a key. The name value of that key is printed in the console, as shown in Figure 12-3.

Alphabetic, numeric, and symbol keys ► printed as they are on the keyboard.

Pressing the Spacebar ► comes out as a space (you can't see the space the spacebar makes in the window, but it's there).

Navigation keys such as the arrows. ► printed out by name; e.g., ArrowUp.

The so-called modifier keys—Ctrl, Shift, and so on ► printed out by name.

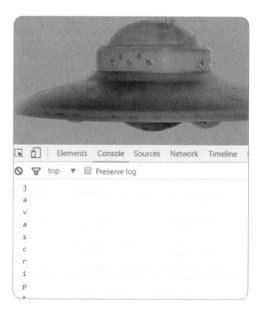

Figure 12-3. Keypress events can be captured and used for controlling your game.

Preventing Default Key Behavior

The keys you press retain any special function they have in the browser, such as F11 for Full Screen. Their name/value appears in the console window, and they have their normal effect in the browser.

If you need to override the default behavior of a key, include the preventDefault property in the event-handler:

```
function getKey(ev) {
 ev.preventDefault();
 console.log (ev.key);
}
```

Preventing Default Key Behavior Only with Certain Keys

Exercise care when using the preventDefault method. When applied to all keys, as shown above, preventDefault essentially disables keyboard access to the browser—this is not something you ordinarily want. You can instead apply the method only with certain keys, while allowing others.

```
if (ev.key == "ArrowUp" || ev.key == "ArrowDown" || ev.key == " ") {
 ev.preventDefault();
}
```

This code checks if the key pressed is ArrowUp, ArrowDown, or the Spacebar. If any of these is true, the default key behavior is prevented.

You might find it easier to use *keycodes* rather than the printable value of the key. The keyboard event allows you to examine the printable key values, as demonstrated above, or the numeric code associated with that key. For example, the following code does the same thing as the previous demonstration but uses the keyCode event property instead of the key event property.

```
var keyName = ev.key;
if (ev.keyCode == 40 || ev.keyCode == 38 || ev.keyCode == 32) {
 ev.preventDefault();
}
```

See the Online Support Site (Appendix A, page 310) for a full list of keyCode values.

Matching Key Values

You can use either the key or keyCode property to match pressed keys with the values you want to examine in your code. I prefer to use a combination:

- keyCode ► for preventing the default behavior of keys I want to capture, because it takes up less space when building if statements that include numerous keys.

- key ► for the actual keys I'm interested in, because by using the descriptive key value, it's more self-documenting.

Here's an example:

```
snipped from: events-keyboard.html
32 document.addEventListener('keydown', function (ev) {
33  var keyName = ev.key;
34  if (ev.keyCode == 40 || ev.keyCode == 38 || ev.keyCode == 32) {
35   ev.preventDefault();
36  }
37  switch (keyName.toLowerCase()) {
38   case "arrowup":
39    console.log ("move up");
40    break;
41   case "arrowdown":
42    console.log ("move down");
43    break;
44   case " ":
45    console.log ("fire");
46    break;
47  }
48 });
```

Add Event Listeners

Line 32 starts the addEventListener for handling keypresses. I'm looking for the keydown event—there's also keyup, which triggers when the key is released, and keypress, which triggers when the key for a (usually) printable character is pressed (keypress ignores the pressing of Alt, Ctrl, Shift, and other keys).

Store Key Value

Line 32 stores the value of the ev.key method in a variable for later use. It's just a mnemonic to remind me that this value contains the name of the key.

Prevent Default Key Behavior

Lines 34 through 36 prevent the default key behavior for ArrowUp, ArrowDown, and Spacebar. I'm using their keyCode values to quickly identify them in the list.

Isolate and Process Key

With the preparation out of the way, you can now match up the key(s) you're looking for and react to them.

- Line 37 ▶ starts a switch statement that compares the value in the keyName variable. To reduce possible errors, this value is converted to all lowercase using the toLowerCase string method.

- Lines 38, 41, and 44 ▶ compare the keyName variable with three expected results: ArrowUp, ArrowDown, and Spacebar (the spacebar is represented in code by the space between the quotes). In fully fleshed-out code, something different happens depending on these three keys.

▶ Using Events with CSS Transitions and CSS Animations

Several events can be triggered in JavaScript as the result of special motion effects created using Cascading Style Sheets. These effects, called CSS transitions and CSS animations, are more fully explored in Chapters 13 through 15 (pages 197–241).

▶ Bonus Examples

Many of the bonus scripts that come with this book demonstrate events of one type or another, but here are several basic examples that will help you hone your event handling skills.

Ruins of Ramic, Lesson 3

Click on any two cards to match them up. The addEventListener method is used to select cards for the matchup.

Sharker, Lessons 1 and 2

Sharker is an update on the old *Frogger* game, where the player helps a shark reach the other side of the road so he can eat the annoying people there while avoiding getting run over. Lesson 1 demonstrates a very basic rendition of the game that responds to keyboard events. Only one lane of cars is active. In Lesson 2, all three lanes contain cars; the movement of the cars is controlled using CSS transitions that contain event listeners.

MAKING YOUR GAME MOVE: AN INTRODUCTION TO ANIMATION TECHNIQUES

Animation is the cornerstone of games. Although not every game is animated, many of them are, and it's this animation that gives players a sense of dynamics and motion.

With the combined power of HTML, CSS, and JavaScript, you have a rich palette of choices for adding animation to your games.

There are four principal ways of animating a two-dimensional scene in a JavaScript-driven game. All of them are detailed in this book:

-   CSS transitions
-   CSS animations
-   Timed events
-   `requestAnimationFrame` method

In this chapter, I provide just an overview of these concepts and then flesh them out in the chapters that follow.

▶ Animating with CSS Transitions

You can add animation to your game without any JavaScript code at all. It's done by using the *transition* style property.

CSS transitions are part of the updated CSS3 specification, which is supported in most modern browsers—those no more than a few years old. The current desktop versions of Chrome and Mozilla Firefox fully support CSS3 transitions.

Take a look at the following two examples to see how it's done. This first version doesn't use a transition. It shows one image abruptly replacing the other when the mouse is positioned over the picture.

snipped from: css-transition-ogre-1.html

```
18 #ogre {
19   position: absolute;
20   width: 600px;
21   height: 600px;
22 }
23
24 #human {
25   position: absolute;
26   width: 600px;
27   height: 600px;
28 }
29 #human:hover {
30   opacity: 0;
31 }
32 </style>
  . . .
37   <div id="mainContent">
38     <img id="ogre" class="image" alt="" src="./assets/ogre.jpg" />
39     <img id="human" class="image" alt="" src="./assets/human.jpg" />
40   </div>
```

Basic Style Rules

Lines 18 through 28 apply basic positioning and sizing rules to the two images used in the example. (The width and height rules are technically not required here, as the images are already 600-by-600 pixels, but I've included the dimensions anyway just as a matter of consistency.)

The :hover Pseudo-class

Lines 29 through 31 define the :hover pseudo-class; when the mouse pointer is over the image of the human, the rule tells the browser to make the picture invisible by setting its opacity to 0 percent.

IMG Elements

Lines 38 and 39 define the two IMG elements containing the pictures.

Running the Example

Place the mouse over the picture of the human, and it immediately changes to the ogre picture.

Now look at the second example, this time using a CSS transition.

snipped from: css-transition-ogre-2.html

```
24 #human {
25   position: absolute;
26   width: 600px;
27   height: 600px;
28   transition: opacity 1.5s;
29 }
30 #human:hover {
31   opacity: 0;
32   cursor: pointer;
33 }
```

Line 28 defines the rule for the transition. It is to affect the opacity of the image and to last for 1.5 seconds.

Line 32 is an optional rule that changes the mouse pointer—it's not required to implement a CSS transition but is included here as a visual cue that something is happening (or will happen). Rather than the usual arrow, you get a pointing finger.

When the mouse is moved over the human, the transition is triggered (see Figure 13-1), making it look like a slow dissolve from person to ogre. The cool Bermuda shorts add to the effect of the transformation!

The transition occurs in both directions: when moving the mouse over the picture, and when moving it out. Each time, the transition creates a dissolve effect of the images slowly fading from one to the other.

See Chapter 14: Creating Motion with CSS Transitions (page 209) for more on using CSS transitions, including enhancing your animations with JavaScript.

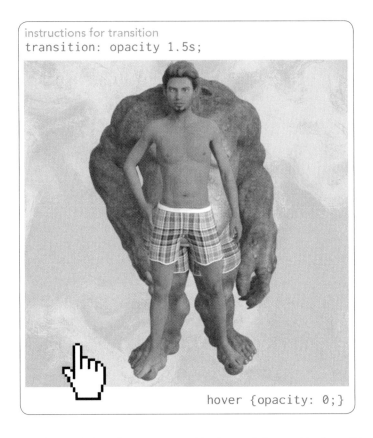

instructions for transition
`transition: opacity 1.5s;`

`hover {opacity: 0;}`

Figure 13-1. Moving the mouse over the image triggers the transition.

▶ Animating with CSS Animations

CSS animations are similar to CSS transitions, but they provide quite a bit more flexibility. They're also a little harder to use, but with some work, you'll master them in no time. As with transitions, you can add animations to your game with or without JavaScript code.

To create an animation, you combine the animation style property, along with a listing of two or more *keyframes*. The object is to move between these keyframes, providing animation. The cycle of movement can happen once, a set number of times, or indefinitely.

On page 202 is an example of a retro-style UFO hovering around in space. The animation bobs the flying saucer up and down in an infinite loop.

snipped from: css-animation-ufo.html

```
12 #mainContent {
13   background-image: url("./assets/stellar.jpg");
14   width: 600px;
15   height: 600px;
16   overflow: hidden;
17 }
18
19 #ufo1 {
20   position: absolute;
21   left: 100px;
22   top: 80px;
23   width: 400px;
24   height:162px;
25   animation: hoverUfo 10s infinite;
26 }
27
28 @keyframes hoverUfo {
29   0%   { top: 80px }
30   50%  { top: 270px }
31   100% { top: 80px }
32 }
. . .
38   <img id="ufo1" class="ufo-large" alt="" src="./assets/ufo1.png" />
```

Style for DIV Container

Lines 12 through 17 define a DIV container for all the action. The background image is set here using the *background-image* property, and so is the size of the DIV element.

Now's a good time to mention a potential headache you may encounter (on many browsers), when using the background-image property. Notice the syntax:

```
background-image: url("./assets/stellar.jpg");
```

Don't do this:

```
background-image: url ("./assets/stellar.jpg"); // No!
```

Be careful not to place a space between url and (characters or else the image may not appear! This is actually how it's supposed to work, but that's no consolation when you can't figure out why your background is blank. Get into the habit of omitting the space and double-checking it first if there's a problem.

Style Rules for IMG Graphic

Lines 19 through 26 set the style for the UFO graphic. The position: absolute property lets you take over the positioning of the image, which starts at 100 pixels from the left and 80 pixels from the top. (Remember: Because the UFO image is inside a container DIV, its position is relative to this container. If you move the left and top of the container, the flying saucer will go with it.)

Animation Style Rule

Of critical interest is the animation property of the UFO graphic, found on line 25. It does three things: defines the name of the animation @keyframes rule to use (in this case, hoverUfo); specifies the total animation time as 10 seconds; and tells the browser to repeat the animation forever.

The Keyframes Animation Rule

Lines 28 through 32 is a @keyframes rule. The rule is given a name—hoverUfo— in order to connect it to the animation rule on line 25. The movement of the UFO contains three keyframes; the keyframes are marked in percentages of completion. By having a start, middle, and end, and by

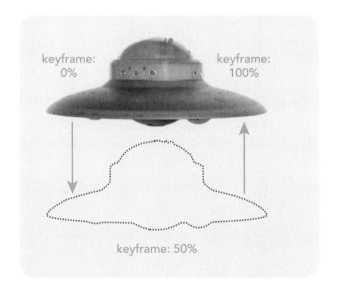

Figure 13-2. Keyframes define the the main positions of animation.

having the end duplicate the start value, the animation will appear to repeat in an endless cycle.

The three keyframes set the top property, which causes the UFO to hover up and down against the deep-space background, as depicted in Figure 13-2.

See Chapter 15: Creating Motion with CSS Animations (page 225) for more on using CSS animations.

▶ Animating with the requestAnimationFrame Method

Animation is really just a sequence of pictures. In each picture, or frame, the position of the subject is moved just a little bit. You get the illusion of motion when the frames play back fast enough. Those (now) old-style movie theaters that used film projectors shuttled the film at 24 individual frames per second (fps). When viewed on-screen, these individual frames looked like seamless motion.

If you've ever tried your hand at computer animation, you know the frame-by-frame process can be resource-intensive, causing jitters and uneven motion. The JavaScript requestAnimationFrame method helps to resolve this virtual logjam by providing a way to animate individual frames in a manner that works directly with the browser's own display engine. This helps to produce the smoothest animation possible.

Under typical circumstances, and assuming a relatively simple animated scene, an animation driven using the requestAnimationFrame method will run at 60 fps. The frame rate may decrease if the computer can't keep up, but the browser does its best to maintain the best animation it can.

In this next example, you see a UFO whizzing past from left to right. It's animated using the requestAnimationFrame method. I've taken the basic page from the *css-animation-ufo-1.html* playground script and removed the CSS animation part. I've added two important properties to the mainContent rule so that the DIV is treated like a framed window.

For the sake of simplicity, the animation runs only once, although there's no technical reason it can't repeat as many times as you like. Because you have specific control of each frame of the animation, you can also combine other movements and changes.

snipped from: request-animation-loop.html

```
12 #mainContent {
13   position: absolute;
14   background-image: url("./assets/stellar.jpg");
15   width: 600px;
16   height: 600px;
17   overflow: hidden;
18 }
19
20 #ufo1 {
21   position: absolute;
22   left: 100px;
23   top: 175px;
24   width: 400px;
25   height:162px;
26 }
   . . .
35  <script>
36    var counter = -400;
37    function animationLoop() {
38      if (counter < 615) {
```

```
39      counter += 5;
40      document.getElementById("ufo1").style.left = counter + "px";
41      window.requestAnimationFrame(animationLoop);
42    }
43    }
44    animationLoop();
45  </script>
```

Control Variable

Line 36 sets up a control variable named counter that is used to keep track of the animation loop and move the UFO from left to right. It starts at –400, which is the width of the UFO. This makes the saucer disappear off the left edge of the mainContent DIV.

Animation Loop

Lines 37 through 43 is the animation loop proper. This loop is repeated until the animation is finished.

▸ **Should the number in the counter variable be less than 615** ▸
the UFO is moved to a new position, as set on lines 39 and 40. The code on line 39 takes the existing value in the counter variable and adds 5 to it. Therefore, the UFO moves to the right five pixels at a time. Line 41 calls the requestAnimationFrame method again, which restarts the loop.

▸ **Should the number in the counter variable be 615 or more** ▸
the animation stops, and the requestAnimationFrame method is not called again.

Line 44 initially calls the animationLoop function the first time the script is loaded. If you forget to include this line, no animation will ever appear.

Note that the code uses window.requestAnimationFrame; window is the top-level object that represents the main browser window. The requestAnimationFrame method "belongs" to this object. On many browsers, the animation will still work without the reference to the window object, but I include it for consistency.

You can read more about using the requestAnimationFrame method in Chapter 17: Extended Animation Techniques (page 257).

▸ Animating with Timer Functions

Before the advent of the requestAnimationFrame method, coders often relied on using JavaScript's various built-in timer functions to play frames of motion. Even with requestAnimationFrame, these timer functions are still often used for basic animation, particularly animation that doesn't need to run as fast as the 60 fps possible with requestAnimationFrame.

JavaScript timers are pretty simple in concept. You can read more about their general use in JavaScript games in Chapter 16: Adding Clocks and Timers (page 243), but for now, it's enough to know there are two types of JavaScript timer functions: *one-shot* and *interval*.

▨ One-shot timer ▶ runs just once after a certain amount of time has elapsed. You can always run the timer again, of course, but it's principal use is to delay an action by some specified duration. To create a one-shot timer, use

```
var myTimer = setTimeout (action, delay);
```

▨ Interval timer ▶ automatically retriggers itself after each time delay—see Figure 13-3. You can stop the timer to end the automatic retriggering. To create an interval timer, use

```
var myTimer = setInterval (action, interval);
```

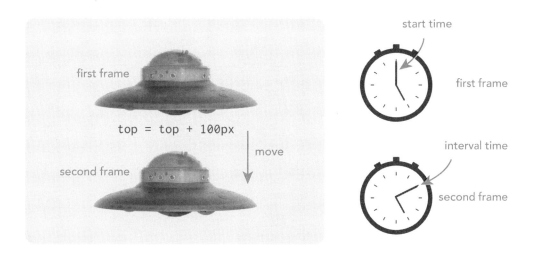

Figure 13-3. The setInterval timer retriggers at regular intervals.

In both cases, the myTimer variable contains a reference to the timer. This reference is used, among other things, to stop the timer from triggering or retriggering.

The setInterval function is more commonly used for traditional animation, so we'll concentrate on just that one for now. Here's a demo of using setInterval to move the flying saucer across the screen in a similar fashion to the previous requestAnimationFrame example.

snipped from: set-interval-animation.html

```
36  var counter = -400;
37  var loopTimer = setInterval(animationLoop, 50);
38  function animationLoop() {
39    if (counter < 615) {
40      counter += 20;
41      document.getElementById("ufo1").style.left = counter + "px";
42    } else {
43      clearInterval (loopTimer);
44    }
45  }
```

The basic script is by and large the same as in the previous playground example, except:

Line 37 ▶ sets up the setInterval timer. The reference variable is named loopTimer, which is used on line 43 to end the animation when the UFO has moved all the way across. The timer calls a function named animationLoop once every 50 ms.

Line 39 through 44 ▶ determine if the loop is repeated. If the counter variable is less than 615, the UFO is moved another 20 pixels to the right. Otherwise, the timer is terminated.

Open both this and the requestAnimationFrame version and compare. You'll likely see the setInterval animation is a bit less smooth. Depending on the objects and speed of the animation, this may not be terribly distracting. Experiment.

▶ Bonus Examples

Many of the bonus games included with this book demonstrate one or more of the animation techniques covered in this chapter. For starters, check out these:

Ruins of Ramic, Lesson 4

Click on any two cards to match them up. This lesson demonstrates, among other things, a self-timed splash screen that fades out when other page elements are loaded. Other CSS transitions and animations are added to rotate each card when it's clicked.

Zombie Girl Dressup, Lesson 3

CSS transitions and animations are added in this lesson to enhance the look and feel of the game. A CSS animation bobs the game title up and down, and a CSS transition is used to enhance the look of a "fly-out" panel that's used for selecting articles of clothing. Each time the panel is opened or closed, a very short transition makes it appear as if the panel is growing or shrinking from the right edge.

PART THREE

STEPPING UP YOUR GAME

CREATING MOTION WITH CSS TRANSITIONS

CSS transitions animate the size, position, or other style properties of an element, from a start value to an end value.

An example is moving the top edge of an element from 100px to 300px. Rather than making the move in one step, causing an abrupt change in location, a transition shows smooth motion between these two start and end values.

In Chapter 13: Making Your Game Move: An Overview of Animation Techniques (page 197), you discovered the basics of CSS transitions. In this chapter, you deepen your understanding of how to use CSS transitions to add action and movement to any HTML element in your game. You also discover how to trigger an event when the transition is finished, vary the time it takes for the transition to elapse, and more.

▶ What CSS Transitions Are ... and Aren't

Think of transitions as "from here to there." All of the motion between "here" and "there" is handled by CSS and the browser. These states, also called *tweens*—for *in-betweens*, an old-cartoon animation term—save you from having to specify every last detail of your animation. You only have to worry about where an element starts and where it ends.

It's important to remember CSS transitions don't solve every animation problem. To repeat: Transitions go from a start point to an end point, and then they are done. Although later in the game you can subsequently retransition the element from 300px back to 100px, this is considered two separate transitions. For repeating or cyclical motion, you're better off using CSS animations, which are covered in the next chapter.

At least for games, CSS transitions are most-commonly used to move something around the screen. This most often involves transitioning the left and/or top style properties of the element. But you're not just limited to movement. You can also change the size of elements, rotate them, fade them in or out, and perform numerous other special effects—all with relatively little code. Many of these techniques are revealed in this chapter.

▶ Properties and Values for CSS Transitions

CSS transitions are created by setting properties. These properties are (typically) defined for a given element in the STYLE block of your script page. Each property controls a certain aspect of the transition. A basic transition might look like the code below:

```
img {
  position: absolute;
  left: 0px;
  transition-property: left;
  transition-duration: 1s;
}
```

It means the transition affects any IMG elements on the page, has a duration of one second, and is triggered whenever there is a change in the element's left style property (see Figure 14-1).

The snipped code from *rocketman-move-1.html* on the next page is a fully working example of a CSS transition where you can watch this in action. To see the transition, click on the rocketman. He slides across the screen by moving the left property of the IMG element from 0px ("from here" point) to 200px ("to there" point).

```
img {

  property starting value
      ┌─────────┐
  left: 0px;

        property to transition = left
      ┌──────────────────────────┐
  transition-property: left;

        duration = 1 second
      ┌──────────────────────┐
  transition-duration: 1s;

}
```

Figure 14-1. To create a transition, specify a style property and how long the transition lasts.

```
11 <style>
12 img {
13   position: absolute;
14   left: 0px;
15   transition-property: left;
16   transition-duration: 1s;
17 }
18 </style>
19 </head>
20
21 <body>
22   <img src="./assets/rocketeer-small.png"
       onclick="this.style.left='200px'" />
23 </body>
```

Here are the four CSS transition properties:

CSS PROPERTY	SPECIFIES . . .	DEFAULT VALUE
transition-property	Which style properties the transition applies to, such as `left`, `top`, `width`, `height`, or `opacity`. Changes in any of these properties triggers the transition.	all (any property change triggers the transition)
transition-duration	The duration of the transition. The value is given as a number plus the time units: 1 s means one second, 1500 ms means 1,500 milliseconds, or 1.5 seconds. You can use decimal values for seconds: 1.5 s is the same as 1500 ms.	0s
transition-timing-function	The timing speed at different phases of the transition. Timing functions, also called easings, can provide a more realistic look to the transitions. More about these later in this chapter.	ease
transition-delay	How long to wait before the transition begins. As with duration, this value is given as a number plus time units.	0s

Default values are applied if you don't define a property. Not all default values are usable—the default value for transition-duration is 0 seconds, for example—which means no transition is displayed. At a minimum, your code should always specify transition-duration.

▶ Transitioning More Than One Property

You can combine two or more properties in a single transition. All of the properties are effected during the transition. For example, suppose you want your rocketman to zoom up, up, and away, like in Figure 14-2. For this, you'd modify the code to:

1. Add a starting point for the top property (200px).

2. Include top as a property to transition on.

3. Include the change of the top property in your code.

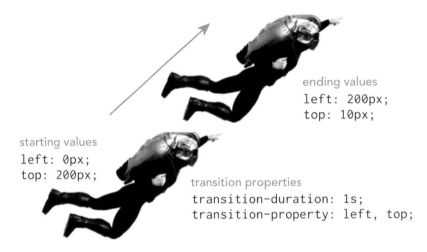

ending values
left: 200px;
top: 10px;

starting values
left: 0px;
top: 200px;

transition properties
transition-duration: 1s;
transition-property: left, top;

Figure 14-2. Combine properties to transition for more complex motion.

snipped from: rocketman-move-2.html

```
11 <style>
12 img {
13   position: absolute;
14   left: 0px;
15   top: 200px;
16   transition-duration: 1s;
17   transition-property: left, top;
18 }
19 </style>
20 </head>
21
22 <body>
23 <img src="./assets/rocketeer-small.png" alt=""
    onclick="this.style.left='200px'; this.style.top='10px'" />
```

▶ Combining Settings in a Single Property

CSS allows a shortcut method for specifying all the properties at once. For this, use the `transition` property and then simply list the parameters you want to use (see Figure 14-3), each separated by a space. Here's an example that combines all four of the above into a single line:

```
transition: width 2s linear .5s;
```

- `width` ▶ specifies the `transition-property`
- `2s` ▶ specifies the `transition-duration`
- `linear` ▶ specifies the `transition-timing-function`
- `.5s` ▶ specifies the `transition-delay`

The all-in-one method is a great timesaver, but it's not as beneficial when you plan on controlling the transitions using JavaScript. The reason: If your code tries to change a single item in the `transition` property, it ends up erasing all the others.

The best approach when you want to manipulate the transition behavior in your JavaScript code is to define all the transition properties separately, rather than all on one line. This gives you the flexibility of altering single transition properties, without the risk of deleting all the others.

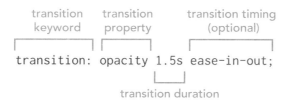

Figure 14-3. Combined transition properties on a single line.

▶ Typical Style Properties to Transition

Quite a few CSS properties are *animatable* for transitions. I'm not going to list them all because you can readily find this information on the Internet. If you're like most coders, you'll probably confine yourself to the same dozen or so animatable properties. Here are the ones I tend to use the most:

STYLE TYPE	PROPERTY
Position	top, left, margin-top, margin-left
Size	width, height, font-size
Border	border-width, border-color, border-radius
Colors	color (for text), background-color (for background shade of elements)
Special effects	opacity, transform (includes rotation and scaling)

▶ Understanding Transition Timings (aka Easings)

During a transition, the speed of change can vary, which provides a more realistic motion effect. Transition timings are a way of specifying how the action between the start and end points of the transition are interpolated. For example, the transition may start out slow, then speed up toward the end, or it may

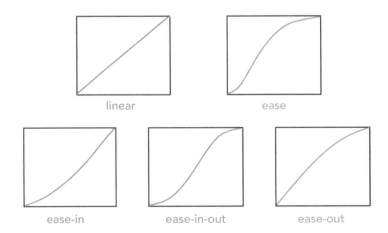

Figure 14-4. These five timings form the backbone of CSS transitions.

maintain the same speed all the way through, by using linear timing. CSS transition timings are also referred to as easings, tweens, or tweeners.

If you don't specify a timing function, CSS defaults to ease, which is a good middle-ground. Graphs make it easier to visualize these timings. The most-commonly use timings are depicted in Figure 14-4.

▶ Triggering the Transition

CSS transitions need to be activated, or *triggered*. In Chapter 13 (page 197), you were introduced to one of the ways to trigger a transition: the :hover CSS pseudo-class. Placing the mouse over the human's picture made him turn into a beach-combing ogre. The actual transition is actually just a change of opacity of the human's picture, giving the appearance of one image "dissolving" into the other.

For games, clicking on things is a common way to trigger a transition. With the click, JavaScript code activates the transition by making a change in the property to be transitioned. For instance, if the transition-property is left, changing the left position of the element somewhere in your JavaScript code activates the transition.

Alternatively, when the properties to change get more complex—you have a whole bowl of them to stir at once—you can activate them as a unit by changing the class of the element. In the STYLE block you define the animatable properties you want to use in separate classes—let's call them .starting and .ending.

Rather than use JavaScript to change all of the properties individually, we can just swap out the class name for the element. This can save time and coding.

snipped from: rocketman-move-3.html

```
17  .starting {
18    left: 0px;
19    top: 200px;
20  }
21  .ending {
22    left: 200px;
23    top: 10px;
24  }
. . .
29  <img src="./assets/rocketeer-small.png" alt="" class="starting"
       onclick="this.className='ending'" />
```

The action takes place on line 29. The initial class for the IMG element is .starting, where the left and top position is set at 0px and 200px, respectively. When the IMG is clicked, the inline JavaScript code changes the class name to .ending. This style has different properties for left and top, so the class name change causes the transition to 200px (left) and 10px (top).

Of course, hovering and clicking the mouse are just two of the things you can do to trigger the transition. Other methods, many of which are detailed in this and later chapters, include:

- After the document loads
- When a particular key is pressed
- Following a timed event or interval
- As part of an animation frame produced by the `requestAnimationFrame` method
- After another transition has completed

▶ Hands-on CSS Transition Motion Example: Planet Pizza

You just got hired to deliver hot pizzas to the colonies of the moon—except they didn't train you on how to fly the delivery rocket. The *Planet Pizza* game tests your skill in landing on the rocky terrain of the moon. Stop the ship just on the crest of the crater, and you land safely. Otherwise, you crash into the eight-mile–deep South Pole–Aitken basin and die a gruesome, horrifying death.

Seriously, it's not all that hard to survive! *Planet Pizza* is a rudimentary variation of the old *Lunar Lander* game, popular way back in the 1970s. This version is kept simple to show you how it uses only CSS transitions to achieve quite workable motion and animation effects.

The *Planet Pizza* playground game is located in its own download on the Bonus Games page, available at the Online Support Site (Appendix A, page 310).

Figure 14-5. The main screen of *Planet Pizza*—help these guys deliver a hot pepperoni pizza to aluminum miners on the moon.

snipped from: planet-pizza-1.html—styles

```
12 #mainContent {
13   position: absolute;
14   background-image: url("./assets/planetscape.jpg");
15   width: 600px;
16   height: 600px;
17   user-select: none;
18   overflow: hidden;
19 }
20
21 #ship {
22   position: absolute;
23   height: 175px;
24   left: 175px;
25   top: 0px;
26   transition-timing-function: ease-in-out;
27   transition-duration: 1s;
28   transition-property: left, top;
29 }
30
31 .panel {
32   position: absolute;
33   height: 600px;
34   width: 600px;
35 }
36
37 .controls {
38   position: absolute;
39   cursor: pointer;
40   width: 50px;
41   height: 50px;
42 }
43 #left  { left: 2px;   top: 450px; }
44 #right { left: 128px; top: 450px; }
45 #up    { left: 65px; top: 455px; }
46 #down  { left: 65px; top: 520px; height: 80px; }
47
48 p {
49 . . .
50 }
```

Styles are important when animating with CSS translations. The STYLE block for *Planet Pizza* consists of several rules for the HTML elements in the game. These consist of

- #mainContent (ID rule): which serves as a DIV container for all the other elements in the game.
- #ship (ID rule): an image containing the spaceship lander.
- .panel (class rule): for the lower-right and lower-left graphical elements.
- .controls (class rule): for the four navigation controls (all created using DIVs).
- Individual ID rules: for the positions of the #left, #right, #up, and #down DIVs.
- p (tag selector): for the "Game Over!" text, which appears near the lower-right portion of the screen.

Of the rules and properties, only a few relate to CSS transitions. These are on lines 26 through 28. The properties specify a timing (easing) function, duration of one second, and the element properties that are to be transitioned left and top.

You need a way to visualize the position of the control DIVs to place them at the desired spots on the background image. Simply add a couple of temporary properties to the .controls rule so you can see the DIVs.

```
background-color: red;
opacity: .5;
```

When these are visible (see Figure 14-6), you can adjust the left and top properties of each control to position them. After positioning, remove the properties to make the DIVs invisible to the player.

Figure 14-6. Make DIVs temporarily visible to align them over graphics.

```
64 <div id="mainContent">
65 <img id="ship" class="image" alt="" src="./assets/ship.png" />
66 <img id="leftpanel" class="panel" src="./assets/leftpanel.png" />
67 <img id="rightpanel" class="panel" src="./assets/rightpanel.png" />
68 <div id="left" class="controls"></div>
69 <div id="right" class="controls"></div>
70 <div id="down" class="controls"></div>
71 <div id="up" class="controls"></div>
72 <p id="result"> </p>
73 </div>
```

The HTML elements consist mostly of DIV containers and several images. The images are placed into the mainContent DIV. The DIV uses a moonscape background image. The two panels are for decoration. They're separate images so that they also can be animated with transitions. This is demonstrated in a follow-up version of *Planet Pizza*. Here is the JavaScript for *planet-pizza-1.html*.

```
77  var gameOver = false;
78  var theShip = document.getElementById ("ship");
79  theShip.addEventListener("transitionend", moveComplete);
80
81  var controls = document.getElementsByClassName ("controls");
82  for (var i = 0; i < controls.length; i++) {
83   controls[i].onclick = function() { shipControl(this) };
84  }
85
86  function shipControl (control) {
87   if (gameOver) return;
88   var left = parseInt(window.getComputedStyle(theShip, null).left);
89   var top = parseInt(window.getComputedStyle(theShip, null).top);
90   switch (control.id) {
91    case "left":
92     theShip.style.left = (left - 35) + "px";
93     theShip.style.top = (top + 15) + "px";
94     break;
95    case "right":
96     theShip.style.left = (left + 35) + "px";
97     theShip.style.top = (top + 15) + "px";
98     break;
99    case "down":
100    theShip.style.top = (top + 120) + "px";
```

```
101    break;
102  case "up":
103    theShip.style.top = (top - 10) + "px";
104    break;
105  }
106 }
107
108 function moveComplete() {
. . . (see game for code)
139 }
```

The working script for *Planet Pizza* consists of four main parts:

Game Setup

Lines 77 through 79 set up the game. A gameOver variable is used to denote when the game has finished. It's a handy way to prevent further play even after the ship has either landed or crashed.

Also here: An event listener is created for the ship graphic. CSS transitions support one event, called transitionend. This listener fires whenever a CSS transition on the ship has ended.

Onclick Listeners

Lines 81 through 84 create onclick listeners for the four controls. The controls themselves are created using small 50px DIVs. All four listeners trigger the same function (shipControl) any time one of these DIVs is clicked on.

Notice the alternative syntax used in this example:

```
controls[i].onclick = function() { shipControl(this) };
```

This is functionally equivalent to:

```
controls[i].addEventListener("click", function() { shipControl(this) });
```

I wanted to show this variation to you because it's a pattern you may encounter in various JavaScript examples found on the web. Both add a listener, but the addEventListener method provides greater functionality should you:

- want to later remove the listener (with removeEventListener)
- attach more than one listener of the same type to the same element

As this script does not employ either of these techniques, either .onclick or addEventListener works just fine.

Notice also the line

```
function() { shipControl(this) }
```

This is one of those famous JavaScript functions-within-a-function. Wrapping the call to the shipControl function in yet another function gives you greater flexibility; in this case, the ability to include the this keyword. With this, the shipControl function can determine which of the four controls triggered it.

The shipControl Function

The shipControl function is defined on lines 86 through 106. When a control DIV is clicked on, this function is executed. The ID of the DIV that was clicked is extracted from the parameter that's passed into the function. Based on this value, the code changes the left and/or top style property of the ship. The left/top position is changed by set amounts, depending on which control was clicked.

- When a new left or top style is specified, the CSS transition properties trigger, causing the ship to animate to its new position.

- Clicking the Down control moves the ship the farthest. It also moves the fastest, because the duration of the transition is still 1 second.

- Clicking the Left or Right controls moves the ship in their respective directions, plus a small amount down.

- Clicking the Up control moves the ship up by only a small change.

The moveComplete Function

For space reasons, the code featuring this function is not included on pages 219–220. Refer to the *planet-pizza-1.html* file for the full code.

Lines 108 through 139 comprise the moveComplete function, which is automatically trigged by JavaScript whenever a CSS transition involving the ship ends (refer back to line 79, when this event listener was created). Each time a transition is completed, the game looks at the ship's left and top style property values, to see if they are:

- Out of bounds ▶ If so, the ship is pushed back into the playfield.

- Within the landing zone (top == 301 to 309) ▶ If the ship is within this narrow space, it has landed, and the game is over. The text "*LANDED*" is displayed in the P element.

Beyond the landing zone (top >= 310) ▸ The ship has gone down too far and crashed. The game is over, and the text *"CRASH!"* is displayed in the P element. Additionally, a replacement transition is created, which spins the ship 250 degrees while moving it down further (see lines 131 through 133)—as if it's fallen off a cliff.

▶ Adding More Transitions for Game Play

Feel free to add transition effects to other elements in your game—whatever it needs to enhance the player's game-play experience. The *planet-pizza-2.html* example builds on the first game but includes a couple of basic tweaks, just to show you how it's done. For space reasons, I won't include all of it here; feel free to review the full code in the *planet-pizza-2.html* playground file to see how it works in its entirety.

snipped from: planet-pizza-2.html

```
.panel {
  position: absolute;
  height: 600px;
  width: 600px;
  opacity: 0;
  transition: opacity 2.5s linear;
}
. . .
  window.onload = function() {
    var panels = document.getElementsByClassName ("panel");
    for (var i = 0; i < panels.length; i++) {
      panels[i].style.opacity = 1;
    }
  };
```

In these added lines, the two graphical panels in the lower-left and lower-right slowly fade in after the game is loaded. This effect is created by adding a single-line transition property to the .panel class and then triggering this transition when the page is fully loaded.

```
document.getElementById("leftpanel").style.transition =
    "opacity .5s linear";
document.getElementById("leftpanel").style.opacity = 0;
```

Similarly, when the game is over, and as a visual cue, the left control panel is dimmed back out. Note that the fully qualified transition property is provided, including the transition property, duration, and timing. The all-in-one property mirrors how the rule was set up in the STYLE block.

Additionally, the *Planet Pizza* playground game set also includes a third script, *planet-pizza-3.html*, which includes CSS animation and other features. Read more about this version in Chapter 15: Creating Motion with CSS Animation (page 225).

As you develop your own games, consider how its various pieces can be enhanced by adding even simple transitions—before, during, and after game play has ended. These little touches go a long way into enhancing the play experience.

▶ Bonus Example:

Check out Lesson 3 of *Sharker*, where CSS transitions are used to not only move cars down the three lanes of traffic, but to move the shark up, down, left, and right. (Note: The "swimming" action of the shark is created by a CSS animation.)

CREATING MOTION
WITH CSS ANIMATIONS

If you read Chapter 14: Creating Motion with CSS Transitions (page 209), you know that CSS transitions create animation by interpolating the size, position, or other style properties of an element from one point to another.

CSS animations do much the same, except that you are not limited to motions with only simple start and end points. With CSS animations, you can specify multiple points and movement will take place between them. This is a big deal: Instead of animating from A–B, you can animate A–B–C–D–E and even back to A. Plus the animation can repeat any number of times that you like—even forever. (Well, at least until you close the browser!)

In this chapter, you'll learn about CSS animations—how they differ from CSS transitions and how you can apply them to your games. Although CSS animations are a little harder to implement than transitions, they offer lots more functionality you don't want to miss.

Properties and Values for CSS Animations

Like CSS transitions, CSS animations are defined by setting style properties, which are normally provided in the STYLE block of your script page. Each property controls a certain aspect of the animation.

Here's a quick example; see also Figure 15-1 for how these properties work with one another.

```
img {
  position: absolute;
  animation-name: moveMe;
  animation-duration: 2s;
}
@keyframes moveMe {
  0%   { top: 100px }
  100% { top: 200px }
}
```

The animation is composed of two parts:

- The animation properties, provided as property/value pairs in the style rule for the element you wish to animate. At a minimum, you need to provide the name of the animation you wish to run and its duration. More about these properties in a bit.

- A @keyframes rule, which contains what can be consider *waypoints* of the animation. This rule is named and matches the name you provided for the animation. This particular animation is pretty simple (just one start and stop point), and does no more than your average CSS transition. But don't worry—you'll soon see how to extract a lot more functionality from CSS animations.

Both the animation properties and the @keyframes rule must be present in the STYLE block, or the animation won't run. The two pieces don't have to be right next to each other, but you'll find doing so makes it easier to build and refine the animation.

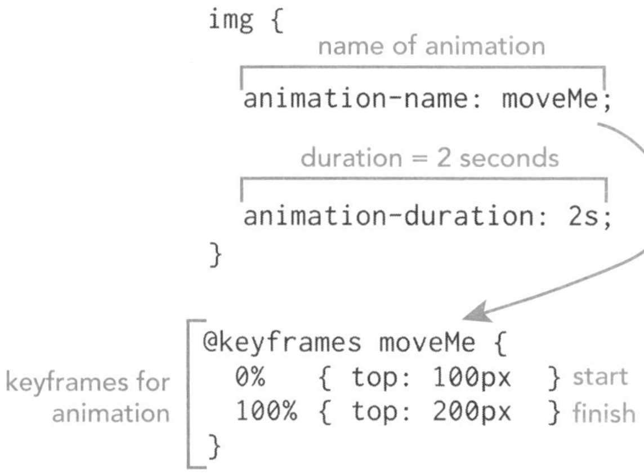

```
img {
              name of animation
  animation-name: moveMe;

         duration = 2 seconds
  animation-duration: 2s;
}

@keyframes moveMe {
  0%   { top: 100px   } start
  100% { top: 200px   } finish
}
```
keyframes for animation

Figure 15-1. Composition of a CSS animation.

There are eight main CSS animation properties:

FORMAT	WHAT IT IS AND WHAT IT'S BEST FOR
JPG	JPG is the workhorse on the graphics format farm, favored because of its flexibility in letting you set the amount of image compression when the file is saved. The more compressed the file, the smaller (in bytes) it is. But at higher compression settings, the image can get degraded, so you must weigh file size against quality.
PNG	PNG images are also compressed, but they use a "lossless" compression format which helps them retain better quality. More importantly, PNG files can have transparent backgrounds, meaning you can overlay a PNG on another image, and the two appear to seamlessly merge. This is commonly used in game design.
GIF	GIF files once played the same role as PNG, including support of a transparent background, but now are mostly just for small icon-sized images. Quality isn't as good as PNG, because the format can only support up to 256 colors, and the transparency can leave a colored outline around the edges.

▶ Combining Settings in a Single Property

It shouldn't come as a surprise that CSS also allows a shortcut method for specifying all the animation properties at once. For this, use the *animation* property and then simply list the parameters you want to use, each separated by a space (see Figure 15-2). Here's an example that combines the four most-commonly used animation parameters on a single line:

```
animation: moveMe 2s infinite linear;
```

moveMe ▶ specifies the animation-name to run (matches an @keyframe rule elsewhere in the STYLE block)

2s ▶ specifies the animation-duration (2 seconds)

infinite ▶ specifies the animation-iteration-count (in this case, repeat forever)

linear ▶ specifies the animation-timing-function

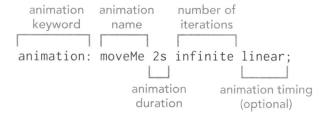

Figure 15-2. Multiple animation properties on one line.

Although the all-in-one method is a great time-saver, if you plan on manipulating any of these values via JavaScript, it's better to use the individual animation properties instead.

▶ Getting to Know the @keyframes Rule

There's a lot of power in the @keyframes rule, more than meets the eyeball. Let's begin by first defining what keyframes are, then how to use them in a CSS animation.

You already know animations are sequences of individual still pictures where there's a slight change in the image for each picture. A keyframe is quite literally a "key" position in this sequence—*key* means important, or crucial. Keyframes show the starting and ending of full motion.

In computer animation, frames between these keys are automatically filled in to create smooth motion. This filling-in, more accurately called *interpolation* or *tweening* (Figure 15-3), may comprise just a few frames, or hundreds of frames. It depends on how far apart (distance as well as action) the keyframes are from one another and the speed of the animation.

The basic @keyframes rule defines just a from and to keyframe—the minimum you need for any animation. To set the animation, simply specify from and to for the two start and end keyframes:

```
@keyframes moveMe {
  from { top: 100px }
  to  { top: 200px }
}
```

This animation moves the top of the element from 100px to 200px.

The alternative is to specify the keyframes using percentage values. Equivalent to from/to is 0% and 100%:

```
@keyframes moveMe {
  0%  { top: 100px }
  100% { top: 200px }
}
```

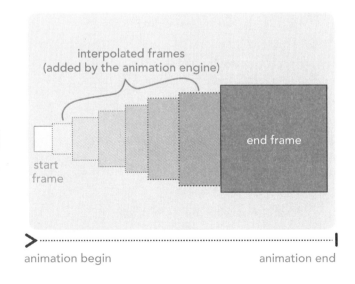

Figure 15-3. With keyframes specified, the browser fills in the rest of the movement.

Using percentage values has more relevance when there's more than just start and end frames. You can divvy up the animation by adding more keyframes. To do this, simply insert middle- percentage values from 1 to 99—see Figure 15-4.

```
@keyframes moveMe {
 0%  { top: 100px }
 50% { top: 200px }
 100% { top: 100px }
}
```

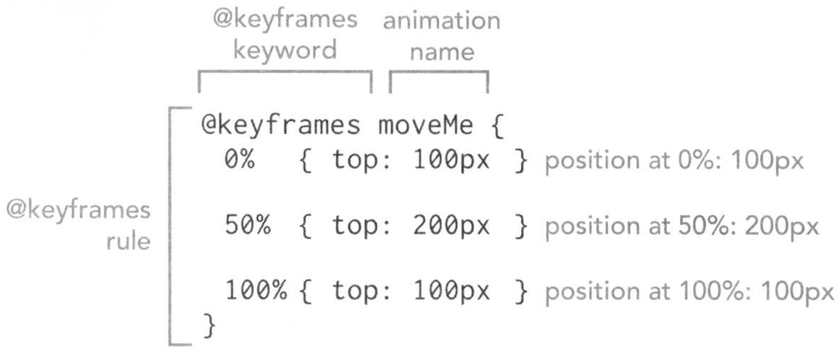

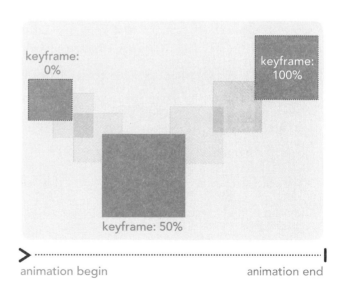

Figure 15-4. Keyframes specified for the start, end, and middle of the animation.

For the first half of the animation— 0 percent to 50 percent—the element is moved from 100px to 200px. In the second half of the animation, the element is moved back to 100px.

Using this approach, you can create full "cycles" of animation, where the action comes back to its starting point. In the previous examples, the animation moves only one way. If you subsequently repeat the animation, the element will jump back to its starting point before the new animation starts.

There's nothing stopping you from adding more style properties within the @keyframes rule.

Simply insert them inside the brackets for each key frame (from/to or percentage). Apply formatting to make the rule more readable. Figure 15-5 shows the effect of the left, top, width, and height style changes on the animation.

Figure 15-5. Combine style properties for more elaborate animations.

▶ Watching CSS Animation in Action

'Nuff talk. Here's a working example of a CSS animation that you can try consisting of a static background image contained in a DIV and an IMG element of a flying saucer from Rigel XII. There is no JavaScript in this animation. The UFO begins hovering just as soon as the page is loaded.

snipped from: ufo-1.html

```
20 #ufo1 {
21   position: absolute;
22   width: 400px;
23   height: 162px;
24   left: 100px;
25   top: 80px;
26   animation: hoverUfo 8s infinite ease-in-out;
27 }
28 @keyframes hoverUfo {
29   0%  { top: 80px }
30   50% { top: 270px }
31   100% { top: 80px }
32 }
. . .
37 <div id="mainContent">
38   <img id="ufo1" class="ufo" alt="" src="./assets/ufo1.png" />
39 </div>
```

All of the animation is handled in CSS on lines 26 and 28 through 32.

Line 26 is the `animation` property, specifying (all on one line) the animation to use:

- `hoverUfo` keyframes rule

- 8-second duration

- infinite looping

- ease-in-out timing

Note that to effect the animation, the saucer IMG element is given the ID of "ufo1", which is defined as a style rule starting on line 20. This is important so that the browser knows what it is you want to animate.

▶ Pausing and Playing Animations

Using CSS or JavaScript, you can make your animations toggle between pause and play. When paused, action stops, and when playing, the action begins again.

The initial animation state—either paused or running—can be set in the CSS rule for the animation. You can then toggle it to the opposite state, either using CSS or with JavaScript. Here's an example of using only CSS to make the UFO start and stop its animation. Move the mouse over the saucer, and the animation-play-state switches to running. Move the mouse outside of the saucer, and the animation pauses again (see Figure 15-6).

snipped from: ufo-2.html

```
20 #ufo1 {
. . .
26   animation-name: hoverUfo;
27   animation-duration: 8s;
28   animation-iteration-count: infinite;
29   animation-timing-function: ease-in-out;
30   animation-play-state: paused;
31 }
32 #ufo1:hover {
33   animation-play-state: running;
34 }
35 @keyframes hoverUfo {
36   0%  { top: 80px }
37   50% { top: 270px }
38   100% { top: 80px }
39 }
```

hover mouse to start/stop animation

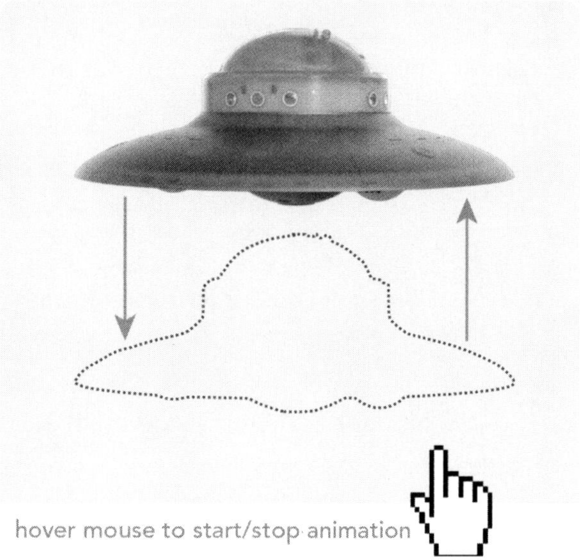

Figure 15-6. Pausing and unpausing animations.

This bit of magic is performed by using the :hover pseudo-class, a special type of class that automatically applies based on certain conditions of the browser. For :hover, this condition occurs when the mouse "hovers" over the element. It's a great way to control animation without having to write any JavaScript code.

▶ Triggering Animations with JavaScript

Of course, you can also use JavaScript code to pause and run animations. In fact, this is likely to be your go-to method of controlling animations because it provides almost limitless alternatives. Two of the most-common methods of triggering animation effects is clicking on something and using timers.

Let's take a closer look at the second method. This version of the UFO script is similar to the last one, where the animation-play-state for the UFO is initially set to paused. Now for the code that makes the animation run:

snipped from: ufo-3.html

```
42 <body onload=init();>
 . . .
48  function init() {
49    console.log ("init");
50    setTimeout(function() {
51      console.log ("delayed running");
52      document.getElementById("ufo1").style.animationPlayState =
         "running";
53    }, 2000);
```

- Line 42 ▶ sets up an event listener for when the whole document has fully loaded. When this happens, the browser executes the init function, starting on line 48.

- Inside the init function ▶ some console.log statements so you can better see the order of things. Open the browser's console window and load the page. You'll quickly see the text "init," which tells you the document has completed its onload event.

- Lines 50 through 53 ▶ set up a timer, using the setTimeout function, which activates two seconds later. You can see that this timer triggers when the text "delayed running" appears in the browser's console.

- Line 52 ▶ sets the animation into its running (playing) state.

▶ Providing Smooth Transitions When an Animation Plays (or Stops)

CSS animations use style properties to create movement and action. A good example is the UFO scripts you've been playing with in this chapter. These animations move the top property of the UFO element up and down.

Now suppose your animation makes a change to a property that is not already in the starting position for the first frame. For instance, the element might be at 50px, and your animation starts at 100px.

What you get is a kind of "jump cut," where the element is abruptly moved from its current 50px position to the initial frame position of 100px. You could try to make sure the element is already in the right place when an animation starts, but that works best when you know absolutely where the starting position is (sometimes you don't).

To the rescue: The animation-fill-mode property. This property literally "fills in" the animation so that the element is always in the right spot when the animation begins. And the same thing for when the animation ends.

Use the *ufo-4.html* script as a playground for experimenting with the animation-fill-mode property. The default value is none—no filling is done, and the animation starts with a sudden, ugly jump. The animation also ends with a jump, as the UFO returns to its original position.

---

snipped from: ufo-4.html

```
32 animation-fill-mode: none;
```

For line 32, try each of the other three options: forwards, backwards, and both. For this particular animation:

- Setting the property to forwards smooths the last frame of the animation so the UFO doesn't bounce back to its original spot. Result: No jump at the end.

- Setting the property to backwards smooths the first frame of the animation.
  Result: No jump at the beginning.

- Setting the property to both smooths both ends of the animation.

The effect of the forwards and backwards properties depend on the animation-direction setting. Unless you're after a specific effect, it's often easier just to set animation-fill-mode to both.

▶ Listening for Animation Events

CSS animations produce three types of events that your code can listen for, and act upon:

- animationstart ▶ triggers when the animation starts. This event can be useful when you've used the animation-delay property to delay the beginning of the animation.

- animationend ▶ triggers when the animation ends. This event only occurs when you have specified a set number of iterations using the animation-iteration-count property.

- animationiteration ▶ triggers when the animation restarts with a new iteration. This event only occurs when you have specified a value of 2 or more using the animation-iteration-count property.

Check out the *ufo-event1.html* playground script. It demonstrates both the animationstart and animationend events. The script sets up a simple 1-iteration animation that moves the UFO up from the bottom of the frame. Open the browser's console window to see the animation event messages produced by the script.

snipped from: ufo-event1.html

```
23 #ufo1 {
. . .
28   animation: hoverUfo 4s 1 ease-in-out 1s;
. . .
43 <script>
44   var ufo1 = document.getElementById("ufo1");
45   ufo1.addEventListener("animationstart", function() {
46    console.log ("animation has started after 1 second delay");}
47   );
48   ufo1.addEventListener("animationend", function() {
49    console.log ("animation ended");}
50   );
51 </script>
```

Line 28 sets up the animation:

- Animation name (matches the keyframes rule name): hoverUfo

- Duration: 4 seconds

- Iterations: 1

- Timing: ease-in-out

- Delay: 1 second

Lines 45 and 48 create the event listeners for the animationstart and animationend events.

Both listeners are defined using the addEventListener method on the ufo1 object element. The handlers for the events are simply console.log messages that provide feedback to you.

When you run this script, the animationstart message appears after a one-second delay, commencing with the actual start of the animation. The animationend message appears when the animation has completed.

▶ Enhanced UFO Playground

For more animation joy, check out the *ufo-event2.html* playground script, which extends this example with several additional features (see Figure 15-7):

- Adding more UFOs, controlled by separate animations

- Combining CSS transitions and CSS animations

- Unpausing and pausing the animation

- Counting animation iterations and triggering programmed transitions

- Responding to click events to retrigger transition effects

The playground script isn't detailed here, but it contains helpful comments so you can follow along with how it works.

Figure 15-7. Animated output of the *ufo-event2.html* playground script.

▶ Using CSS Animations with Sprite Sheets

One of the most exciting features of CSS animation are the full-motion graphics implemented with sprite sheets. A *sprite sheet* is a single graphics file that contains multiple individual frames. Motion is depicted when the frames are displayed in rapid succession. Think of it as a modern version of a stick-figure cartoon in a flip book.

Figure 15-8. Sprite sheets are collections of individual frames.

By stuffing all the frames in one file, sprite sheets are a better use of resources, because the animation doesn't need to load a bunch of separate images before playback can begin. This is especially important when accessing files from a web server, where it can take time to download larger files.

Figure 15-8 shows a portion of a sprite sheet of a waving cartoon alligator. The sheet contains frames that are played back in succession to simulate the waving motion. Animating a sprite sheet is nearly the same as any other CSS animation, except for a few special properties and settings, which I will cover momentarily.

Below is an example of a sprite sheet demonstrating the whirling globe of Earth. The sprite sheet contains twenty-six individual frames in a single row. When animated, the thing just spins and spins and spins, because the animation-iteration-count property is set to infinite. A portion of the sprite sheet that produces this animation is shown in Figure 15-9.

snipped from: planet-animation-1.html

```
20 #thePlanet {
21   background-image: url("./assets/Planets2-SpriteSheet.png");
22   position: absolute;
23   left: 20px;
24   top: 20px;
25   width: 260px;
26   height: 260px;
27 }
28 .planet {
29   animation: play 2s steps(26) infinite;
30 }
31 @keyframes play {
32 from { background-position:  0px;  }
33  to { background-position: -6760px;  }
34 }
     . . .
```

Figure 15-9. Individual pictures in a sprite sheet.

Take special note:

- Specify the exact width and height of each frame in the properties for the element (in this case, 260px for both width and height). If you get the size wrong, you'll cut off the frame, or see bits of the next frame with the current one.

- Specify the number of frames in the sprite sheet by using the steps property.

- Indicate the from-to range of the image as the background-position property in the @keyframes rule.

- The from keyframe is set to 0px, and the to keyframe is set to the negative value of the width of the entire sprite sheet.

Remember to specify the to key frame as a negative value. The reason: In effect, you are sliding the sprite sheet toward the left in order to bring the images on the right of the sheet into view. When you move something leftward, you use negative values.

▶ Going Further with Sprite Sheets

We're not quite done with sprite sheets. You'll often want to pause and unpause the animation, monitor animation events such as animationiteration, and even restart it from a hard stop. Check out the *planet-animation-2.html* playground script. It demonstrates all these.

snipped from: planet-animation-2.html

```
28 .planet {
29   animation: play 2s steps(26) 4;
. . .
43 <script>
44   var planet = document.getElementById("thePlanet");
45   planet.addEventListener("click", planetClick);
46   planet.addEventListener("animationstart", animationStart);
47   planet.addEventListener("animationiteration", animationIteration);
48   planet.addEventListener("animationend", animationEnd);
49   var iteration = 0;
50
51   function planetClick() {
52     thePlanet.className = "";
```

```
53    setTimeout(function () {
54      thePlanet.className = "planet"
55    }, 2);
56    thePlanet.offsetHeight;        // Restart hack for Mozilla
57    iteration = 0;
58  }
59
60  function animationStart() {
61    console.log ("Animation has started");
62  }
63
64  function animationIteration() {
65    iteration++;
66    console.log ("Animation has iterated: %s", iteration);
67  }
68
69  function animationEnd() {
70    console.log ("Animation has ended");
71  }
72 </script>
```

Sprite Sheet Setup

Line 29 sets up the animation. It's the same as in the previous example, except that the number of iterations has been modified from infinite to a set value of 4.

Event Listeners

Lines 45 through 48 set up a series of listeners: click for registering mouse-clicks on the planet image and the three specialty animation events to trigger when the animation starts, ends, and iterates.

Global Variable

Line 49 sets up global variables used elsewhere in the script. This iteration variable monitors the number of times the animation has looped (iterated).

Planet Click Event

Lines 51 through 58 respond to when the planet is clicked. The code in this function restarts the animation from the beginning. To do this, it uses a hack discovered some time ago by intrepid JavaScripters that first removes the class name from the thePlanet element and adds it back after a very brief (two millisecond) delay. This hack-jogs the image and causes the browser to reload the animation so that it begins again.

Animation Events

Lines 60 through 71 contain functions that are called when one of the three animation events—animationstart, animationiteration, or animationend—occur. Each function displays a message in the browser's console window. The animationIteration function advances the value of the iteration variable so that the console message includes this information.

You might have noticed that I created both an ID and a class for the planet image. Basic styles go into the #thePlanet rule, and only the animation property goes into the .planet rule. In many cases, this separate treatment isn't required—you could combine everything into the #thePlanet rule.

But CSS animations can get tricky—as you can see in the *planet-animation-3.html* playground script—like when you wish to restart an animation that has ended. The process requires a work-around (aka "hack").

The work-around employed in this script requires removing the class name of the element, then inserting it again. This has the end effect of reestablishing the animation in the element. By including only the animation property in the class style, the only stylistic elements being reset are those associated with the animation.

▶ Integrating CSS Animation and CSS Transitions

It's a true no-brainer to combine CSS animation with CSS transitions. Although both produce motion, they work independently, and they use different property values so there's no chance of one setting clobbering another.

One great way to combine the power of these two engines is to add sprite sheet animations to transition effects. The sprite sheet provides cyclical animation, whereas the transitions enhance the play action with smooth motion effects.

To see this concept in action, let's return to the *Planet Pizza* game first introduced in Chapter 14: Creating Motion with CSS Transitions (page 209). Recall that this game

Figure 15-10. The updated *Planet Pizza* game.

creates fluid animation of a spaceship landing on the surface of the moon using only CSS transitions. With just a couple extra lines of code and a properly-formatted sprite sheet, you can add an animated exhaust plume that blazes while the rocket lands. See Figure 15-10 for a screenshot.

And while we're at it, why not enhance the game in a couple other ways. The *planet-pizza-3.html* bonus game adds these features:

- An animated exhaust plume that can be displayed or hidden, depending on game play.

- A timer that makes you land the spaceship before fuel runs out.

- Synchronization between the game start and the activation of game controls (in the Chapter 14 version, you can begin playing while the panel instruments are still fading in—boo, cheater!).

You can review the new additions to the game by opening the *planet-pizza-3.html* file in the Atom editor. Refer to the code for details on these enhancements and what they do.

Careful: Capitalization Matters!

Among the most frustrating gotchas of working with CSS style sheets is that the names of things are case-sensitive. An element with the class `myClass` is distinct from `myclass`. This rule also applies to animation names. Be sure the `animation-name` property matches the one you've provided in the `@keyframes` rule. For example, this won't work

```
animation: playBlastH .4s steps(6) infinite;
…
@keyframes playblastH …
```

because the `animation-name` is specified as `playBlastH` (with a capital B), while the `@keyframes` rule uses `playblastH` (lower-case b). For this reason, try to use a consistent naming scheme whenever creating CSS styles.

▶ Bonus Examples

CSS animation is used in a number of the bonus games included with this book; some use just animations, and others combine with CSS transitions. First at bat: Check out Lesson 4 of *Sharker*, where the shark is animated with a swimming action. This animation comes from a sprite sheet containing twenty-eight frames.

For more advanced examples of CSS animation, see also:

- Multiple transition and animation effects are used in Kaylee Saves the World. These include transiting marauding Martians on and off the screen; displaying a "zap" effect when an alien is shot; and an animated laser blast using a sprite sheet.

- Kitteh in Space is a classic "side-scroller" game where a background slides from right to left, giving the illusion of motion. This is accomplished with CSS animation. Other features of the game, such as tumbling rocks and laser blasts, use CSS animation and CSS transitions.

ADDING CLOCKS
AND TIMERS

The world runs on time. And so do many games and scripts. With JavaScript, you can set timed events that occur at regular intervals, delay an action for a certain amount of time, or even impose a time limit for your player to complete a task. It's all done with timers—special JavaScript functions that, quite literally, operate like clockwork.

Which brings us to this chapter, in which you'll learn about JavaScript timers: What they are and how to use them. JavaScript timers are surprisingly simple in how they work, but as you'll read, they offer lots of cool features and options that aren't always obvious right off the bat.

one-shot timer

▶ Types of JavaScript Timers

JavaScript supports two types of built-in timers: *one-shot* and *interval*.

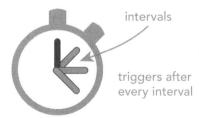

interval timer

- A *one-shot* timer provides a set delay, firing once after the delay has expired.

- An *interval* timer fires repeatedly, with each firing after a specified delay.

Figure 16-1. JavaScript's two timers: one-shot and interval.

The delay for both timers is set in milliseconds—1,000 milliseconds to one second. To delay for half a second, for example, you'd set the timer for 500 milliseconds.

 The standard shorthand for milliseconds is **ms**. Throughout this book and the example scripts, you'll see references to things like 2,000 ms, which means 2,000 milliseconds, or two seconds.

Each type of timer has its unique set of uses. One-shot timers are handy when you want to delay a single action.

Interval timers, on the other hand, are handy for use in such things as count-up or countdown timers (0–60, or 60–0 seconds, for example). They're also frequently used as so-called "game loops," where the various actions of the game are continuously triggered. *Kaylee Saves the World*, as well as several of the other example games, use this type of timer, too; in *Kaylee*, aliens pop out from behind cars and other props at timed intervals, and the player must shoot at them before they disappear.

▶ Using setTimeout: Creating and Using a One-Shot Timer

The JavaScript setTimeout function creates a one-shot timer. The syntax is

    var timerID = setTimeout (action, delay);

timerID ▶ a variable that references the timer. You can use this reference for managing the timer should you need to. For example, you can cancel the timed action if it hasn't occurred yet.

action ▶ the code you want to execute when the timer triggers.

delay ▶ the time delay, in milliseconds, before the action is triggered.

snipped from: setTimeout-1.html

```
17   console.log ("Waiting 3 seconds for the timer to trigger . . .");
18   var myTimer = setTimeout( function() {
19     console.log ("Timer has triggered.");
20   }, 3000);
```

The timer is specified on lines 18 through 20. It's formatted the way it is for clarity—it could all be on one line. The timer action is an inline (so-called *anonymous*) function that simply prints a line of text to the browser's console window. On line 20, the time delay is set to 3,000 ms, or three seconds.

It's not uncommon for the action to be fairly involved, with many lines of code. In these instances, it's usually easier to move the action to its own named function and then call the function from the timer (see Figure 16-2).

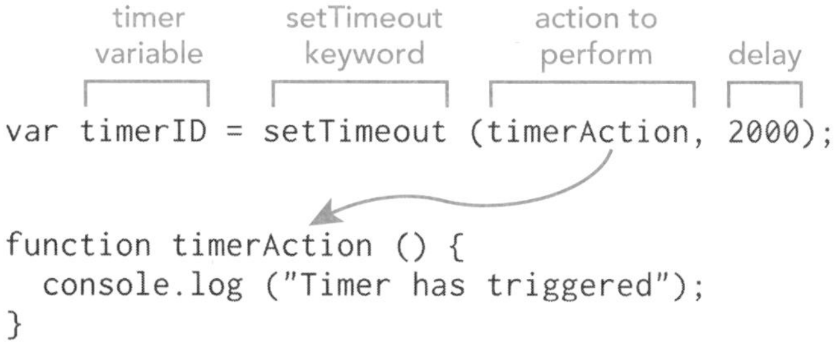

```
        timer        setTimeout      action to
       variable       keyword        perform        delay

var timerID = setTimeout (timerAction, 2000);


function timerAction () {
  console.log ("Timer has triggered");
}
```

Figure 16-2. One-shot timer using setTimeout.

snipped from: setTimeout-2.html

```
17  console.log ("Waiting 3 seconds for the timer to trigger . . .");
18
19  var myTimer = setTimeout(timerAction, 3000);
20  function timerAction () {
21    console.log ("Timer has triggered.");
22    console.log ("This code is in a function named timerAction.");
23  }
```

The timer is created on line 19, this time with a call to a function named timerAction.

The timerAction function itself is defined on lines 20 through 23. This approach makes it easy to add as much code to the function as you'd like.

When you call a function in JavaScript, you normally include a set of parentheses after the function name, like so:

```
callThisFunctionNow();
```

This causes JavaScript to immediately execute the code in the callThisFunctionNow function when this line of the script is reached. When working with timers, remember that calls to functions do not include the () parentheses.

▶ Using setInterval: Creating and Using an Interval Timer

The JavaScript setInterval function creates a repeating interval timer; check out Figure 16-3.

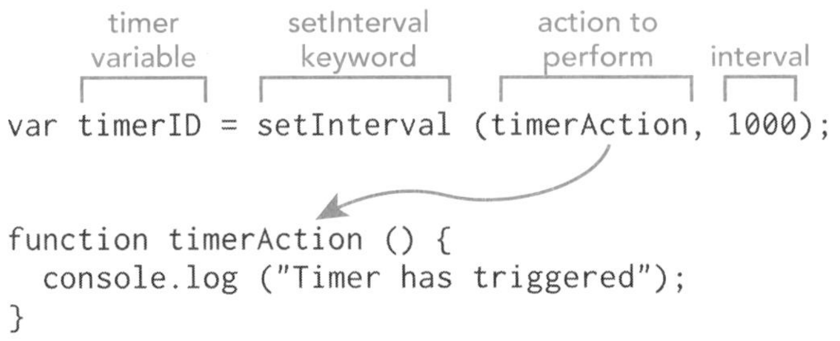

```
         timer        setInterval     action to
         variable      keyword        perform      interval
         ┌────┐       ┌────────┐     ┌──────┐      ┌──┐
    var timerID =  setInterval (timerAction,  1000);

    function timerAction () {
      console.log ("Timer has triggered");
    }
```

Figure 16-3. Interval timer using setInterval.

The syntax is

```
var timerID = setInterval (action, delay);
```

As you can see, the syntax is exactly the same as with setTimeout. The main difference is the reliance on keeping track of the TimerID variable. I pick this up again in a moment.

The next example shows setting the interval to 2,000 milliseconds.

snipped from: setInterval-1.html

```
17  console.log ("Waiting 2 seconds for the timer to trigger . . .");
18
19  var myTimer = setInterval(intervalAction, 2000);
20  function intervalAction () {
21    console.log ("Timer has triggered.");
22  }
```

The interval timer is established on line 19. After an initial 2,000 ms delay, the timer calls the intervalAction function, defined on lines 20 through 22.

Whereas setTimeout fired the timer only once after the 2,000 millisecond delay, here setInterval repeatedly fires the timer every 2,000 ms.

▶ Clearing the Interval Timer

With setTimeout, you'll only occasionally need to terminate a set timer before it's triggered, but stopping an interval timer is a common requirement. This is done with the clearInterval function:

```
clearInterval (timerID);
```

Here is an example of clearInterval in action. When the page is loaded, the interval is repeated every two seconds. This process is repeated twice, at which point the timer is cleared and does not repeat again.

snipped from: setInterval-2.html

```
17  var counter = 0;
18  console.log ("Waiting 2 seconds for the timer to trigger . . .");
19
20  var myTimer = setInterval(intervalAction, 2000);
21  function intervalAction () {
22    console.log ("Timer has triggered.");
23    console.log ("Waiting for retriggering . . .");
24    counter++;
25    if (counter > 2) {
26      console.log ("Timing has ended.");
27      clearInterval (myTimer);
28    }
29  }
```

A counter variable is set up on line 17 to keep track of the number of times the interval timer has triggered.

The counter variable is incremented by 1 on line 24.

If the value in the counter variable is greater than 2, clearInterval clears the timer, which stops it from further retriggering.

▶ Creating a Clock using setInterval

Setting a time limit adds a sense of urgency to games, so clocks are a common component to many types of games, especially those entailing lots of action.

snipped from: setInterval-clock-1.html

```
14   <p id="clock"> </p>
15   <script>
16    var counter = 0;
17    var timeLimit = 10;
18
19    var myTimer = setInterval(intervalAction, 1000);
20    function intervalAction () {
21     document.getElementById("clock").innerText = counter + " seconds.";
22     counter++;
23     if (counter > timeLimit) {
24      document.getElementById("clock").innerText = "Time is up!";
25      clearInterval (myTimer);
26     }
27    }
28   </script>
```

Clock Display

The P element on line 14 serves as a readout for the timer. It's given the unique ID name clock so that it can be referenced later in the script. Note: The text   inside the P element means a non-breaking space, and it is a way to format the element with content that won't initially show.

Timing Variables

Two variables control the action of the clock: counter and timeLimit.

- counter ▶ keeps track of the number of seconds elapsed.

- timeLimit ▶ specifies the number of seconds when the time is up (here specified as 10 seconds).

Clock Function with setInterval

The setInterval function on line 19 specifies an interval of 1,000 ms, calling the intervalAction function at each interval.

The intervalAction function is on lines 20 through 27. Inside the function, the counter variable is incremented by 1 and the text of the P element is updated on line 21.

Checking the Time

Line 23 is an if test: If the value in counter is greater than the timeLimit, the clock has expired and the game is over.

▶ Creating a Countdown Clock

Countdown clocks—where time starts at some value and goes down to 0—are easy to construct. Although you could revise the code to decrement the counter variable down to zero, a one-line change is all that's usually needed:

```
21 document.getElementById("clock").innerText =
   (timeLimit - counter) + " seconds.";
```

You can experiment with this approach in the *setInterval-clock-2.html* playground example. The timer still counts up, but what's displayed to the player is a countdown.

Alternatively, you can rewrite the code to create a pure countdown. The revised code is a little shorter, too.

snipped from: setInterval-clock-3.html

```
16 var timeLimit = 10;
17
18 var myTimer = setInterval(intervalAction, 1000);
19 function intervalAction () {
20  document.getElementById("clock").innerText = timeLimit + " seconds.";
21  if (timeLimit == 0) {
22   document.getElementById("clock").innerText = "Time is up!";
23   clearInterval (myTimer);
24  }
25  timeLimit--;
26 }
```

▶ Using Multiple Timers in a Game

JavaScript supports a nearly unlimited number of timers in one script. You can create multiple timers, each firing at different times and executing different code. By carefully selecting the time delays, this gives the appearance of lots of seemingly random action.

When creating multiple timers, be sure to assign them to unique variables. This is as easy as:

```
var timerID1 = setInterval . . .
var timerID2 = setInterval . . .
var timerID3 = setInterval . . .
```

Each timer is associated with a different ID; each ID is contained in a separate variable.

When using either setTimeout or setInterval, if you know you never need to manage the timer (such as stop it if before it's fired again), you can leave out the variable assignment:
setTimeout(timerAction, 3000);

That said, for coding consistency, you may want to always include the variable assignment, even if you don't use it.

▶ Adding a Random Factor to the Time Delay

Games are more interesting when things appear to be random. Imagine a blackjack game where the cards are dealt in the same order every time. You would play that game a couple of times, then move on.

With a short piece of JavaScript code, you can produce random numbers that can be used for all sorts of tasks, including generating random time delays for the setInterval and setTimeout functions. It's all done with the Math.random method.

```
var myRandomNumber = Math.random();
```

The result is a number from 0 to 1, like so:

```
0.30585089563905776
```

That's obviously not a value you can use with either `setInterval` or `setTimeout`, which expects millisecond time delays. You can (partially) fix this by multiplying the randomized result by multiples of one thousand. For example, this code returns a *floating point* (number with a decimal value) between 0 and 1,000:

```
var myRandomNumber = Math.random() * 1000;
// Example value 839.093690314558
var myTimer = setTimeout(timerAction, myRandomNumber);
```

The process: Fetch a random number and then use that value as the delay, for `setTimeout` or `setInterval`.

Ideally, you want to provide whole numbers to the timer functions, exclude a value of 0 (no delay), and even specify minimum and maximum delays. This is a perfect job for a user-defined function. Here's one that does all three of the requisite improvements:

```
function getRandomInt(min, max) {
  return Math.floor(Math.random() * (max - min + 1)) + min;
}
```

To use this function, call it by specifying the minimum and maximum values you want. Suppose you want a time delay between 1,000 and 3,000 ms:

Method 1:

```
var myRandomNumber = getRandomInt(1000, 3000);
var myTimer = setTimeout(timerAction, myRandomNumber);
```

Method 2:

```
var myTimer = setTimeout(timerAction, getRandomInt(1000, 3000));
```

Both do the same thing. The difference is that in Method 1 you assign the random number to a variable (which you can use with `console.log` for troubleshooting purposes) and then use that value in the `setTimeout` function.

You can experiment with randomized delays with the *setTimeout-random.html* playground script. Try different minimum and maximum values for the `getRandomInt` function call. Open the browser's console window to see the results of the script.

snipped from: setTimeout-random.html

```
19 var myRandomNumber = getRandomInt(1000, 3000);
20 var myTimer = setTimeout(timerAction, myRandomNumber);
      . . .
```

▶ Using CSS Transition/Animation Events as Timers

Both CSS transitions and CSS animations provide events that are automatically triggered within JavaScript upon completion of the transition/animation movement. You can use these events as a method of creating timers. The timer triggers when the transition or animation ends, or when the animation begins a new iteration.

Recall from Chapter 14: Creating Motion with CSS Transitions (page 209) that transitions are set up as a CSS property. In the *rocketman-move-1.html* script, the rocketeer moves when he's clicked:

snipped from: rocketman-move-1.html

```
11 <style>
12 img {
13   position: absolute;
14   left: 0px;
15   transition-property: left;
16   transition-duration: 1s;
17 }
18 </style>
. . .
21 <body>
22 <img src="./assets/rocketeer-small.png" alt=""
     onclick="this.style.left='200px'" />
23 </body>
```

The transition is defined on lines 15 and 16: It lasts one second (1s) and is triggered by any change in the left style property. This change occurs thanks to the onclick listener added to the IMG element. Upon the click, the left property is changed to 200px. Instead of abruptly changing the left property, the transition creates a smooth motion.

By adding an event listener for when the transition ends (see Figure 16-4), your code can receive a signal that is useful as an elapsed timer.

duration = 1 second

```
transition-duration: 1s;
```

clicking triggers
timed transition

```
<img src="./assets/rocketeer-small.png"
        onclick="this.style.left='200px'" />
```

JavaScript code
executes at end
of transition

```
rocketeer.addEventListener("transitionend", timer);
function timer() {
  console.log ("The transition has ended");
}
```

moves in 1 second

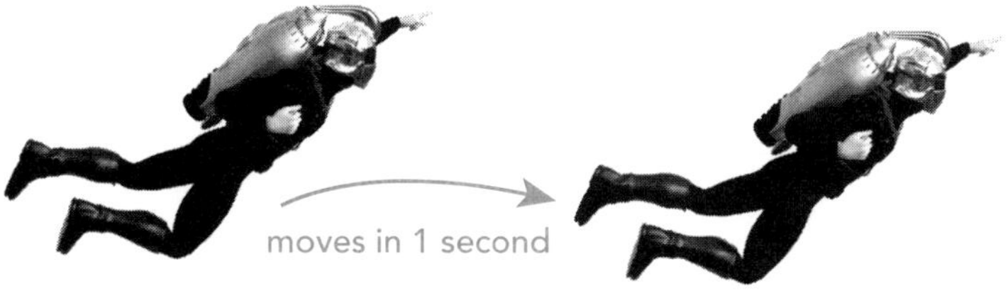

Figure 16–4. A CSS transition used as an elapsed timer.

snipped from: rocketman-move-eventtimer.html

```
22 <img id="rocketeer" src="./assets/rocketeer-small.png" alt=""
   onclick="this.style.left='200px'" />
23 <script>
24  var rocketeer = document.getElementById("rocketeer");
25  rocketeer.addEventListener("transitionend", timer);
26  function timer() {
27   console.log ("The transition has ended");
28  }
29 </script>
```

Line 22 ► changed to provide a unique identifier to the IMG element: The rocketeer ID is used on line 24 to reference this element in code.

Line 25 ► tells JavaScript to listen for the transitionend (end of transition) event on the rocketeer element.

When that event occurs ► the code executes the function defined on lines 26 through 28.

Where this is helpful: Rather than define a transition and a setTimeout timer, you can combine the two. This saves some code but also allows you to synchronize the two events together. For instance, at the termination of the transition, your game could produce a sound (see Chapter 19: Adding Sound [page 287) or launch some other animated sequence.

▶ Using Timers for Animation

Before the requestAnimationFrame feature was added to modern browsers, games were often animated using the setInterval function as a way to time individual frames of action and display them to the player. The technique is still used today, especially when the frame rate of the animation is low—under 10 frames per second or so.

The technique of using timers for animation is discussed in more depth in Chapter 17: Extended Animation Techniques (page 257).

▶ Bonus Examples

See the following bonus games for examples of
countdown/count-up timers that control play duration:

Planet Pizza, Lesson 3

A timer displays the remaining fuel of a spaceship. If
the fuel is depleted before the ship can land, the game
is over and the ship crashes.

Pipeworks

A timer controls the level of rising water in a reservoir.
The player must complete the puzzle before the
reservoir fills up.

EXTENDED ANIMATION TECHNIQUES

Motion is the lifeblood of games, and it's a good thing that JavaScript supports numerous ways to achieve it.

In previous chapters, you learned about several methods, some of which don't even require any code. In Chapters 14 and 15, you learned about creating motion with CSS transitions and CSS animations, respectively, and how to create decent animations using timers that trigger at regular intervals.

But these are not the only methods at your disposal. In this chapter, you'll learn how to go further with the requestAnimationFrame method, taking direct control of the frame-by-frame images that make up the motion graphics.

You'll also learn how to combine the requestAnimationFrame method with something called SVG graphics so movements of your animated characters and other objects can follow any arbitrary path. And you'll discover better ways to use the JavaScript setInterval timer for animations that don't require a high frame speed.

▶ The requestAnimationFrame Method Revisited

In Chapter 13: Making Your Game Move (page 197), you were introduced to the requestAnimationFrame method, or *RAF* for short. RAF provides a way to animate individual frames that integrates with the browser's own display engine. This helps to produce the smoothest animation possible.

Depending on a number of performance factors, an animation driven by RAF runs at 60 frames per second (fps). Among the many causes for reduced frame rate are:

- The computer is under battery power. The browser may detect this and switch to a power-saving mode that includes lower performance.

- The animation consists of many elements. The more things to animate, the longer it can take.

- The computing device is not capable of a higher frame rate. This can be the case with certain underperforming tablets, for example.

For RAF to do its magic, you need only create a user-defined function. Inside this function, you add a call to itself, thereby creating a self-perpetuating loop (don't worry; there are ways to stop the loop). To get the animation started in the first place, you merely add another call to the function somewhere in your script. See Figure 17-1 for an overview of the basic process.

```
function timer() {
    var ufo = document.getElementById("ufo");
    ufo.style.left = counter + "px";
    window.requestAnimationFrame(timer);
}
```

function then re-calls itself
to keep animation going

```
timer();
```

first call starts animation

Figure 17-1. Using the requestAnimationFrame method.

Remember the flying UFO example back in Chapter 13 (page 197)? It used RAF to animate a flying saucer across the screen. That playground script included a way to stop the animation when the UFO traveled far enough. Here's the relevant code repeated again for your convenience:

snipped from: request-animation-loop.html

```
36   var counter = -400;
37   function animationLoop() {
38    if (counter < 615) {
39     counter += 5;
40     document.getElementById("ufo1").style.left = counter + "px";
41     window.requestAnimationFrame(animationLoop);
42    }
43   }
44   animationLoop();
```

Implementing the RAF Animation Loop

The actual `requestAnimationFrame` method comprises lines 37 through 43. In it, the UFO is translated to the right 5 pixels at a time. RAF works by "calling itself," as demonstrated in line 41. By calling itself, the loop keeps going.

Starting the RAF Animation Loop the First Time Around

I'm using a named function for the animation loop, and I've called this function `animationLoop`, to keep its purpose obvious. Because of the way the function is constructed, code inside it won't execute unless you first call the function from the main body of the script. This is what line 44 does. As JavaScript processes the script, line 44 triggers the first iteration of the `animationLoop` cycle.

Stopping the Animation

A `requestAnimationFrame` loop will continue as long as the loop keeps calling itself. Line 38 continues the loop as long as the position of the `left` edge of the UFO is less than 615px. When the saucer slides past this point, the code no longer calls the `requestAnimationFrame` method, and so the animation stops.

▶ Changing Frame Rate and More

RAF updates the animation frame about 60 times per second (commonly referred to as *fps*, or *frames per second*). For some animation, that may be too fast. You have a couple of options for slowing the frame rate, depending on the type of animation you're doing.

If you're moving an object (probably the most common type of animation), you can vary the distance per frame to speed up or slow things down. For example, instead of moving five pixels at a time, you can slow the move by incrementing by a smaller number:

```
counter += 5; // Original value
counter += 2; // Apparent speed is about halved
counter += 10; // Apparent speed is doubled
```

Implement a frame-rate component with the `requestAnimationFrame` method. This allows you to select an approximate frame rate of *up to* 60 fps. You can't go over 60 fps, but you can choose anything slower. The frame rate can even be less than 1 fps.

Check out the *request-animation-loop-enhanced.html* playground script. It contains several enhancements over the basic RAF demonstrator, including—just for fun—adding a second saucer, making the animation restart itself, and incorporating a frame-rate control.

```
38 <div id="mainContent">
39  <img id="ufo1" class="ufo" alt="" src="./assets/ufo1.png" />
40  <img id="ufo2" class="ufo" alt="" src="./assets/ufo2.png" />
41 </div>
42
43 <script>
44
45  var fps = 1000 / 20;
46  var newTime, oldTime = 0;
47
48  var counter = -400;
49  function animationLoop(timestamp) {
50    newTime = timestamp;
51    if (newTime - oldTime > fps) {
52      if (counter < 615) {
53        counter += 5;
54        document.getElementById("ufo1").style.left = counter + "px";
55        document.getElementById("ufo2").style.left = counter + 30 + "px";
56      } else {
57        counter = -400;
58      }
59      oldTime = oldTime += fps;
60    }
61    window.requestAnimationFrame(animationLoop);
62  }
63  animationLoop();
```

Animated Objects

Three graphics are used: A static background image and two flying saucers. The static background is part of the mainContent DIV, and the saucers are added on lines 39 and 40.

Frame-Rate Selection

The frame-rate selection is on line 45. The expression *1000 / n* returns the time interval between frames, in milliseconds. Changing the second operand sets the fps. The calculation *1000 / 20* results in a value of 50 (ms).

A lower number sets a lower frame rate and, of course, a higher interval. An fps of 1000 / 10 is 100 ms between frames.

Frame Control

The frame control comprises lines 50 through 51 and line 59.

The requestAnimationFrame method itself gives you a time stamp value since it last started. This value, also in milliseconds, is passed into the animationLoop function using the timestamp argument. This value is then used to set an oldTime (previous) and a newTime (current) value.

The difference between these time values (line 51) is the elapsed interval since the previous pass through the loop. If the interval is greater than the fps interval, the code on lines 52 through 60 is executed. This code updates the position of the saucers.

Line 59 updates oldTime so that it's equal to the previous oldTime plus the fps interval.

Whether or not enough time has elapsed to update the animation, line 61 calls the requestAnimationFrame method again, setting things up for the next loop.

▶ Animating with SVG

Many games use simple animation, where movement is either up-and-down or side-to-side. And that's fine, but what about more complex movement, such as zigzags, or curves? It could be done by defining "phases" in the animation where a character first moves in one direction and then the other. Having to write code for each change in direction is a thankless task, and it makes for difficult modifications down the road.

A better approach: *Scaled vector graphics*, or *SVG*. You may have already heard of SVG—it's a type of graphic image that is defined using lines and geometric *shapes* rather than bitmap pixels—see Figure 17-2 for a collection of common SVG graphics objects. Programs like Adobe Illustrator® and Inkscape create vector images and SVG format files.

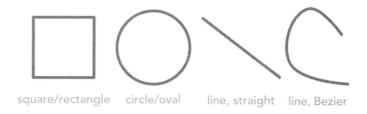

square/rectangle   circle/oval   line, straight   line, Bezier

Figure 17-2. Common SVG graphics objects.

Where SVG comes into play is using the vector—be it a line, circle, square, or squiggly—as a *path*. ("A path! A path!" for you *Monty Python* fans.) Using relatively simple script, add this code inside a requestAnimationFrame loop. You can have an object trace the path, giving your animations nearly infinite possibilities of motion.

Let's see how SVG path-following works by looking at the *svgsimple.html* playground file. This script contains just a couple of pieces:

▨ A simple SVG path using the special `<svg>` tag ▸ This path becomes a kind of guide rail that controls the movement.

▨ A small object to travel the path ▸ It's an IMG of a small rock. Nothing special.

▨ A short animation function where the animation takes place ▸ This function is used in coordination with the requestAnimationFrame method.

snipped from: svgsimple.html

```
12 #mainContent {
13  position: absolute;
14  background-color: #fafad2;
15  width: 750px;
16  height: 250px;
17 }
18
19 .path {
20  stroke-dasharray: 10;
21  stroke: black;
22  stroke-width: 1;
23  fill: none;
24 }
25
26 .curves {
27  position: absolute;
28  overflow: hidden;
29  margin-left: 0px;
30  margin-top: 0px;
31  width: 750px;
32  height: 250px;
33 }
34
35 .rock {
36  position: absolute;
37  width: 20px;
38  height: 20px;
39 }
. . .
45  <div id="mainContent">
46
47   <div id="curve1" class="curves">
48    <svg class="curves">
```

```
49      <path class="path" d="M 0,185 C 91,7 395,0 575,195" />
50     </svg>
51    </div>
52
53    <img id="rock" class="rock spinccw" alt="rock" src="./assets/rock.png" />
54   </div>
55
56   <script>
57
58    var rock = document.getElementById("rock");
59    var curve = document.getElementById("curve1");
60    var path = curve.getElementsByTagName("path")[0];
61    var speed = 3;
62    var curPos = 0;
63
64    function animate () {
65     var length = path.getTotalLength();
66     curPos = curPos + speed;
67     var point = path.getPointAtLength(curPos);
68
69     rock.style.left = point.x + "px";
70     rock.style.top = point.y + "px";
71     if (curPos < length) {
72      window.requestAnimationFrame(animate);
73     }
74    }
75    animate();
76
77   </script>
```

See Figure 17-3 for how the script looks in action.

Figure 17-3. With SVG, objects can be made to follow any path.

Element Styling

Lines 12 through 39 define styles to use with the HTML elements on the page. Take note of the path class: This class visually displays the SVG path that is drawn with the SVG element (discussed on page 261). The visual display isn't necessary for the animation to work—it's just there for reference.

Some basic styling is needed for the path, or else the browser will apply an unattractive default appearance. At a minimum you will want to use fill: none;.

Element Definitions

Lines 47 through 54 define an SGV path inside a DIV container and an IMG element displaying a 20-by-20px rock. The rock is meant to follow the SVG path. The DIV has an ID so it can be referenced.

Setup Code

Setup code is provided on lines 58 through 62. The rock, path, and curve variables hold references to their respective HTML elements, so they don't have to be re-fetched each time the animation frame is repeated.

- The speed variable ▶ controls the "steps" of the rock object as it is animated. The lower the number, the slower the animation.

- The curPos variable ▶ holds the current position of the rock as it's animated along the SVG path.

Animation Loop

Lines 64 through 74 is the animation loop. It begins by getting the total length (in pixels) of the SVG path. (I elected to put this line inside the loop, but as it doesn't change over the course of the animation, it could really be a part of the setup code.)

The script then updates the curPos variable to find the next point on the path to go to. The curPos variable holds a number that starts at 0 and increments until it reaches the total length of the path.

To locate the actual spot on the path to move to, the script uses the getPointAtLength method, which is unique to using SVG. The point variable that results from this method is a simple object with .x and .y properties. These properties are used to update the position of the rock using the lines:

```
rock.style.left = point.x + "px";
rock.style.top = point.y + "px";
```

The animation needs to know when to end; this is the job of the if statement on lines 71 through 73. As long as the current positon (curPos) of the rock is less than the length of the path, the animate function is called again, which results in a new animation frame.

Starting the Animation First Time Through

Line 75 executes the animate function when the page is loaded. From there, the function is repeatedly called via the requestAnimationFrame method until the rock has reached the end of the path.

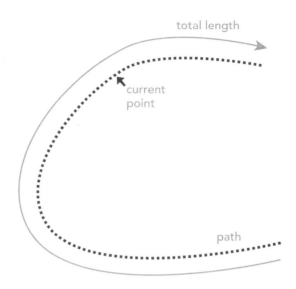

Figure 17-4. Using the getPointAtLength method to follow an SVG path.

To run the demonstration, simply load the page and watch the rock follow the path. Try experimenting with different *speed* value to see what effect they have on the animation playback. You can replace the d= attribute on line 49 of the code to make a different vector. To start, try small changes in the values and reload the page to see what effect these changes have.

The path in the demo code is a Bezier curve with two control points.

```
d="M 0,185 C 91,7 395,0 575,195"
```

The first number following M is the starting point (0,185). The values are X/Y coordinates. This is where the path begins. The three numbers following the C are the first control point (91,7), the end control point (395,0) and the final end point (575,195).

If hand-editing Bezier curve paths isn't your bag, there are several online SVG path generators you can try. See the Online Support Site (Appendix A, page 310) for a list of some of my favorites.

Or, if you have Adobe Illustrator®, Inkscape, or another program that generates SVG files, you can use it to draw the shape you want, save the file, and then open it in a text editor. Pick out just the d= path that defines the vector. Just be sure the program hasn't added a default offset to the values, or else the path will not start and end where you expect.

▶ Using Timers for Animation

JavaScript's setInterval function provides a simple yet effective mechanism for animating objects. It's not as robust as the requestAnimationFrame, but it's still a viable choice for simpler tasks, especially those with a fairly low frame rate. And that's just how we'll use it in the *timerinterval-animation1.html* playground script, where an object is moved across the screen using a setInterval timer. The object is a DIV with an image background and is shown in Figure 17-5.

Figure 17-5. Using a setInterval timer for a relatively slow frame animation.

snipped from: setinterval-animation1.html

```
20  #ogre {
21    position: absolute;
22    background-image: url("./assets/ogre-static.png");
23    margin 0;
24    left: 0px;
25    top: 170px;
26    width: 84px;
27    height: 80px;
28  }
   . . .
34    <div id="ogre"></div>
38    var ogre = document.getElementById("ogre");
39    ogre.style.left = "750px";
```

```
   . . .
38  var ogre = document.getElementById("ogre");
39  ogre.style.left = "750px";
40  var timerID = setInterval(walk, 10);
41  function walk() {
42   var left = parseInt(ogre.style.left);
43   if (left > 0) {
44    ogre.style.left = parseInt(ogre.style.left) - 1 + "px";
45   } else {
46    clearInterval(timerID);
47   }
48  }
```

Character Style

The #ogre character is defined in lines 20 through 28. It's a simple DIV (line 34) with a background image. The ogre DIV is itself tucked into a container DIV (not shown here). The container DIV has a width of 750px.

Set Start Location

After getting a reference to the ogre DIV, on line 39 the script forces the image to 750px, which is beyond the width of the container DIV, effectively making it look like the ogre character is coming into view.

Trigger Timer

Line 40 starts an (automatically retriggered) interval timer, which sets off the walk function every 10 ms. This is used later to stop the timer when the ogre gets to the other side.

Timer Loop

The animation loop spans lines 41 through 48 and comprises the walk function. This function first gets the current location of the ogre and subtracts 1 pixel from it.

If the current position is greater than 0, the script moves the ogre to the new location.

If the current position is 0 (or less), then the timer is cleared using the clearInterval function on line 46. This causes the animation to stop, because the timer is no longer retriggered.

The *setinterval-animation2.html* playground script is essentially the same, but it also incorporates CSS animation to provide a walk cycle for the ogre. This provides a more realistic animation—the ogre's legs move in a walking cycle while its body also slides across the screen.

```
20 #ogre {
21   position: absolute;
22   background-image: url("./assets/ogre.png");
23   margin 0;
24   left: 0px;
25   top: 170px;
26   width: 84px;
27   height: 80px;
28   object-fit: none;
29   object-position: -0px 0;
30   animation: play 2s steps(19) infinite;
31 }
32 @keyframes play {
33 from { background-position: -1520px; }
34   to { background-position: 0px; }
. . .
47  var timerID = setInterval(walk, 30);
```

Line 22 sets a different background image to the ogre DIV. This image is a *sprite sheet*, which consists of multiple individual frames of the ogre in various walk poses.

Line 30 sets up the CSS animation by specifying:

- The animation is to use the play @keyframes rule to read the sprite sheet

- The full walk cycle is to take two seconds

- There are nineteen frames (*steps*) in the sprite sheet

- The animation is to repeat indefinitely

The play @keyframes rule specifies the from and to positions. See Chapter 15: Creating Motion with CSS Animations (page 225) for more details on animations using @keyframes.

The animation is slowed down a little—to 30 ms between frames—to better correspond to the speed of the walk cycle.

Play with the settings in the *setinterval-animation2.html* demo to see how different values for the play @keyframes and setInterval timer affect the look of the animation.

Figure 17-6. The *Ogre!* game uses SVG animation.

▶ RAF, SVG, and setInterval Animation—Play Ogre!

Time to toss some rocks at those slothful ogres that have been walking on your lawn. The *Ogre!* game demonstrates all of the three primary techniques outlined in this chapter:

- SVG for animating along complex paths.

- The requestAnimationFrame method to do the rock-tossing animation.

- A setInterval timer to animate moving the ogre across the play field.

Add a little bit of CSS animation to display an animated walk cycle for the ogre. As noted on the previous demo, the walk cycle is comprised of nineteen poses in one sprite sheet file. The combination of the CSS walk cycle and the horizontal slide of the ogre DIV using setInterval give a full animation effect, belying the simplicity of the coding involved. See Figure 17-6 for a screen shot.

Here are the main points in the *Ogre!* game:

mainContent Container

A container DIV named mainContent holds all of the game elements: Explanatory text, score text, walking ogre character, multiple SVG paths, and the hurled rock.

Ogre Character

The ogre character is a sprite sheet containing nineteen frames. Each frame is a different walk pose. CSS animation is used for the ogre's walk cycle. The ogre's movement is provided by a setInterval timer that literally slides the animated image from right to left.

SVG Paths

A set of five different SVG paths are hard-coded. Each path is enclosed in a DIV container. Later in the script, JavaScript picks one of these paths for the rock trajectory. (The track of the paths is normally hidden for game play; by altering the CSS styling rules, the tracks can be made visible for development purposes.)

HTML for a sample SVG path:

```
<div id="curve4" class="curves">
 <svg class="curves">
  <path class="path" d="M0,188 C91,7 396,-6 575,197" />
 </svg>
</div>
```

Rock Image and Animation

A small 20px rock image is used as a projectile to launch against the approaching ogre. Included in the style rules for the rock is a simple CSS animation that slowly spins the rock, giving it more realism.

```
.spinccw { animation: spinccw 4s linear infinite; }
@keyframes spinccw { 100% { transform:rotate(-360deg); } }
```

Explanatory Text

Two P elements are added for explanatory text. One element is used as instruction and "Game Over" feedback. The other holds the score: The number of ogres left to invade (there are five total), and the number of ogres that have been hit by rocks.

Track Object Constructor

Ogre! uses a user-defined JavaScript object to control the track and its animation. The object, called PathTrack, encapsulates all the functionality to manage one or more tracks simultaneously. *Ogre!* only uses one (randomly selected) track at a time. But the more sophisticated PathTrack object is included because it's also found in the *Kitteh in Space* example game, which involves more tracks and simultaneous target objects.

Collision Detection

When a rock hits an ogre, the collision is detected using a short bit of code common to many of the arcade-style games in this book. The code, contained in a function called isCollide, checks whether any part of Object A is within Object B. If so, that's a collision, and it's duly noted that a rock has struck an ogre. When that happens, the ogre is removed from the play field, and another takes its place.

Hurling a Rock

A mouse-click event listener is added to the mainContent DIV so that whenever it's clicked, the throwRock function is executed, which lobs another rock toward the approaching ogre.

- The game limits only one rock in the air at a time.
- The track (one of five) is selected at random.
- The throw speed (from 5 to 12) is selected at random.

Ogre Counting, Game Scoring, and Game Over

The resetOgre function handles adding a replacement ogre onto the game board. A user-defined object, game, keeps track of several game-related variables, including the number of ogres left to play and the number of ogres that have been hit. These values are decremented or incremented accordingly.

If all the ogres have been depleted—the game.ogres value == 0—then the game is over. The P explanatory text element is updated to say "Game Over!," and the mouse-click event listener is removed to prevent hurling more rocks.

The updateScore function handles updating the P scoring element, which displays the values of the game.ogres and game.hits properties.

USING NUMBERS
AND MATH IN GAMES

$$E=mc^2$$

It's really just a simple math formula, but Albert Einstein's famous equation forever changed the way we think of the universe.

Math and numbers are an integral part of our lives. Even those of us who aren't good at math (go ahead, raise your hand!) have to deal with it on a day-to-day basis. There's no escaping numbers and mathematics.

It's no surprise that games (and other kinds of scripts) often make heavy use of math. Fortunately, whether or not you have an aptitude for numbers, employing the power of math in JavaScript is pretty simple.

In this chapter, you'll learn about JavaScript's built-in math functions and how to use numbers to solve all kinds of programming tasks. You might not be able to use JavaScript to answer all the remaining questions about special relativity, but it comes in handy when calculating game scores, keeping track of nasty villains, shuffling cards, and more.

▶ The Joy of JavaScript Numbers

If you have experience with another programming language, you may have encountered a dizzying array of *number types*—8-bit integers, 16-bit integers, signed and unsigned integers, floats—the list continues.

JavaScript simplifies all that and, internally, supports just a single numeric type. This one type can represent both *whole* (integer) and *floating-point* numbers:

    Integer ▶ a whole number, such as 0, 15, 107, –1005. Integers can have either positive or negative values.

    Floating point ▶ a number with a decimal point: 3.1416, or –1001.919. Floating-point values (*floats* for short) can be positive or negative.

Inside your computer, integer or floating-point JavaScript numbers are stored using 64 bits of data (recall from basic computer study that a bit is the smallest indivisible unit, representing 0 or 1). This allows a maximum JavaScript number value of 2 raised to the 53rd power. From a technical standpoint, all numbers in JavaScript are considered floating-point. This means 42 is really more like 42.0000 (. . . etc.).

To assign a number to a JavaScript variable, simply type the number, without quotes:

```
var myNumber = 5;
var myNumber = 3.14;
```

If you enter the number with quotes, the value is a string instead. Although it may *look* like a number 5 in the browser's console window or when displayed on a web page, JavaScript considers a 5 within quotes a text character, rather than a true number. This is an important distinction, as you'll see in the next section.

When dealing with large numbers, you can use exponents as shorthand. Examples:

```
var myNumber = 987e5;          // Result: 98700000
var myNumber = 987e-5;         // Result: 0.00987
```

▶ Be Watchful of Combining Numbers with Text

JavaScript is what's known as a typeless language, meaning that its data is not required to be defined as a certain data type. In some other languages, if you want to store an integer number, you have to tell the program an integer is the type of data to expect. Same for floats, strings, and other data types.

Being a typeless language, JavaScript is considered easier to learn and use, but this convenience comes at a price. Sometimes it does seemingly crazy things if you unwittingly try to combine different kinds of values. This is never more apparent than when dealing with numbers and with text strings that look like numbers. For instance:

```
var myText = "42";
var myNumber = 42;
console.log (myText);
console.log (myNumber);
```

When the values are printed in the browser's console window, they'll look (almost) identical:

42
42

Assuming you're using Google Chrome, if you look closely at the numbers, you'll see the two values are actually in different colors: Black for the text version of "42," and dark blue for the number version of 42. These colors tell you the values are actually different types.

For some routine scripting chores, whether the value is a text string or a number doesn't make much difference. When used as display data for the player, for example, 42 is "42." Where the difference can make a huge impact is when you want to perform arithmetic with the value, or when you want to compare values to see if they match.

Let's try adding the two values together. At first glance, you might think the result is 84, but you'd be wrong (see Figure 18-1):

$$42 \quad + \quad "42" \quad = 4242$$

number   string

Figure 18-1. Using the + character with a number and string.

```
var myText = "42";
var myNumber = 42;
console.log (myText + myNumber);        // Result: 4242
```

JavaScript knows it can't add a string value to a number and still have a number as the result. So it automatically coerces (*promotes*) the myNumber value to also be a string value. Adding "42" to 42 gives you "4242."

The best way to avoid this situation is to make sure that any values you intend to use in arithmetic operations are actual numbers. When this isn't possible, you can do your own coercing. Here's one method:

```
var myText = "42";
var myNumber = 42;
console.log (Number(myText) + myNumber);          // Result: 84
```

Using Number(myText) forces JavaScript to respect your intended promotion of the string to a number, and you get the sum of the values.

Exercise care when coercing values. If myText can't resolve to an actual number, the Number function will return *NaN*, for *Not-a-Number*. That means the result will also be NaN. Here's an example of a coercion that will fail:

```
var myText = "42a";
var myNumber = 42;
console.log (Number(myText) + myNumber);          // Result: NaN
```

If you suspect the value might contain non-numeric characters, which is surprisingly common, use the parseInt function instead. The parseInt "parses" the value, using a set of rules to toss away non-numeric characters.

```
var myText = "42px";
var myNumber = 42;
console.log (parseInt(myText) + myNumber);          // Result: 84
```

Akin to parseInt is parseFloat. It does the same job as parseInt, but with floating-point values. Use parseFloat it in the same way as parseInt.

▶ Tips for Converting Numbers to Strings

From time to time, you'll have reason to convert a number to a string. You might do this in order to use the number value with some function or method that requires a string. Fortunately, it's quite simple: Add the toString method after the variable:

```
var myNumber = 42;
console.log (myNumber);                   // Blue text in console window
console.log (myNumber.toString());        // Black text in console window
```

Look closely at the result in the console window, and you'll see the first value is printed in blue (number) and the second in black (string).

▶ Performing Arithmetic with Numbers

A key requirement in many games is to calculate numeric values for things like the final score, or for keeping track of the number of ghouls the player has successfully terminated. Most game math can be performed using the five basic arithmetic operators:

CALCULATION		EXAMPLE
Addition	+	100 + 5.91 // Result: 105.91
Subtraction	~	100 - 5.91 // Result: 94.09
Multiplication	*	100 * 5.91 // Result: 591 . . .
Division	/	100 / 5.91 // Result: 16.92047 . . .
Modulus division (remainder)	%	100 % 5.91 // Result: 5.439999

The main thing to keep in mind when using any arithmetic operators is that the values on both sides of the expression should be numbers. This provides the most consistent results. Recall from above that when using the + operator to add a number to a string, JavaScript will *coerce* the number into also being a string:

```
var value1 = 50;
var value2 = "40";
console.log (value1 + value2);          // Result: 5040
```

But when using the other math operators, you get correct results:

```
console.log (value1 - value2);          // Result: 10
console.log (value1 * value2);          // Result: 2000
console.log (value1 / value2);          // Result: 1.25
console.log (value1 % value2);          // Result: 10
```

This seemingly inconsistent behavior of the math operators is not inconsistent at all. It comes from the + symbol being *overloaded* to act in two different scenarios. The + is used to both combine strings together and to add numbers. When combining a string and a number, JavaScript simply assumes you want to treat both values as strings.

The other symbols are not overloaded—they work only as math operators. So for these operators, JavaScript knows that if a string value can be converted to a number, it'll do so and calculate the result for you.

Okay, with all this said: Despite JavaScript's smarts, good coding practice recommends—whenever possible—that you cast the values to the type you want to use before JavaScript coerces them to another type. That helps to avoid unexpected results and ensures the code is working the *way* you intend. Refer to the section, "Be Watchful of Combining Numbers with Text" earlier in this chapter (page 274) for more details on instructing JavaScript how you want string number values to be interpreted.

▶ Keeping Track of Scores and Other Game Values

Tallying or *totalizing* is the process of keeping track of changing values in a game or other script. Many games maintain just a simple total score, where all the successes and failures of the player are formulated and displayed. You can use a single variable for that:

```
var totalScore = 100; // Initializes the starting score at 100
```

Then, during game play, the number is incremented as the player moves from one stage to the next. To increment or decrement the score by 1, you'd use:

```
totalScore++;        // Increments the score
totalScore--;        // Decrements the score
```

Or if by a value other than 1:

```
totalScore += 10;    // Increments the score by 10
totalScore -= 10;    // Decrements the score by 10
```

can also be expressed as:

```
totalScore = totalScore + 10;
totalScore = totalScore - 10;
```

In some cases, specific actions by the player result in incrementing or decrementing by different amounts:

```
var queen = 100;
var alien = 50;
var friend = -50
totalScore = totalScore + queen; // Totalize score when alien queen is hit
 // or
totalScore += queen;
```

Preset values are defined for different character types—hitting the alien queen is worth 100 points, but it's only 50 points for the average alien. If the player hits a friend, that *costs* 50 points.

It's not uncommon to keep track of several scoring mechanisms and to totalize the result based on ever-changing metrics. For this, a user-defined object is the preferred method. The object stores numerous values, each identified with a unique name. The object serves the same purposes as individual variables but makes it easier to keep all score-related values together as a single unit.

Recall from Chapter 6: Getting Started with JavaScript: Part 1 (page 91) that the basic structure of a user-defined object is:

```
var objectName = {
 property: value,
 property: value,
 . . .
 property: value
}
```

objectName is the name of the object you created, and the property: value pairs each specify a unique property and its value. Properties can be updated at any time.

In the following playground example, a score object holds all the relevant values needed to calculate the score in real time. Several pieces of information are stored:

- The relative "hit" values for three types of targets: Queen aliens, regular aliens, and friends. The hit values specify how much the score is increased (or decreased) depending on which type of character is shot at.

- Separate totals of how many of each target has been hit.

- A running total calculating the overall number of hits of target types.

To access any property of the object, use objectName.propertyName dot notation.

```
16  var score = {
17    total:    0,
18    queen:    100,
19    alien:    50,
20    friend:   -50,
21    queenHits: 0,
22    alienHits: 0,
23    friendHits: 0
24  }
25  score.queenHits += 1;
26  score.alienHits += 3;
27  score.friendHits += 1;
28  score.total += score.queen * score.queenHits;
29  score.total += score.alien * score.alienHits;
30  score.total += score.friend * score.friendHits;
31  console.log(score.total);
```

In this hard-coded example, I've incremented the number of hits to the queen, alien, and friend totalizer values. The score total is then calculated by adding up the three types of hits, each multiplied by their relative scoring weights. See the result by opening the browser's console window.

- There is 1 queen hit, for a subtotal of 100.

- There are 3 alien hits, for a subtotal of 150.

- There is 1 friend hits, for a subtotal of –50.

Added together, the resulting total score is 200.

Remember that objects can also contain methods. As you learned in Chapter 6, a method is merely a built-in function of the object that executes some code. You can revise the script to include a calculate method and call it whenever you want to totalize the score:

```
24    calculate: function() {
25      this.total += this.queen * this.queenHits +
26      this.alien * this.alienHits +
27      this.friend * this.friendHits;
28      return this.total;
29    }
34  console.log(score.calculate());
```

▶ Rounding Off Numbers

Some calculations result in floating-point numbers, when you really want whole values—for example, *5 / 2 = 2.5* is a floating-point number. JavaScript supports several built-in methods for converting numbers with a decimal point component into whole-number integers.

METHOD	WHAT IT DOES	EXAMPLE

Math.round()	Rounds off the value; values under .49 are rounded down, and values .5 and over are rounded up	Math.round(5.41) // Result: 5
		Math.round(5.94) // Result: 6

Math.ceil()	Rounds up the value to the nearest whole number	Math.ceil(5.41) // Result: 6
Math.floor()	Rounds down the value to the nearest whole number	Math.floor(5.41) // Result: 5

Which one should you use? All have appropriate applications. Some suggestions:

When it's only necessary to return the whole part of the value, I prefer to use Math.floor—5.99 is still just 5.

If the number might be less than 1 (example: 0.5), and you don't ever want a result of 0, use Math.ceil. In this way, the result will always be 1 or greater.

For general number rounding following traditional rules, use Math.round.

▶ Getting a Random Number

Many games involve a random factor. By making each game different, it's more fun to play again and again. This random factor can be created by generating a random number each time the game is played. JavaScript supports such a random-number generator using the Math.random method:

```
var myRandomNumber = Math.random();
```

The result is a floating-point value from 0 to 1, like

```
0.4076283438737409
```

For most applications, you want to create a whole-number random value. You can do it by first multiplying the Math.random result to make it greater than 1 and then using one of the rounding functions noted in the previous section.

```
var myRandomNumber = Math.floor(Math.random() * 100);
// Example value: 7
```

All this is the perfect job for a general number-maker function, since generating random-numbers is such a common chore in making games. You can specify a minimum and maximum value so that any generated random-number will be within your specified range.

```
function getRandomInt(min, max) {
  return Math.floor(Math.random() * (max - min + 1)) + min;
}
```

Place this function anywhere in your script to use it. When you need a random number, call the function by specifying the minimum and maximum values you want. Suppose you're looking for values between 1 and 100:

```
var myRandomNumber = getRandomInt(1, 100);        // Example result: 41
```

Or other examples:

```
var myRandomNumber = getRandomInt(1000, 2500);    // Example result: 1432
var myRandomNumber = getRandomInt(-1, -10);       // Example result: -6
```

▶ Shuffling an Array (Like for Playing Cards)

Playing cards need to be shuffled before they can be dealt, or else every round of baccarat, gin, or Go Fish is the same, every game. Playing cards can be represented as arrays of numbers—a deck of 52 cards requires an array of 52 elements. The process of creating the deck and shuffling it goes like this:

1. Create an empty array.
2. Fill each array element with a number, ranging from 1 to 52.
3. Shuffle the deck by randomizing the order of the array elements.

Here's an example 52-card deck-maker and shuffler, which I've used in several of the example games that accompany this book. This demonstrator creates a deck with 52 cards, then shuffles the deck. Both the pre- and post-shuffle arrays are printed in the browser's console window so you can compare the action of the shuffle.

snipped from: cardshuffle.html

```
16  var arr = [];
17  shuffleCards();
18  console.log (arr);    // Shuffled deck
19
20  function shuffleCards() {
21   arr = [];
22   var starting = 1;
23   while(starting < 53){
24    arr.push(starting++);
25   }
26   console.log (arr);  // Pre-shuffled deck
27   shuffle(arr);
28  }
29
30  function shuffle(array) {
31   var currentIndex = array.length, temporaryValue, randomIndex;
32   while (0 !== currentIndex) {
33    randomIndex = Math.floor(Math.random() * currentIndex);
34    currentIndex -= 1;
35    temporaryValue = array[currentIndex];
36    array[currentIndex] = array[randomIndex];
37    array[randomIndex] = temporaryValue;
38   }
39   return array;
40  }
```

Line 16 ▶ creates an empty array, named arr, for the card deck.

Line 17 ▶ calls the shuffleCards function, which itself spans lines 20 through 28.

Line 21 ▶ empties the arr array (in the case of playing a new game), while lines 22 through 25 add 52 elements to the array. Each element is assigned a numeric value, from 1 to 52.

Line 27 ▶ calls the shuffle function, which spans lines 30 and 40. The shuffle function is a terrific all-purpose *array disorganizer*.

Lines 18 and 26 ▶ print the full contents of the arr array into the console window, so you can verify the result of the shuffling (see Figure 18-2).

Ghoul's Blackjack also demonstrates how to convert the values 1 through 52 into card values and suits. The technique uses the result of modulus division:

```
var cardVal = (arr[currentCard] % 13); // 0-12 for card values
var suit = arr[currentCard] % 4;    // 0-3 for card suits
```

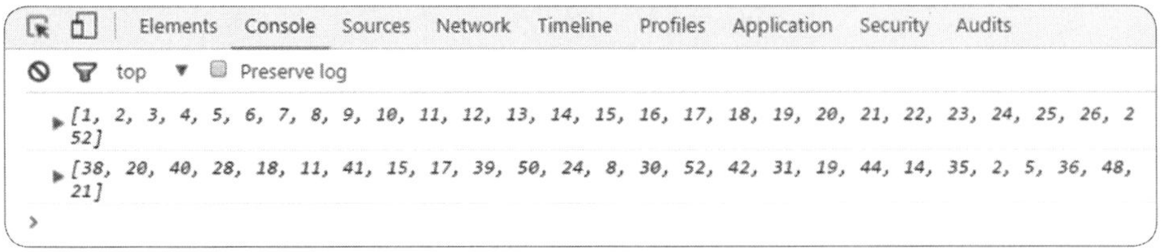

Figure 18-2. View the shuffled cards in the console window.

Elsewhere in the script, the `cardVal` value is simply converted to a card numbered between 2 and 10, jack, queen, or king. The `suit` value is converted to one of four suits: Diamond, heart, club, or spade. See the *Ghoul's Blackjack* game for more insight in how this is done.

Storing Values for Future Game Play

Your games can keep track of player settings and high scores, even when the player quits the browser and returns to the game at some later date. One easy-to-use method is called local storage. It is a mechanism for keeping, and later fetching, simple string values.

Local storage data comprises two parts: name and value. Both are text strings.

Name is an identifier you provide; you later use this name to retrieve the data.

Value is the data you want to associate with the name.

To set a value, use the `localStorage.setItem` method, and specify the name and value you wish to use:

```
localStorage.setItem("MyGame_highScore", "100");
```

This sets the (string) value of 100 to `MyGame_highScore`. To later retrieve this value, use the `localStorage.getItem` method:

```
var highScore = localStorage.getItem('MyGame_highScore');
```

When executed, the `highScore` variable contains the string "100."

To round out the `localStorage` methods if you no longer want or need the name/value pair, use `localStorage.removeItem`:

```
localStorage.removeItem("MyGame_highScore");
```

Try out the *localstore.html* playground script for a complete routine that both fetches and then sets the high score. The code checks to see if there's an existing `MyGame_highScore` name/value already set.

snipped from: localstore.html

```
17  var highScore = localStorage.getItem('MyGame_highScore');
18  if (highScore !== null) {
19    console.log ("The previous high score is: %s ", highScore);
20  } else {
21    console.log ("High score has not yet been set");
22  }
23  highScore = '100';
24  localStorage.setItem("MyGame_highScore", highScore);
```

Line 17 fetches the MyGame_highScore name/value and assigns it to the highScore variable.

Line 18 checks if the value in highScore is null; if it is not, the code prints the current value of MyGame_highScore in the browser's console. Otherwise, the code tells you the high score has not yet been set.

Lines 23 and 24 set the highScore for the next time the script is run.

For your testing, you can append the line localStorage.removeItem("MyGame_highScore"); to remove the MyGame_highScore name/value and try the script again.

Local storage is a relatively new feature to web browsers and is part of the HTML5 specification. As all of the games in this book are intended to be played on an HTML5–compliant browser, such as modern versions of Google Chrome, we can make the assumption that all players will use a compatible system.

That said, you can add this code if you feel the need to explicitly test for local storage support:

```
if (typeof(Storage) !== "undefined") {
  // Your storage code goes here
} else {
  // No Web storage support; i.e., do nothing.
}
```

Place any local storage code in place of "Your storage code goes here."

When using local storage, keep in mind that values are always stored as strings. This can have ramifications when storing numbers like high scores. For use in your game, you probably want to convert these string values to actual number types. As discussed at the start of this chapter, you can use

```
var highScore = Number(highScore);
```

or

```
var highScore = parseInt(highScore);
```

Either will convert the string value to a full-fledged number. (Note: If the value you are storing is a floating point, you can use parseFloat instead of parseInt.)

ADDING SOUND

Imagine Pac-Man without that famous theme song, or Donkey Kong without its lively sound effects.

Sound is an integral part of many games. In years long past, integrating sound with JavaScript required a browser add-in, and you'd never know if the player had installed it.

Today, with HTML5, sound is directly supported in JavaScript through an *application programming interface*, appropriately called the *Web Audio API*.

Want the sound of a laser blast when your character zaps the bad guys? You can do that. Or how about chirps and bleeps when the player correctly guesses the answer? You can do that, too, and more. Read this chapter to find out how.

▶ Ways to Add Sound to Games

Sound management in JavaScript is complex and involved science. But fortunately, there are several freely available, open-source JavaScript libraries that make incorporating sound into your games a cakewalk. Rather than deal with all the vagaries of the Web Audio API—a task that's daunting for even seasoned JavaScript coders—these handy add-in libraries make short work of adding sound, music, and effects to your games.

I'll be talking about two JavaScript audio libraries that just so happen to share confusingly similar names:

sound.js

This is a "micro" library that encapsulates playing sound files as well as synthesized sound effects. In this book, I only use *sound.js* for its sound effects abilities. The library isn't fancy, but it has lots of nifty features that invite experimentation.

SoundJS

Part of a collection of open-source JavaScript libraries, *SoundJS* offers a robust framework for playing pre-recorded (WAV, WP3, OGG) sound files.

These JavaScript libraries are included with the examples for this chapter and with any demo game that requires them. Be sure to also check out the Online Support Site (see Appendix A, page 310) for links to these and other useful JavaScript sound resources.

XMLHttpRequest and Sound Libraries

I selected *SoundJS* because it has several methods of playing sounds, depending on whether you are running your scripts from a web server or from your local computer.

When running scripts from a web server, *SoundJS* uses the Web Audio API and the XMLHttpRequest method to fetch sound files. XMLHttpRequest is designed to improve server performance, but it's not compatible when combined with local files running in Google Chrome. As much as possible, I wanted the examples and demonstrations for this book to be playable on Chrome simply by opening them from your own desktop computer without requiring a web server.

When running scripts from your own computer, *SoundJS* falls back to a secondary method, known as HTML Audio. This method allows sound playback when running local scripts in Chrome.

▶ A Very Brief (and Simple) Web Audio API Demo

Before diving headfirst into the sound libraries, let's take a quick moment to look at a simple (okay, *very* simple) demonstration of the Web Audio API. It will give you a basic insight for what's happening under the hood.

The *basic-api.html* demo plays a short and sweet *audio sprite*, a 250-millisecond (quarter-second) "blip." The sound is wholly synthesized inside JavaScript and the browser and consists of a 440 hertz (Hz; cycles per second) sine wave. To hear the sound again, reload the page.

snipped from: basic-api.html

```
16    var audio = new AudioContext();
17    var osc = audio.createOscillator();
18    osc.frequency.value = 440;
19    osc.type = "sine";
20
21    var volume = audio.createGain();
22    volume.gain.value = .5;
23    osc.connect(volume);
24    volume.connect(audio.destination);
25
26    osc.start();
27    osc.stop(audio.currentTime + .25);
```

Building the Context

Web Audio API uses *contexts*, a kind of foundation that builds the framework from which sound is produced. Line 16 defines such a context for the Web Audio API platform. This context is then used to spawn other required parts of the audio-playback mechanism.

Creating an Oscillator to Produce the Sound

Line 17 uses the audio context to create an *oscillator* node source, which is a way to produce synthesized sounds. Oscillators are just one type of source supported by the audio context. Oscillators generate electrical signals at various frequencies within the range of human hearing.

Lines 18 and 19 define the type of sound to produce on the oscillator: Specifically, a 440 Hz sine wave tone.

Adjusting the Volume

Lines 21 through 24 interject a volume control into the sound playback. Web Audio API sound can be quite loud, especially when playing synthesized effects. It's always nice to include some kind of volume control. Line 22 sets the *gain* (volume) to half. A value of 0 is muted, and 1 is full.

Playing and Stopping the Sound

Line 26 starts the oscillator, whereas 27 tells the script when to turn the oscillator off. The code

```
audio.currentTime + .25
```

means to turn off the sound after a delay of 0.250 seconds (250 ms).

Discover more about Web Audio API by messing with the values in this basic demo. For line 19, try these variations:

```
osc.type = "sine";
osc.type = "square";
osc.type = "sawtooth";
osc.type = "triangle";
```

Try adjusting the gain from .5 to some other number between 0 and 1, and experiment with the time delay on line 27. If you leave out line 27 entirely, the tone will never shut off.

To change the pitch of the tone, change the numeric value on line 18. This value is in Hz. A tone of 440 is usually referred to as *Concert A* pitch, which is the A right above middle-C on a piano. For reference, middle-C has a frequency of about 261.6 Hz. Try plugging that number into the script to see how it sounds.

Sine waves are one of several common audio waveform shapes. Others supported by the Web Audio API include triangle, square, and sawtooth, as shown in Figure 19-1. Each shape confers its own distinctive timbre to the sound. For example, sine waves tend to sound smoother, while sawtooth waves tend to be harsh and "jagged," just as their name suggests.

▶ Using the sound.js Library to Generate Synthesized Sound Effects

The *sound.js* library can play both audio files and generated (synthesized) sound effects. The library comes with an example page that demonstrates its various capabilities. To simplify things, I modified it so it contains only the synthesizer portion. I've also reformatted a few things to make it consistent with the other examples that accompany this book. Otherwise, I've kept the sound effect examples just as they are in the original.

The *soundefx.html* playground script demonstrates pressing keyboard buttons to create four different sound effects.

KEY	EFFECT
1	Laser blast with echo
2	Upward "whistle" connotes a character jumping
3	Bomb explosion (or force-field effect, or . . .)
4	Quick three-note cadence with rising pitches

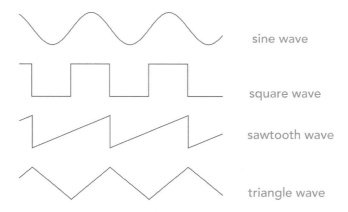

sine wave

square wave

sawtooth wave

triangle wave

Figure 19-1. Comparison of sound wave types.

snipped from: soundefx.html

```
11 <script src="./assets/sound.js"></script>
19 . . .
20  <script>
21
22   var num1 = keyboard(49),
23    num2 = keyboard(50),
24    num3 = keyboard(51),
25    num4 = keyboard(52);
26
27   num1.press = function() { shootSound() };
. . .
30   num4.press = function() { bonusSound() };
31
32   //Shoot
33   function shootSound() {
34   soundEffect(
35     1046.5,                 //frequency
36     0,                      //attack
37     0.3,                    //decay
38     "sawtooth",             //waveform
39     1,                      //Volume
. . .
89   //Bonus points
90   function bonusSound() {
91    soundEffect(587.33, 0, 0.2, "square", 1, 0, 0);        //D(5)
92    soundEffect(880, 0, 0.2, "square", 1, 0, 0.1);         //A(5)
93    soundEffect(1174.66, 0, 0.3, "square", 1, 0, 0.2);     //D(6)
94   }
```

Include *sound.js* file

Line 11 includes the *sound.js* library file in the *soundefx.html* script. The library file is located in the *assets* subfolder.

Define Keypress Events

Lines 22 through 30 set up four keyboard listeners to trigger the four sound effects. These listeners trigger when pressing the number 1, 2, 3, and 4 keys. Each key calls a different sound function (lines 27 through 30).

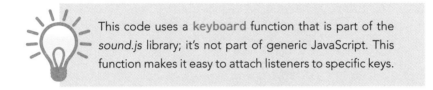

This code uses a **keyboard** function that is part of the *sound.js* library; it's not part of generic JavaScript. This function makes it easy to attach listeners to specific keys.

Example Sound Function: shootSound

To use the *sound.js* library for generated sounds, define the sound by specifying a number of parameters, such as the frequency of the sound, the amount of the attack and decay (see Figure 19-2), volume, waveform type, and so on.

These parameters are used with the soundEffect function that is part of the *sound.js* library. Calling soundEffect with the parameters you've specified is what actually generates the sounds.

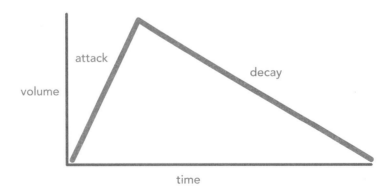

Figure 19-2. Attack and decay determine how quickly the volume rises and falls.

Bonus Sound: Stringing Audio Sprites Together

Lines 89 through 94 show how to string multiple sound effect sprites together to make a type of "melody." In this case, the sounds create a familiar three-tone "twinkle," used to indicate that the player has earned bonus points. The sounds are simply emitted one after the other with little or no delay between them.

Notice that only some of the parameters are provided. The soundEffect function in the *sound.js* library applies default values for any missing parameters.

Playing with Values to Make New Sounds

Use the *soundefx.html* playground script to experiment with making other sounds using the *sound.js* library. Start with one of the first three sprites (shoot, jump, explosion), and try different values for the parameters. Keep an original copy of the *soundefx.html* file in case you want to return to the original values.

Sound.js uses the Web Audio API to generate sound using the oscillator node source, just like in the *basic-api.html* script from earlier in the chapter. To learn more about what each of the parameters do, check out the documentation for the Web Audio API—see the Online Support Site (Appendix A, page 310) for links. The docs are a bit on the heavy side, so supplement your reading with lots of hands-on experimentation.

Also open the sound.js file itself in the Atom editor. Scroll down to the soundEffect function. The library is well documented, and you can learn a lot just by reading the comments.

▶ Using the SoundJS Library to Play Prerecorded Sound and Music Files

The *SoundJS* library (remember, different from *sound.js*) plays audio files in a variety of formats, including Windows WAV, MP3, and OGG. *SoundJS* includes its own *pre-loader* so that the sound files are pre-loaded when the page is ready to go.

As noted earlier, unlike many other sound-file libraries currently available, *SoundJS* provides a fallback for running your scripts in Google Chrome when accessing local files on your computer. It's also a well-crafted library with a robust set of features that includes:

- Automatic selection of file format based on browser type
- Sound volume control
- Ability to repeat sound once, set number of times, or indefinitely
- Playback events, such as when a sound file finishes

When writing this book, I used an in-development version of the *SoundJS* library. The then-current version (0.6.2) had some issues that were corrected in the development version. Software can change, and future versions of the library may be different. A copy of the *SoundJS* library I used for this book is included in all examples and demo games that reference it.

The *soundjs-audio.html* playground script lets you test playing back sound files with the *SoundJS* library. Accompanying the script is the *SoundJS* library itself, plus two sound files, each in two different formats: MP3 and OGG. You select the sound file to play by pressing the number 1 or 2 key on your keyboard.

KEY	EFFECT
1	*Boing* cartoon sound. Sound files: *boing.ogg, boing.mp3*
2	*Splat* cartoon sound. Sound files: *splat.ogg, splat.mp3*

The *SoundJS* library automatically selects which format of the sound file to play based on the requirements of the browser used. By including both OGG and MP3 file formats, your script is usable in a greater variety of browser platforms, should this be important to you.

snipped from: soundjs-audio.html

```
10 <script src="./assets/soundjs-NEXT.combined.js"></script>
   . . .
18   window.addEventListener("load", init);
19   window.addEventListener("keydown", soundPlay);
20
21   function soundPlay(ev) {
22    if (ev.keyCode == 49) { createjs.Sound.play("boing"); } // 1
23    if (ev.keyCode == 50) { createjs.Sound.play("splat"); } // 2
24   }
25
26   function init() {
27    if (!createjs.Sound.initializeDefaultPlugins()) {
```

```
28      console.log ("Error loading SoundJS");
29    } else {
30      console.log ("Success loading SoundJS");
31      createjs.Sound.addEventListener("fileload", playSound);
32      createjs.Sound.alternateExtensions = ["mp3"];
33      createjs.Sound.registerSounds(
34      [ {id: "boing", src: "boing.ogg"},
35        {id: "splat", src: "splat.ogg"} ],
36        "./assets/");
37    }
38  }
39
40  function playSound(ev) {
41    console.log("Preloaded:", ev.id, ev.src);
42  }
43  </script>
```

Include *soundjs* file

Line 10 includes the *soundjs-NEXT.combined.js* library file into the *soundjs-audio.html* script. The library file is located in an *./assets/* subfolder, so the library file includes a reference to this subfolder.

Define Page Load Event

Line 18 creates an onload event for the *soundjs-audio.html* script. When this event fires—which occurs after all HTML elements and coded have been loaded—JavaScript calls the init function, which readies sound playback.

Define keydown Keypress Events

Lines 19 through 25 set up two keyboard listeners to trigger the two sound files. These listeners trigger when pressing the number 1 or 2 keys. Each key plays a different sound asset (lines 22 and 23) using the createjs.Sound.play method, which is part of the *SoundJS* library. More detail on this in a minute.

Initialize Sound Playback

Lines 26 through 38 set up the sounds you wish to use with *SoundJS*. The code first checks with the *SoundJS* library that there is a plugin compatible with your browser. Assuming there is, *SoundJS* loads up the primary sound files, *boing.ogg* and *splat.ogg*; in case the browser is not able to play OGG files, *SoundJS* reverts to MP3 format (line 32).

SoundJS uses ID names for the sounds you want to play. You must provide a unique ID for each primary sound file. In the test code, the ID for *boing.ogg/mp3* is boing; the ID for *splat.ogg/mp3* is splat.

Validating Sound File Loading

Lines 40 through 42 serve only as a means to validate that the sound files have been loaded. This is not code you need for a finished game, but it's handy when developing your project.

Playing a Sound

To play a sound loaded by *SoundJS*, use the library's `createjs.Sound.play` method and specify the ID (not the filename) of the sound file you want. For instance,

```
createjs.Sound.play("boing");
```

plays the *boing.ogg/mp3* sound file.

Playing Multiple Sounds/Overlaying Sounds

Although the *boing* and *splat* sound effects are short, you can hear by pressing the number 1 or 2 key very quickly that the sounds play in rapid succession, even overlapping one another. This shows how *SoundJS* allows multiple sounds at the same time. You could, just as an example, play both *boing* and *splat* at the same time with this:

```
if (ev.keyCode == 49) {
 createjs.Sound.play("boing");
 createjs.Sound.play("splat");
}
```

Applying Options to the `createjs.Sound.play` Method

SoundJS supports a number of options for the `createjs.Sound.play` method. Two of the most-commonly used options set the volume of the sound and specify the number of times to repeat the sound.

To set the loudness of playback, add the `.volume` property, and specify a volume from 0 (muted) to 1 (full):

```
createjs.Sound.play("boing").volume = 0.3;
```

To set the number of repeats, add a second parameter to the method and specify the number of loops you want:

```
createjs.Sound.play("boing", {loop: 2}); // Plays twice
```

Or to play indefinitely:

```
createjs.Sound.play("boing", {loop: 'infinite'});
```

And you may combine these two options:

```
createjs.Sound.play("boing", {loop: 'infinite'}).volume = 0.3;
```

▶ Getting Recorded Sounds

Now that you know how to play recorded sounds in JavaScript, you need to rustle up a bunch to use in your games. Options: Record your own sounds, or find them readymade.

Finding, Recording, and Editing Your Own Sounds

You can record music, sounds, and sound effects for your games with a smartphone, your desktop computer and sound card, a digital sound recorder, or even an old-fashioned tape deck. The overriding factor is using a quality microphone. The better the microphone, the better the recording.

If you're serious about the sound design in your games, consider a portable, stand-alone digital sound recorder. The recorder sports one or two microphones (for monophonic or stereo sound) and records to a flash card. You can do basic editing in the recorder or transfer the sound files to a desktop PC and use a more robust sound production application (see below).

Considerations for best quality:

- `Chose recording environments that are quiet` and don't exhibit a lot of reverberation. The best recordings isolate the sound you want without a lot of background clutter.

- `Avoid recording outside or in areas with lots of wind.` The gusts of air will cause a thumping sound in the recording.

- `Watch the audio level!` If it's too low, you'll need to boost the audio in your sound editing software, and that'll introduce noise. If it's too high, the signal may overdrive the recording equipment and sound distorted.

- `Make a series of recordings of the same thing` so you can pick the best one.

Finding Readymade Sounds

Stock sounds are pre-recorded audio files housed in online sound libraries. The best ones are for commercial use and cost lots of money.

A terrific source of free pre-recorded music and sound effects is Freesound.org, where I got many of the sound files for this book. You can search for sounds by category and subject matter, and filter based on numerous tags.

Whether you record your own files or use readymade, you'll likely need to modify them using a sound-editing program. Using the editor, you can trim quiet parts from the start and end of the file, change volume, pitch, or speed, and introduce special effects.

On the free side, just about everyone's favorite is Audacity®. It can both read and make WAV, AIFF (more commonly used on Apple Macintosh), OGG, and MP3 files (for MP3 you need a separate MP3 codec, which you can download). Audacity lets you do all the same vital editing tasks as expensive commercial products, and it has an easy-to-use interface.

While free, many of the sound files on Freesound.org are copyrighted. They are provided with the Creative Commons license. Uploaders can choose the specific terms of the license. For greatest flexibility, I opted only for CC0 (Creative Commons 0) files, which have been deeded to the public domain and have no use restrictions. For other ready-made sources, there are a few collections, like the now out-of-print Hanna Barbera Sound FX CD, that come with professionally made sounds but are not intended for commercial use. They're fine if you're just writing games for yourself and family.

On the paid side, there's Pro Tools® and Sound Forge®, among others. Professional sound tools tend to be expensive and offer a feature set that's likely to be far more than you need to produce game sounds. However, you might already have one of these for other projects you do.

▶ Useful Links for Sound

Try these links for the libraries and tools detailed in this chapter:

- `freesound.org` ▶ open-source sound effects and music
- `www.audacityteam.org` ▶ open-source sound editing and conversion software
- `createjs.com/soundjs` ▶ *SoundJS* sound library (play sound files)
- `github.com/kittykatattack/sound.js` ▶ *sound.js* sound library (play sound effects)

▶ Bonus Examples

Find more sound examples in these bonus games:

Ruins of Ramic, Lesson 5

Synthesized sound (using *sound.js* library) is used
when cards match.

Kitteh in Space

Sound- file playback (using *SoundJS*) is used for
the spaceship, laser blasts, and when obstacles hit.

Kaylee Saves the World

Sound-file playback (*SoundJS*) is used for alien
ship landing, blaster explosion, and Martians
dissolving.

Pirate's Cove Word Guess

Sound-file playback (*SoundJS*) is used for
reinforcement of right and wrong answers.

FIXING ERRORS: TROUBLESHOOTING AND DEBUGGING

Nobody's perfekt. And no script of any complexity is 100 percent correct right off the bat.

Mistakes and coding go hand-in-hand. In programming circles, a *bug* is an error in code that causes a wrong or incomplete result. When you *debug* a program, you locate those pesky mistakes and correct them so that your code runs smoothly.

Some bugs come right out and bite you, making their presence obvious simply by keeping your otherwise beautiful game from even running. The problem is easy to spot, and the fix easy to make.

But not all bugs are self-evident. You must sometimes sift through your code to find the gremlins lurking within. This part of debugging involves systematic *troubleshooting*, a methodology of problem-solving that some first-time coders find difficult to conquer. But conquer you must if you want your scripts to run at peak performance.

Fortunately, Google Chrome and most other desktop PC browsers give you a head start with a console window that provides feedback about your scripts. If you've been following along with the examples in this book, you've been employing the console all along. But it's worth a recap, and there are a few more features of the console you'll likely want to know about.

▶ Displaying the Console

As a reminder, to display the console in the current version of Google Chrome, press Ctrl+Shift+I (on the Macintosh, press Cmd+Shift+I). The console window appears.

There are other tools in this window besides the Console tab. There's also Elements, Sources, Network, and others. Other than a few of these tabs, I don't get into the other tools in this book, but that doesn't mean you can't experiment with them to see what they do. You can't hurt your code or the browser by playing.

The console displays three general types of information:

- Console text ▶ output from your scripts using the console.log method.
- Error messages ▶ generated by the browser. These are mistakes in code that you must fix for the script to work properly.
- Warning messages ▶ generated by the browser. These are less critical than errors and are often advisory in nature. Whether you need to act on them depends on the message. As a general rule, you should strive for clean no-error/no-warning console output when playing your games.

The console window displays line numbers indicating where the text, error, or warning has occurred (see Figure 20-1). With an editor program like Atom, you can load your script into the editor and use its line numbering to correlate the actual code with the indicated line number.

Figure 20-1. The console displaying an error.

▶ Outputting Status Text to the Console

Throughout this book I've used the console window as a means for scripts to communicate with you. With just one line of code, you can print status messages that show what your script is doing at that point. Sprinkled throughout the code, these messages can be a useful development technique that shows you're on the right track. They're also useful for troubleshooting should a problem occur.

In review: The basic console text message is printed using the console.log method:

```
<script>
 console.log ("Congrats, the code has reached this part!");
</script>
```

To see the result, open the console window and load the page.

> The console.log method is considered "experimental" and is not supported in all browsers. In fact, on some older browsers, it might break your script and prevent it from properly running. If you wish to create games for older browsers, you should make sure that any console.log code is removed (or at least commented out).

Sometimes you want to combine a message with a value stored in a variable. You can combine these pieces of information using the + string concatenation operator (see Figure 20-2):

```
var x = 100;
console.log ("The value of x is " + x); // Prints: The value of x is 100
```

```
var x = 100;
console.log ("The value of x is " + x);
prints
The value of x is 100
```

Figure 20-2. Add a variable to a string to show its value.

When you have more than one variable to print with the message, you may instead want to use *substitution strings*. Here's a basic example with just one value (as a variable), to show how it works, as shown in Figure 20-3.

```
var x = 100;
console.log ("The value of x is %s", x);
// Result same as above
```

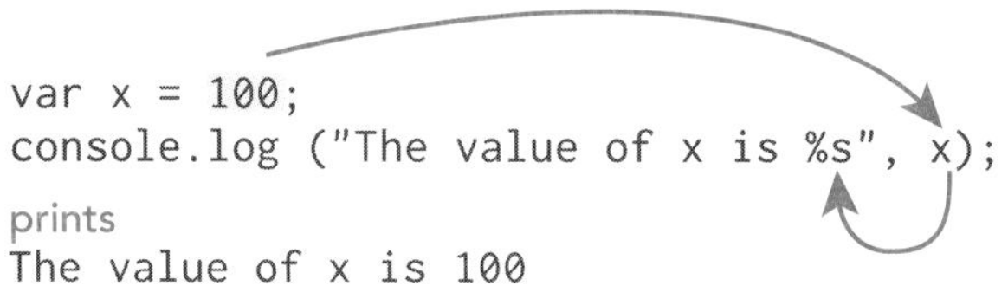

```
var x = 100;
console.log ("The value of x is %s", x);
prints
The value of x is 100
```

Figure 20-3. Using the %s substitution character.

The %s is the substitution string. It matches up with the parameter(s) list that follows (separated by a comma). To include more than one substitution string, simply use multiple %ss, and append more values at the end of the console.log method. You should have one %s for every parameter.

```
console.log ("x=%s, y=%s, z=%s", 1, 2, 3);
// Prints: x=1, y=2, z=3
```

You can also print a list of items by simply separating them with commas. Each value is separated by a space in the console window.

```
var val1 = 1;
var val2 = "hello";
var val3 = 19.87;
console.log (val1, val2, val3);
 // Prints: 1 "hello" 19.87
```

Feel free to intersperse text with those commas:

```
console.log ("Counter: ", val1, ", Message=", val2, ", Cash in bank", val3);
 // Counter: 1 , Message= hello , Cash in bank 19.87
```

▶ Printing Objects and Arrays in the Console

Printing lone text and numbers in the console is simple enough. But what if the data is in an object or array? Neither presents a problem: You can specify a particular object property or array element, or you can look at the whole structure, simply by using the name of the object or array in the console.log method.

Here's an example of checking values in an array:

```
var myArray = [1, 2, 3];
console.log (myArray[1]); // Element 1 only
console.log (myArray); // All elements
```

Here's the result of this code in the console window:

```
2
> [1, 2, 3]
```

The array is indicated by the clickable arrow. Use the same technique for objects.

▶ Understanding the Types of Errors

Errors in programming code generally fall into one of three categories:

Syntax Errors

A *syntax error* is a mistake in the formation of the code itself. Writing something like

```
If (myVar == 5)
```

results in a syntax error because there is no If statement; the correct form is if (all lowercase). Syntax errors are generally shown in the console as

```
Uncaught SyntaxError: <reason>
```

where <reason> is the suspected cause of the error and the line number where the error occurs. Most syntax errors appear when the script is initially loaded into the browser.

Note that JavaScript doesn't always get the line number right, or even the exact cause of the error. Sometimes the actual reason is caused by something else, located at a different part of the script. Use the line number only as a general guide.

Runtime Errors

Runtime errors are not usually caught by JavaScript when the page is first loaded but instead when the script executes. The error occurs when, and only when, the problem code is run. For example, suppose your code contains the following fragment somewhere in it. The myNumber variable has been defined but the myVar variable has not.

```
var myNumber = 5;
if (myNumber == 6) {
 myNumber = myVar;  // myVar not defined, but the code is never run
}
```

Because the if expression fails (5 does not equal 6), JavaScript never gets to the code

```
myNumber = myVar;
```

and so no error is raised in the console. But alter the if statement to read myNumber == 5, and the browser complains with

```
Uncaught ReferenceError: myVar is not defined
```

This is a good example of a runtime error—an error that only pops up after the script has been parsed.

Logic Errors

Logic errors are mistakes in coding that are silent—the console rarely, if ever, tells you about them. Instead, they keep to themselves and simply cause your code to not work as expected.

A common logic error is mistyping variable names:

```
var myVar = 5;     // This is the variable you want
myVart = 10;       // Oops, wrong name
```

Ordinarily, JavaScript allows this type of mistake, believing you intended to create two variables, one named myVar and the other myVart. Later in your code, when you attempt to use the myVar variable, it'll still contain 5 rather than the expected 10.

But there's good news! This type of error can be identified by adding a setting to your JavaScript code. Just include

```
"use strict";
```

at the top of the code, and these (and a few other more obtuse) "silent" errors are caught and identified in the console window.

Stepping Through Code with the Debugger

Some JavaScript code zooms by so fast, it's hard to know what it's doing. Wouldn't it be nice if you could slow it down a bit and take a look under its hood one step at a time? You can by using the debugger.

debug-breakpoint.html

Open the *debug-breakpoint.html* playground page in Chrome and then display the console window. Now click on the Sources tab. In the Sources tab you will see all the markup for the page, including the JavaScript section. The browser will automatically stop at the first line of code, which says

```
debugger;
```

This tells the browser you want to use its built-in debugging feature (see Figure 20-4).

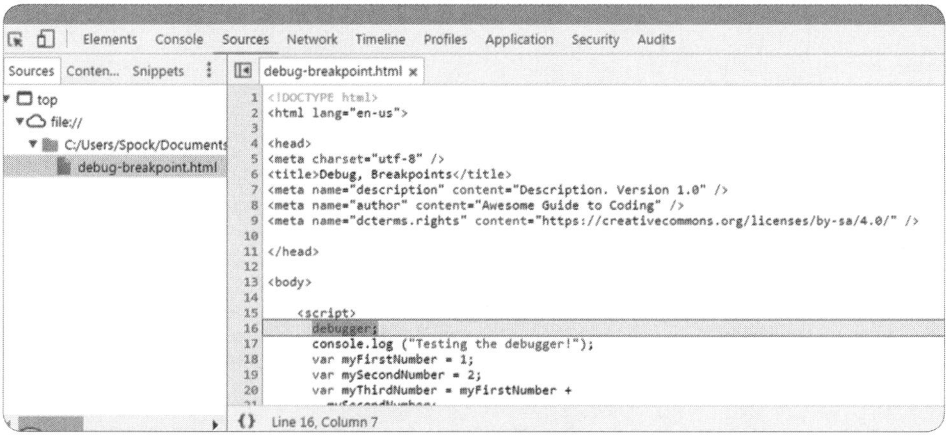

Figure 20-4. Chrome's debugging feature.

Clicking the Resume Script Execution button (or pressing F8) resumes code execution. Because you've not told it otherwise, in one quick flash, the browser runs through the script until it ends.

Setting Breakpoints in the Sources Window

Suppose there are one or two places in your code that are giving you problems. You already know where they are, but you're unsure of all the context of the code up until then—*context* is all the variables and values that have been set up and assigned to that point.

Before resuming script execution, click the mouse on a line number just to the left of the code—see Figure 20-5. This inserts a breakpoint, a blue arrow that indicates that the code will run to that line and stop. (If you make a mistake and add a breakpoint you don't want, just click on it again, and the breakpoint will go away.) For now, click on line 20 to add a breakpoint to that line.

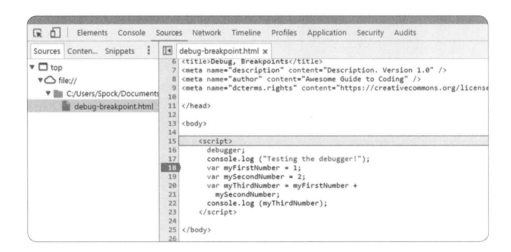

Figure 20-5. Adding a new breakpoint.

Press F8 (or click Resume Script Execution). Code execution runs up to line 20 and stops again. Click on the Console tab to see that the text message "Testing the debugger!" has been printed. Click back to Sources.

Reload the page. Hover the mouse over the variable assignments. Pop-ups appear to show the values assigned to the variables. Variables assigned up to the breakpoint should hold values; the current line and below should show *undefined*.

Click beside line 22 to add a second breakpoint there and press F8 to resume script execution. This time, all variables should be assigned, and by hovering the mouse over them, they should all contain the values they are supposed to.

Complete the script to its termination by pressing F8 one last time.

Breakpoints remain even after you edit the source code and reload the page. If you modify the source in a way that changes line numbers, clear the old breakpoints and add them in again.

Setting Breakpoints in Code

You can also add breakpoints in code, simply by inserting more debugger; statement lines. At each debugger; the browser will stop.

Stepping Through Code One Line (Function Call) at a Time

If you want to study your code in more detail, you can step through it one line at a time. It's actually not one "line," but one complete function call. Lines can span more than a single function call, so the distinction—while not critical to understanding how to debug JavaScript—is important to keep in mind.

Begin by inserting a debugger; instruction at the point where you want the script to stop. Then instead of pressing F8 (*Resume Script Execution*), press F10 (*Step Over Next Function Call*).

Continue pressing F10, and the code now steps one line/function at a time.

Cleaning Up after Debugging

After you have successfully debugged your script, remember to go through and remove those debugger; instructions. Or at least comment them out.

As long as the Inspect pane is not visible, Chrome will ignore the calls to debugging; and your code will run normally. But should the console, sources, or other window be open, the browser will once again pause at those breakpoints, making your game stop in its tracks.

Going Further with the Chrome Debugger

The debugging feature built into the Chrome browser is incredibly powerful, requiring a book of its own to cover everything it can do. That's not the point of this book, so I'll leave the discussion here, which gives you plenty to play with.

▶ Now It's Up to You!

In the last 20 chapters, you've learned what you need to create your own action-packed JavaScript games. You're well on your way to becoming a coding maestro! But don't let your discovery end here. Play and practice to extend what you've already explored.

Remember: Over a dozen bonus game examples are provided as part of this book, ranging from puzzles to blackjack to a first-person shooter. All are available for free download from the Online Support Site—no ads, no pop-ups, no registration required. Check out the Appendix A (page 310) for details.

USING THE ONLINE SUPPORT SITE

The book comes with an Online Support Site, where you can download all of the playground scripts and bonus games, plus find useful references, tips, and how-to on JavaScript and game coding. There is no cost to use the support site. It's ad-free and does not require user registration. Visit at: buenacreek.com.

▶ You'll Find . . .

Playground examples ▶ Separated into chapters, these examples can be downloaded so that you can play along while you read. Feel free to make changes to the scripts just to see what happens. Experimenting is the best way for you to learn!

Free bonus games ▶ Discover more scripting techniques with over a dozen free bonus games developed exclusively for this book, like *Kitteh in Space*, *Kaylee Saves the World*, and *Ghoul's Blackjack*. Just download to your computer and play. Each game comes with a *readme* file that explains how it works.

Links to the best online references ▶ Wander the web no more with my hand-picked links to authoritative JavaScript reference sites.

Book updates ▶ Changes, corrections, enhancements, and alternative approaches.

All source code is provided in zip archive file format for easy downloading. Each zip may contain one or more constituent files inside it. To use these files, the archive must be unzipped to a new folder.

Modern operating systems including Windows and Macintosh OS X, provide their own built-in means for unzipping archive files. Refer to the manufacturer's instructions or online help forums for your exact computer model, as it often depends on the version of the operating system you use.

Be sure to unzip the files to a folder where you have full user-access rights. Otherwise you may not be able to save the files or make changes to them.

▶ Backup Support Site

All playground scripts and bonus-game source code for this book may also be found at the following GitHub repository, should the main *buenacreek.com* site be unavailable for whatever strange reason:

github.com/gamerscoding/bookexamples.

WHERE TO PLAY AND PUBLISH YOUR GAMES

So you've written a game and now you want to play it
and maybe even publish it for others. You have several options.

▶ Game Files On Your Computer

The easiest way to play any JavaScript code—games or
otherwise—is to copy all the files to a folder on your
computer and access them directly using a web browser.
This is called *local file access* or *offline access*.

All of the playground examples and bonus games
that accompany this book were designed to be run
locally in the Google Chrome web browser, using files
on your desktop or laptop computer.

However, not all scripts you may find on the
Internet may be so cooperative. Just so you know:

- Code that requires *interaction with a web server*
  may not run, because there is no server to connect
  to. This includes programming functions that
  request data from the server after all of the other
  web page files have been downloaded. This is a
  common technique used to fetch individual sound
  files, for example.

- Code that *breaks a security model* imposed by the
  browser will not run, as the code is assumed to be
  "tainted." Modern browsers like Chrome can
  be very picky about where files are from. This is
  to protect you, as an Internet user, from being
  affected by malware spread by bad websites.

You can determine if there's a problem in accessing
the code by opening the browser's console window.
Check for any error messages that indicate a security or
policy violation.

You have two options when running code locally
that is designed for access from a web server:

- Try a different web browser. As of this
  writing, Mozilla Firefox isn't quite as testy when it
  comes to local file security. During development
  of this book, scripts that refused to run in Chrome
  usually ran just fine in Firefox. However, since
  security policies can change from one version to
  the next, this may not always be the case, so never
  count on it as a permanent solution.

- Use Chrome in Local Files Mode. You can
  tell Chrome to ease up on its security model by
  starting it with a special flag setting. This *allow-file-
  access-from-files* flag instructs Chrome to suppress
  the security policy affecting fetching local files
  from your own computer.

This is very important, so please
read: Telling Chrome to ignore
its local-file policy can decrease
your online protection against
malware. I recommend making
this change only with a separate
desktop shortcut to the Chrome
browser. Run this version of
Chrome only when developing
and testing your own code. When
you're ready to surf the Internet,
quit all instances of Chrome, then
start your regular version.

The exact instructions for setting local-file access varies depending on the operating system and is known to change from time to time. So rather than list the instructions here, I provide the necessary how-to on the Support Site for this book (see Appendix A).

▶ Game Files On a Local Web Server

Some scripts (though none included with this book) just absolutely require a web server. Or maybe you don't want to circumvent Chrome's security policy but still want to access local files from your own PC. It can be done by running your own web server. Okay, so the whole idea of turning your computer into its own web server may seem complex and replete with dangers, but it's actually fairly simple, with a number of alternatives you can try.

The first thing you need is web server software. If you're using OS X or Linux, a good one is already included—it's part of the Python programming package. If you're using Windows, you can download Python (it includes the web server) and quickly install it to your computer.

Get Python

Start first by downloading the full Python distribution, available here: *www.python.org/downloads/*. This is only necessary if you're using Windows. OS X and Linux come with Python already installed.

Choose the 2.x version. While it is a little older, it'll suit our purposes just fine. It also conforms to the Python found in (as of this writing) current versions of Macintosh OS X and various Linux distributions. Note that the instructions that follow won't work for the 3.x version, so be sure yours is the 2.x variety.

Install Python

After downloading, install the Python files into their own folder. For ease of use, create a main folder right off of the drive—in Windows, use c:\python\. You'll probably need administrator rights to install Python, so be sure you have full access rights before proceeding.

Open a Command Window or Terminal

The best way to run the Python server is to open a command window (Windows) or Terminal (Macintosh OS X, Linux).

Windows:

1. Click Start, and in the Search box, type *run*. The Run window opens.
2. Type Cmd and click OK. The command window opens.
3. Navigate to the folder containing the script(s) you wish to run. Skip to "Navigating to the Script Folder" at right for more info.

Macintosh OS X:

1. Click the Spotlight-search magnifying glass in the upper-right corner, then type *terminal*.
2. Double-click on the Terminal application to open it.
3. Navigate to the folder containing the script(s) you wish to run. Skip to "Navigating to the Script Folder" at right for more info.

Linux:

1. The exact instructions for finding and running the terminal program depend on the desktop-user interface you are using, so check your system's help pages for more information. In Ubuntu Unity, for example, you can choose Dash, More Apps, Accessories, and Terminal. Other desktop interfaces may have similar methods.
2. Navigate to the folder containing the script(s) you wish to run. Skip to "Navigating to the Script Folder" at right for more info.

Navigating to the Script Folder

Before starting the Python web server from the command window or terminal, you need to first navigate to the folder on your computer where you scripts reside:

- For Windows, type:
  `cd \path\to\files`
  where `\path\to\files` is the scripts folder.

- For OS X and Linux, type:
  `cd /path/to/files/`
  where `/path/to/files` is the scripts folder.

Starting the Python Server

You're now ready to start the Python web server. Assuming the Python files are in a main folder named *python*, from the command window or terminal, type all on one line:

- `\python\python -m SimpleHTTPServer 8080` (for Windows)

- `python -m SimpleHTTPServer 8080` (for OS X and Linux)

If everything is working properly, you should see the following message in the terminal: Serving HTTP on 0.0.0.0 port 8080 . . .

Access Your Server From the Browser

Open Chrome (or other browser) and type the following in the address bar:

- `http://localhost:8080/`

All the files in the folder containing your script(s) should be listed. Navigate to the script you want, and click it to run.

Stopping the Server

When you're done using your server, stop it by returning to the command window or terminal, and pressing Ctrl+C (Cmd+C on Macintosh). It may take a few moments for Python to respond and quit the server. You may close the command window or terminal if you're done with it.

View the Python Documentation for More Options

Naturally you can do more with the Python web server. Be sure to consult the online documentation for a thorough discussion.

▶ Game Files On a Public Web Server

A local web server is just that—it's local only to you and those on your local network. If you want friends and family to play your scripts, you need to load them onto a public web server.

Check out any good Internet reference on how to set up a web server; the process is far too involved to do it justice here. In any case, here are some tips to help you get started:

- If you attend school, the school may provide space for publishing web pages. Ask your instructor.

- Some Internet service providers are still offering free web space. It pays to check.

- You can rent web server space for as little as a few dollars a month. However, you usually also need your own domain name, which you must obtain from a domain registrar such as GoDaddy.

With a bit of work, you can have other computers connected to your local area network (LAN) and access your local web server. If your computer is connected to the Internet via a router, you have a LAN. Access is limited to only those computers connected to the same LAN. The exact process for setting up servers for LAN connection is beyond the scope of this book. But if you're interested, you can search online to investigate the various methods available to you.

Free web and blog pages are only occasionally useful for publishing your games, as the specialty servers they use may prevent the inclusion of JavaScript code. This is for security reasons. Check the FAQ for the site to determine if they allow custom JavaScript.

▶ Running Games on a Mobile Device

Your options are more limited if you want to play games on a mobile device, such as an Android or Apple iPad tablet. The best method is to upload the scripts to a public web server and then access that server with the device.

Important note: The example scripts and bonus games for this book were designed for Google Chrome. For best results, be sure to install an up-to-date version of Chrome on your mobile device. Chrome is available for Android and Apple iPad devices.

For Android devices, local file access is also permissible using a browser such as Google Chrome. The general steps are:

1. Use a file-manager app (one should be included with the table) to create a new */documents* directory in the internal memory of the device (skip this step if there's already such a directory).
2. Copy the script files from your desktop/laptop PC to a flash media card.
3. Load the media card into the tablet.
4. Use the file manager app to move the files from the media card to the *documents* directory you previously created.
5. Open the desired script into the browser.
6. The last step is often easier said than done. Different tablets—even those running similar versions of the Android OS—differ in how to access local files from a browser. On some Android devices, you can often type one of the following to display a page of files in the *documents* folder:

```
file:///sdcard/documents/
file://localhost/mnt/sdcard/documents/
```

▶ Running Games on Other Devices

Other devices require a different address in the browser. You'll need to research the method based on the particular operating system, version, and make of device you own.

Try tapping on a script file to open it in the browser. If that opens the script into another application (such as a text editor), rather than Chrome, it means the default app for the *.html* file type is set to something else. You can usually open the script into the browser with one of the following:

- Enter the full name of the script, including its folder, in the browser's address bar. In the file listing, tap the link and hold. Wait for the Open in New Tab popup, and choose it.

- Install a file manager app that allows you to select local files to open in the browser.

- For Apple iOS devices, opening local files in a browser represents a much larger challenge due to security limitations imposed by the operating system.

- While there are some hacks and work-arounds (which don't always work and may require "jailbreaking" the device) probably the best overall method is to load the scripts to a web server—public or local—and access the scripts via the Internet.